ECONOMICS AND THE IDEA OF MANKIND

ECONOMICS
AND
THE IDEA
OF
MANKIND

EDITED BY BERT F. HOSELITZ

Under the Auspices of the Council for the Study of Mankind

COLUMBIA UNIVERSITY PRESS NEW YORK & LONDON 1965

GERHARD HIRSCHFELD

Foreword: On the History of the Council for the Study of Mankind

AS THE READER glances through these pages, he will find that the authors give their principal attention to two basic challenges. New conditions have been created by the advance of science and technology. If we are to adjust to them successfully, we need new insights; perhaps the mankind perspective will provide them. Also, certain questions can be answered only if mankind is considered as a functioning whole, among them disarmament, the gap between the haves and the have-nots, population, food, and automation.

While the authors focus largely upon these two basic points, their primary purpose is not to come up with final or even tentative answers. It is rather to try to understand first the general nature and then the precise meaning of the problems posed by these and other challenges.

These objectives are exactly what the founders of the Council for the Study of Mankind had in mind when they met in the spring of 1952 to consider the idea of mankind. They hoped that understanding would gradually grow into clarification of the procedure and determination of the direction in which ultimate action might be most promising. As this volume on economics, along with volumes on other disciplines, is sponsored by the Council for the Study of Mankind, the reader may want to know more about the organization—how it began, how it approached the concept of mankind, what it has accomplished, and what it anticipates in the way of results. I hope that the following account will help answer these and related questions.

Like many others, I had been bothered for some years by my inability to understand this age of crisis. We speak of mankind, but actually we do not know what mankind signifies, what part it is playing now, and what part it might play in the future. By "mankind" I mean the totality of man and his society. Obviously, if we hope to deal effectively with the problems that confront all people regardless of race, creed, color, or nationality, we must know what mankind means. Some of the scholars I approached shared my concern. It was with this background that we met in Chicago to discuss the idea of mankind. The original group consisted of Adolf A. Berle, Herbert Blumer, Richard P. McKeon, Charles Morris, Robert Redfield, Quincy Wright, and a few others. The first meeting was followed by many others.

From the first, there was a common understanding on mankind, but the interpretations varied. The concept of mankind exists and always has existed, said some, but not mankind as a configuration, said others. Actually, the awareness of mankind is true only of the present age, since communication has become worldwide only in the last twenty years. Concern with peace is more urgent and of a different nature today. A single mistake in diplomacy can cause more damage than the atom bomb.

It might be useful for an understanding of the Council's evolutionary process to give a bit of the flavor of these discussions, which have extended over a number of years.

If we say that the human race is threatened with extinction, we imply a biological concept of mankind, which is incorrect. The threat is to civilization. The destruction of mankind would not mean the destruction of all men but rather of the common values that bring them together. A concept of mankind cannot avert extinction. The concept will emerge out of investigating the problem of conflict itself.

Some questioned the value of a concept of mankind. They preferred specific questions: What is true of mankind everywhere? What is the universal nature of humanity? How may mankind conceive of itself as a unit? How might one think of mankind as that to which one is loyal and responsible? Basic positions were set forth in reply. There is a concept of mankind underlying all experience and thought, much as "human nature" underlies and relates concepts of human nature set forth in psychology, anthropology, sociology, and literature. Related to the concept is the variety of perspectives that men take to communities, mankind being the most inclusive earthly community. The concept has at least three distinct practical applications. Because of scientific and technological advance, mankind is emerging in a set of aspirations that can be pursued more effectively than ever before. Another aspect takes the form of new bonds of community. A third is found in the appearance of new values.

Concern was expressed as to what might grow out of the formulation of a concept of mankind. Is our aim to see mankind as an entity? "Entity" is a disturbing word. Entity has never existed. It would be more accurate to speak of different levels of mankind.

Rather than entity, we sought to clarify the idea of unity. How is the unity of mankind to be conceived? Might unity create a closed society in which variety and individuality would be neglected? How would unity help or hinder the ends of nations, institutions, cultures, and civilizations? Should mankind function as an organized whole and if so, on what basis, for what functions, and for what purposes? Mankind as a whole is probably just as capable of misfunctioning as national states are. Most likely, it would hinder some of the ends of groups and individuals, but it could equally well advance others. While some individuals and institutions might have a primary loyalty to the whole of mankind, it would not even be good for mankind if all had mankind as their primary loyalty. However, individuals and groups can act in the light of the awareness of mankind and in this way modify their actions without losing their distinctive nature and function.

Progress toward unity means progress in changing values. The problem today is that we have value systems, for example, Christianity and Islam, but they have not unified the human race; they have split it. No body of values remains static. Systems of values change, and the realization of these values changes as well. The problem is: Can we create a value system as comprehensive as the human race? We can if we start building on positive values rather than through an analysis of faults. The breakdown of institutions is more alarming than the crisis of the atom. The appeal should not be on fear but on the aspiration of the ages. The goal would be to transform our functional way of living to a human one. The progress that is needed is purely an artistic or creative job—assembling what is known and is being done to give man a new concept or ideal for a world community.

And so the discussion went. As the reader will see from these brief excerpts taken from the early discussions, there existed no consensus concerning the concept of mankind and related issues. We shared a sense of the potential practical importance of the problems under consideration. Perhaps even more important was the feeling that the discussion raised questions and suggested ideas that set us thinking. These questions and ideas, we felt, applied to our own special studies as well as to the large problems of cultural and political cooperation. This test in problems in which we had special knowledge, and the accompanying indications that the lines of inquiry had large scope of theoretic and practical application, was the irresistible pull to further inquiry despite differences of approach and difficulties of stating problems and communicating hypotheses.

Awareness of mankind and action oriented toward the needs and values of mankind rather than of some segmental group seemed essential instruments to the solution of the problems of world crisis. To use these instruments, we needed to understand their development and application, and therefore we thought to formulate the concept of mankind. Briefly, we did not seek the concept in the sense of ideological agreement in a doctrine or philosophy but in the sense of a framework within which to discuss common actions, associations, attitudes, and values. We did not want to become a pressure group advocating a program of world society or government at one extreme nor a sect promulgating a dogma of salvation at the other. We wanted to advance the discussion of common ends and associated action. We felt that the unity of mankind in cooperative action does not depend on a unity in ideas and beliefs; on the contrary, it depends on a pluralism that would provide the energy and diversity of ideas to constitute an active and ever-growing unity.

In putting the various theories to a test, we decided to hold a series of weekend conferences that would seek to relate various disciplines to the concept of mankind. It was thought that such conferences would serve to clarify the problems involved in the study of mankind as they relate to each discipline, to induce the participants to re-examine in a new light their own knowledge and theories, and to enable them to make use of this new awareness and possibly of new insights in their teaching and writing. We also hoped that a series of papers might be prepared after each conference and published in book form.

Such a conference was held on "Economics and the Idea of Mankind" at the Massachusetts Institute of Technology in November, 1960. Similar conferences have been held at other universities on philosophy, education, science, law, nationalism, history, and technology. The conferences and subsequent activities were made possible by foundation support. Clarence Faust, President of the Fund for the Advancement of Education; Frederick Burkhardt, President of the American Council of Learned Societies; Leslie Paffrath, President of the Johnson Foundation; and Adolf A. Berle, Chairman of the Twentieth Century Fund, were among the first to encourage and to support the work of the Council. Since then, the Rockefeller Foundation, the Corning Glass Works Foundation, and other foundations have joined in the support of the Council.

The conferences yielded results. Increasingly, the insights

gained in the discussions were applied by the participants in lectures and seminars, for example, in series held at the College of the University of Chicago, at Boston University, at the New School for Social Research, and at other educational institutions. Discussion groups on the idea of mankind were organized at the University of Chicago and are now being formed at other colleges and universities. Substantial papers have been prepared and are now being published in book form. The first book, *Education and the Idea of Mankind*, was edited by Robert Ulich, Professor of Education, Emeritus, Harvard University.* This book, *Economics and the Idea of Mankind*, is the second in a series which is to include volumes on anthropology, history, mental health, the humanities, technology, law, art, and other subjects—all related to the idea of mankind.

To aid the high school teacher in the social studies to give his students an idea of the meaning of world interdependence, a series of monographs is being prepared. Those on world history, education, and science have been completed, while others on philosophy, technology, and anthropology are scheduled for early completion. Educational radio and television programs are gradually being developed.

While all these activities are designed to further and broaden the understanding of the idea of mankind as it relates to our institutions, cultures, and disciplines, perhaps the most significant gain has been scored in the new understanding of that idea. I should list that understanding in three categories:

First, whether we look at a problem from the national-parochial or from the mankind perspective makes a basic difference in understanding that problem, therefore, in its correct eval-

* New York: Harcourt, Brace & World, 1964.

uation. World history from the national point of view sees India mostly from the deck of a gunboat and begins the history of Japan with Commodore Perry's arrival. From the point of view of mankind, world history is not the rise and fall of nations but the ceaseless flow and intermingling of cultures and civilizations. From the one point of view, the problems of education are Federal aid, high school drop-outs, and desegregation; from the other, they are widespread illiteracy, lack of facilities for the training of teachers, and practically no funds for even a minimum system of education in Asia, Africa, and other parts of the world. What applies to history and education applies equally to economics.

Second, the idea of mankind requires both a horizontal and a vertical perspective. No discipline can operate effectively and constructively any more within and by itself. Productive and progressive scholarly work in one discipline must be done in cooperation with other disciplines. Again, the reality of an interdependent world requires that the disciplines (as other parts of society) extend to the largest of all social units—mankind. They do not do so today. There exists probably no discipline (if indeed any part of society) that in its operation and development is guided by the interests of the whole of mankind as seen from the point of view of mankind.

Third, if anything effective is to be done about the opportunities and the problems of the totality of man and his society, it can be done only by the parts that make up that totality. The obstacle to the realization of an orderly world does not lie in the existence of nations, institutions, disciplines, and cultures but in the exclusive nature of their identity and orientation. They are guided primarily by their own interest. Notwithstanding its peaceful intentions, a nation will go to (nuclear) war if it feels that its basic values, be these democracy or communism, are in mortal danger. The interest of the nation is ranked above that of mankind. The same attitude applies to other segments of society, if in lesser degree.

The need is for nations, disciplines, cultures, and institutions to make room for the awareness of the interdependence of mankind as an overarching concept and to make their decisions in the light of that awareness. In this way, individuals and groups can modify their actions without losing their distinctive nature and function. Applied to economics, the primary aim would not be to try to set up a mankind economy but to extend the economic functions and organizations to include the mankind dimension, indeed, to convert their often monopolistic character, such as tariffs and investments, to what in effect they are—parts of a greater system in which they have certain autonomous rights but also some overarching responsibilities. If they are to make a contribution to the realization of an orderly world, they can do so only as parts of that whole.

It will be noted that this book on economics is not done actually by members of the Council but by a group of experts recruited largely from outside the Council. This is equally true of other projects—books, lectures, seminars, monographs, discussion groups. The method explains how a group consisting of a small staff, an executive committee, board of directors and advisers, and a few hundred scholars (fewer than are found in any medium-sized university) can engage in such a comprehensive and far-reaching program. The Council acts as a catalyst. It confines itself to stimulating interest in the idea of mankind and to designing methods by which it might be studied and taught. Other groups and institutions, better equipped than the Council, will take up the further development and clarification of the idea. This book, along with the others, is a test as to how well the collaboration between the catalyst and the executor of an idea works.

And is it not the idea that after all will be decisive in the struggle for the understanding of mankind? What the Council is doing to work toward the attainment of an orderly world has been tried a thousand times. Although aided by millions of people, by large sums of money, and by outstanding leadership, the effort has not succeeded in creating that world or even in bringing us closer to it. Is not the assumption warranted that future efforts will be just as futile unless they are supported by a radically new approach such as the broader understanding and the mankind perspective of which we have spoken before?

We in the Council feel that our search for the idea of mankind has been useful and rewarding. We have found profitable questions to ask and have been able to clarify many of the questions. In developing our inquiry, we have also laid the groundwork for a widely supported campaign to fight today's widespread ignorance of the idea of mankind and its meaning for our nation, for our economy, for our institutions, and, last but not least, for ourselves, for our families, and for our communities.

If this effort is successful, it will create a widespread awareness of the interdependence of the human society. It will expand the horizon of knowledge to a point where the fundamental problems of the totality of man and his society can be approached upon the basis of world-wide discussion of universal values and the formulation of policies. It will make it possible to consider specific problems in the framework of mankind. It will provide a sound basis upon which we may reasonably expect to be able to resolve these problems.

The Directors of the Council for the Study of Mankind express their gratitude to Adolf A. Berle, Chairman, August Heckscher, Director, and the Trustees of the Twentieth Century Fund. Their support made possible the conference on "Economics and the Idea of Mankind," which was held November 25–27, 1960, at Endicott House, Massachusetts Institute of Technology, as well as the preparation of these papers.

BERT F. HOSELITZ

Introduction:
Purpose of the Book

A STUDY of economics during the last two centuries will show that at different periods during that time economists have been concerned with different important problems. International trade, the protection of economic advancement of a given country, conditions of capital investment, the role and participation of large labor groups, and other important problems of this kind as well as more general theory were widely discussed at different periods, and important economists contributed to them. But the problem of economic conditions of world-wide peace and the economic unification and adjustment of mankind as a whole are ideas that have only very recently begun to provoke some viewpoints and even some theories. In the last few years, especially since the end of World War II, economists have contributed greatly to a better understanding of the functioning of human societies on various economic and social levels, but only very few of them have actually addressed themselves to one of the main problems that has faced for a long time and today does face humanity: how could and how would mankind function as a whole on the level of production, distribution, and consumption? This problem has become, and is continuing to become, increasingly severe in the present world, since effective distances between all parts of the world have been greatly shortened, communication between people who previously were ignorant of one another has become thorough and intense, and the main economic centers of the world have become meeting places of peoples of all races, languages, and nationalities.

Although world trade has not grown as much as some governments wanted to see it increase, its distribution has become more highly differentiated and has affected more countries importantly. Political regions that were colonies until recently have become independent countries and must find methods of expanding their economic relations—whether trade, capital movements, or learning more advanced production methods—with other countries, some on a similar and many others on a higher economic level. International agencies have been created that in some form or another have developed concerns of world-wide economic interrelations and comparisons. The United Nations and many other related international agencies are operating on practical and theoretical problems that are closely associated with the study of the interrelations of mankind. But, although questions of world population movements, migration, economic interaction, capital movements between countries, developmental processes in different nations, world health, world agricultural developments, international labor problems, and many other questions are examined, discussed, and explored by the United Nations and agencies related to it, the complete and extensive study of the economics of mankind as a whole has as yet been little expounded, and the knowledge of this subject is as yet hardly developed. It is true that its significance will not be denied by persons whose interest in the United Nations and its associated and related agencies is strong, but the theoretical and related applied study of the economics of mankind has not yet been made a subject of work to be done by the United Nations or related agencies. It may be hoped, however, that if this subject is made more popular, if its importance is stressed and discussed more widely, its significance and implication for the United Nations and its related agencies will be clearly recognized, and studies on various aspects of the economics of mankind may be fostered by these organizations and their members.

A proper procedure of the study of this field will take place, however, only when some existing approaches that have to do with the international economic problems or the relations of various countries will be changed into a more general system of the study of the economics of mankind as a whole. In the customary approaches, the problems of the economic interaction of different parts of the world and different sectors of mankind have been treated as aspects of interregional or international trade. Economic theories developed from these forms of interaction appeared to work fairly well, notably if the somewhat unusual conditions of the world economy during the nineteenth century were taken as a norm and if, in addition, this norm was idealized by the elimination of ideas and generalizations on the theoretical and speculative level of "frictions," "discontinuities," and other "imperfections" in international economic relations.

With the developments of recent years, notably with the rise of new aspirations for economic progress in the underdeveloped countries, these solutions have become increasingly less satisfactory, and a new approach to the economic problems of mankind has to be sought. Much of the current discussion that surrounds such questions as the liberalization of international trade, the improvement of the conditions for capital investment abroad, and even the extending of technical and economic aid among governments or international organizations is couched in terms derived from classical theory of international economic relations and is based on certain more or less implicit assumptions that were customary in that body of theoretical and applied economics. Thus, for example, mobility of certain factors of production across international boundaries, wide differentials in income levels between countries, and, above all, differences in culture and social stratification—which in turn affect economics motivations and attitudes—have remained unexplored or have received relatively inadequate treatment in the economic literature.

For this reason it is hoped that new insights can be gained by a new approach. It is not the purpose of this book to create a new theory of international or interregional economic relations. It is rather to apply the existing theories to an approach that starts from the assumption that mankind may function as an integrated whole and to explore the conditions under which this alternative would be possible and what economic results could be postulated if this assumption were to become a reality. It should be noted that this problem is not quite the same as that of studying the economic problems of a large and variegated country, although there are some similarities in the two tasks. Income differences, differences in production techniques, and differences in consumption standards and consumption patterns all over the world are too great to allow the mere application of the economic principles developed for one country to the analogous problems of mankind. More-over, there are certain questions that become vital only if mankind is considered as a functioning whole. Among them are such problems as alternatives for armament production, the reconciliation of wide income and productivity differences that are ultimately based on different cultural norms and social attitudes, and the difficulties arising from very different rates of population growth in various parts of the world.

The main emphasis of this book will be placed on these and similar problems. Although in some instances care must be taken to avoid utopian speculation and although blueprints for many features of functioning mankind economy cannot be made, the propositions in the chapters of this book will, it is hoped, clarify two major questions: (1) What are the chief characteristics of an economy embracing all mankind? (2) What measures may be taken to bring the world closer to such a result? Only the solution of these problems will, in the last resort, tip the precarious balance between war and peace that is now with us.

Contents

ECONOMICS AND THE IDEA OF MANKIND

I

ERSKINE MCKINLEY

Mankind in the History of Economic Thought*

MANKIND is afflicted with the pain of many poverties—spiritual, emotional, and material. These need not coincide. In the belief, however, that spiritual and emotional poverty can more easily be alleviated in the absence of material poverty, some men have pondered the question of material wealth. What material things do men value, how is the sum of these valued objects to be increased, and how is this increase distributed among those making it? Some have felt it necessary to apologize for philosophizing about these baser aspects of life. Others have asserted that spiritual values are themselves generated and developed by the mode of organization in which material values are produced. Even those who reject the latter belief explicitly accept as true that, at least in this life, spiritual values cannot be

* I am indebted to the editor and several fellow contributors for criticisms of an earlier draft of this essay. I am grateful also to A. W. Coats and my colleague Herbert Geyer, with whom I have been discussing some of the concepts for several years. Arlene Daniels of the Palo Alto Medical Research Foundation provided me with many excellent criticisms. I assume full responsibility for the errors of fact or mistaken inference which I am sure remain.

generated until man is able to obtain the minimum needs for survival. Thus, "economists . . . are the trustees, not of civilization, but of the possibility of civilization."[1] Indeed, one would like to accept the conjecture that the very word "civilization" was first used by an economist, the elder Mirabeau, and as well, his definition of it as "l'adoucissement de . . . moeurs." He believed that "C'est du sein des sociétés adoucies . . . qu'est née la conception de l'humanité."[2]

If mankind is to be defined as the sum of all human beings born or to be born into the world, then it might seem almost impious to ask what can be predicted of any one of them, much less all of them. Yet with no more impiety than that of the Psalmist who wondered, "What is man, that Thou are mindful of him?" are the questions here raised: What concept of man has been held by economists in their analysis of the behavior of any individual man, and to what extent have they universalized their concept of the individual to mankind? Here arises a subsidiary question: How have economists defined the term "all men"? That is to say, given a map of the world as they knew it and their conception of the evolution of the species, how would they have defined mankind over the universe of living creatures? This is an important question even today, since we seem given to dehumanizing those who differ from us. Western Europeans at the time of the Crusades divided the known world into Christendom and the rest. A living creature became a part of humanity only when he possessed a soul, and Limbo had to be invented for the known virtuous who antedated Christ. Until comparatively recently, living creatures could be regarded as

---

[1] John Maynard Keynes, quoted in Roy F. Harrod, *The Life of John Maynard Keynes* (New York: Harcourt, Brace & World, 1951), p. 194.

[2] The conjecture and quotation are from John U. Nef, *Cultural Foundations of Industrial Civilization* (London: Cambridge University Press, 1958), p. 79.

a part of mankind only if possessed of property and political freedom. Even today there seem many who retain this attitude.[3]

While economists have often not been explicitly concerned with the specific nature of mankind, one may make reasonable inference about their views on the subject because their economic writings often contain material of relevance to the question. Were one to have asked Adam Smith, "What is man?" he might well have replied without thinking that man is that collection of beings whose chief end is to know God and to enjoy Him forever. He might have been shocked that anyone could infer from his writings that he held, perhaps, a different idea. If one wants to infer from the writings of economists what views they might have held about the nature of mankind, it is advisable to restate the question in the following way:

1. What have been economists' theories of the psychology of the individual? What is the nature of the atoms composing society? Do men enter the world with the same or differing innate endowments? Is man a completely rational being? In positing rationality, does one rule out the possibility of explaining irrational behavior within the same system?

2. How did economists see man as reticulated in a social structure? Can or do the atoms defined in question (1) achieve a condition of social equilibrium?

The very use of the term "equilibrium" implies that question (2) involves the analysis of a stationary society. If the economic process is to be regarded as part of the historical process, economists have had to ask:

3. How did it come about that we are where we are, and

---

[3] Compare Knut Wicksell, *Lectures on Political Economy* (London: Routledge and Kegan Paul, 1934), I, 3ff.

are there patterns of history that can lead us with safety to predict how, at least in its economic aspects, it will all come out?

The unit of analysis, the individual, was not, I think, of very great interest to Plato, believing as he did that every man is a very poor rendering of the idea. Since there is no reason to assume identical flaws in each poor copy, it easily follows that men are born as much with differing innate instincts and abilities as with differing physical characteristics. It is not necessary to agree with the assertion that Plato believed in more than one universal man, one of Greek man and "one each of the various barbarian races." [4]

The Hebraic doctrine sharply dichotomized Jew and non-Jew, and the identifying characteristic of the former, to have been chosen by God, made him the inheritor of the earth. The Christian doctrine, on the other hand, making all souls equal in the sight of God, offered to Christians an even more dazzling patrimony, eternal life in heaven. It would seem that the earthly behavior of the Christian ought to consist in giving away all his goods and, forsaking all others, in rejecting the world for the contemplation of God. Such an interpretation was, in fact, made by some and in part by others, but of the latter a few, such as Aquinas, directed at least minor attention to the nature of man, the social order, and worldly, even economic, affairs. Some historians of economic thought maintain that the Scholastics wrote for the instruction of confessors. Hence, they were more concerned with the relationship between the individual and God than with political and social relationships except as these affected the first. Steeped as they were in the belief in original sin and the universal tendency to transgress, it

---

[4] K. R. Popper, *The Open Society and Its Enemies* (London: George Routledge and Sons, 1945), I, 21, 237ff.

is no wonder that Aquinas in the *Summa Theologica* can say that certain commercial practices, control of which came under the civil law, are lawful yet sinful.[5] Tawney points out that

There is no place in mediaeval theory for economic activity that is not related to a moral end, and to found a science of society upon the assumption that the appetite for economic gain is a constant and measureable force, to be accepted, like other natural forces, as an inevitable and self-evident *datum*, would have appeared to the mediaeval thinker as hardly less rational or less immoral than to make the premise of social philosophy the unrestrained operation of such necessary human attributes as pugnacity or the sexual instinct.[6]

Yet so much had Scholasticism altered by the end of the seventeenth century that economic affairs, particularly speculative and commercial activity, were the subject of considerable examination. "The Economic Man of later times put in an appearance in the conception of 'prudent economic reason' . . . the intention of gaining in every legitimate way." [7] But by this time, about the mid-seventeenth century, such an idea was becoming a commonplace in the writings of the "consultant administrators and pamphleteers" and the Mercantilists.[8] In the debate between the Nominalists and the Realists, Aquinas seems to have taken one version of Aristotle's somewhat ambiguous interpretation of Plato's theory of universals, while Occam, a Nominalist, in denying the reality of any universal, took another. Occam has also been called the first Protestant in his attitude towards limitation on the temporal power of the

[5] For example, Questions 77 and 78 in the *Summa*.
[6] R. H. Tawney, *Religion and the Rise of Capitalism* (Harmondsworth, Middlesex: Penguin Books, 1938), pp. 44–45.
[7] Joseph A. Schumpeter, *History of Economic Analysis* (New York: Oxford University Press, 1954), p. 99.
[8] The quoted phrase is Schumpeter's heading for Chap. 3, *ibid.*, p. 143.

Papacy. It is thus no accident that Luther's knowledge of Scholasticism was derived from Occam, for Protestantism fostered the individualism that grew up with and was required by relatively free capitalism and the new nation-state for which the successors to the Scholastics were beginning to provide advice. Roscelin (*fl.* 1050) called the universal a *flatus vocis* and "flatly denied . . . the existence of humanity." [9] His follower in extreme Nominalism was Occam (*d.* 1349). Such a Nominalist position, had it gained widespread acceptance, must have made any study of man impossible, beyond, of course, the simple listing of names. At the same time, the Nominalist attitude, if it did carry through the Reformation, served to emphasize the compelling need for an understanding of how individualistic anarchy is, in fact, socially constrained. It is perhaps wrong to equate individualism and Nominalism and oppose to them Realism and what might be called "Universalism." I do so to emphasize that if one accepts a divine order in society, man's duty is to conform, and there is no need to inquire in "scientific" fashion how the order emerges from the acts of individuals. Thus, the analogy with natural science:

These [Scottish] moral philosophers believed that a science of man must concern itself at base with the irreducible element in man, e.g., his "original nature." This was a conscious effort on the part of philosophers to provide an analogue to the chemist's "elements." [10]

The most extreme Nominalism would have to deny that men have any "irreducible element" or least common denominator.

---

[9] Patrick J. Foote, S.J., in his introductory chapter in Michael W. Shallo, S.J., *Scholastic Philosophy* (Philadelphia: Peter Reilly, 1926), p. 6. The statement about Luther's knowledge of Occam is to be found at p. 21.

[10] Gladys Bryson, *Man and Society: The Scottish Inquiry of the Eighteenth Century* (Princeton, N.J.: Princeton University Press, 1945), p. 242.

If economists were to model their methods on the natural sciences, especially physics, then they, like scientists, would have to "search for basic units and entities which are not divisible in themselves," [11] and more particularly the ultimate or irreducible building block of the universe to which all matter that obeys scientific laws, that is, all matter, can be reduced. In a social science this unit must be that of which society, the universe, is built—the individual. This is at least true if one accepts Aristotelian logic or Newtonian mechanics, that the whole is equal to the sum of its parts. I believe that Hegel would have denied this. Thus, "Hegelian absolute mind is really the postulation of an absolute 'perspective' which somehow differs from and yet includes all finite perspectives." [12] Hence, the whole cannot be learned by an analysis of its parts except in the ultimate synthesis of all the parts into the truth that transcends them.

The Mercantilists looked on man "as an egoist animatable and directable through his desire for gain." [13] The earlier Mercantilists also regarded men as units of production and, at least the laboring classes, as animatable primarily by near starvation.[14] Even so, since new men were new hands for the production of wealth and the manning of armies, they were, so to speak, welcome. Petty in 1672 reckoned the loss of Irishmen in the rebellion at 10,335,000 pounds (counting them, as slaves and Negroes were, at 15 pounds the head rather than as Englishmen

[11] Walter A. Weisskopf, *The Psychology of Economics* (Chicago: University of Chicago Press, 1955), p. 53.

[12] Charles W. Morris, *Six Theories of Mind* (Chicago: University of Chicago Press, 1932), p. 60.

[13] Joseph J. Spengler, "The Problem of Order in Economic Affairs," in Joseph J. Spengler and William R. Allen, eds., *Essays in Economic Thought* (Chicago: Rand McNally, 1960), p. 15.

[14] Compare A. W. Coats, "Changing Attitudes to Labour in the Mid-Eighteenth Century," *Economic History Review*, Second Series, XI (1958), 35.

at 70 pounds apiece). Children he put at 5 pounds.[15] The acute observation has been made that

The temper which views all things in their theory rather than in their historical setting must also see little, as it gazes upon human institutions, but failure and futility, and as it contemplates human actions, little but departures from rational norms. It is just in this comparison between actual things and their theory that satire consists, and the dry light of Cartesianism threw upon the deformities of actual humanity just the kind of illumination which is necessary to evoke the satiric comparison.[16]

The calculations of Petty and others like him evoked one of the most savage pieces of satire ever penned, Swift's *A Modest Proposal for Preventing the Children of Ireland from Being a Burden to Their Parents or Country*, in which he, with calculations similar to Petty's and the utmost seriousness of manner, advocates that Irish children be raised for the butcher's block and tanning factory. This should have finished the sort of calculation that assigns a money value to human beings as capital or as consumer goods. It is, in fact, a recurring aberration.

The Physiocrats, who with Adam Smith represent economists of the Enlightenment, seem in general to have accepted the notion of the individual set forth by Hobbes and Locke: the mind of the new-born baby is a blank tablet upon which the environment alone can act. Thus, when Quesnay's disciple Mirabeau, the elder, wrote

As to the native disposition of peoples, I venture to say that it is something which is more real and perhaps more insurmountable than the influence of climate. The different families which in a short time populated the three parts of the world bore with them from

---

[15] He does this, among other places, in his "Political Anatomy of Ireland," in *Tracts: Chiefly Relating to Ireland* (Dublin: Boulter Grierson, 1769), p. 315.

[16] Basil Willey, *The Seventeenth Century Background* (New York: Doubleday Anchor Books, 1953), p. 96.

the beginning, each on its own part, an absolutely different native disposition, doubtless derived from that of the chief of the tribe, and perhaps relative in the sight of Providence to the diversity of the courses they were destined to take.

Quesnay struck out all the words after "derived" and substituted

from the behaviour and the manner of life to which the different nations devoted themselves in order to procure their subsistence and to conform to the advantages and disadvantages of the places and circumstances to which they were subjected.[17]

Such a notion is, of course, fundamental to the near worship of reason that characterized the Enlightenment generally. The idea that the newly born organism reacts by purely tropistic responses but "learns" additional automatic responses is essential to the utilitarian philosophy upon which liberalism must ultimately be based. I mean by this that to the utilitarian, if each individual is to count as one in the adding up of pleasures, then the same stimulus must evoke the same degree of pleasure or pain in each individual. It seems further that the almost credal belief in educability of man implies the same, coupled as this belief was, if not with Locke, at least with "associationism." Further, the demand theory, or, as they would have had it, the value theory of Jevons and the Austrians, is atomistic in that utility is experienced by the individual wholly in proportion as he acquires more of a commodity, not as a function as well of the quantities possessed by others. Incorporating the latter notion—a social notion—presents major if not insuperable difficulties. Smith, however, did not regard men as wholly appetitive

[17] Quoted from Ronald L. Meek, *The Economics of Physiocracy: Essays and Translations* (Cambridge, Mass.: Harvard University Press, 1963), pp. 67–68. Concerning this and the passage immediately following, compare Homer W. Smith, *From Fish to Philosopher* (New York: Doubleday, 1961), p. 204.

but as also capable, through sympathy, of altruism. Indeed, he attempted to reconcile these apparently conflicting elements. If the irreducible element has internally conflicting motives, how does it achieve a balance between them? But since in Smith, as in others, the conflict is resolved in the individual only in a social setting, discussion will be deferred.

The German historical school was concerned primarily with man in social interaction and, professedly nonanalytical in reducing the society to its irreducible elements, had no need of a theory of individual psychology. Whether they had such a theory I cannot say, but we know at least that their rejection of Smith's atomism, universalism, and perpetualism indicated that they found his unacceptable. Marx's view is better discussed under question (2), since those psychological traits which differentiate men from nonhuman animals are the products of the mode of production. In fact, to Marx the problem was not to discover universally valid psychological laws but rather to change the environment, within which and only within which such laws could be valid. "The point was to discover the real character of society, to explain the meaning of human alienation (man's *summmum malum*), not as an abstract and philosophical, but as a social and concrete phenomenon." [18]

At the same time that Marx and Engels were to flabbergast the bourgeoisie, Stanley Jevons and the Austrian school, drawing on the man-machine idea of the Enlightenment, were developing the marginal analysis of value, which is the core of neoclassical or orthodox allocation theory.[19] If Marx stood

---

[18] Ralph Miliband, review of T. B. Bottomore and Maximilian Rubel, *Karl Marx, Selected Writings in Sociology and Social Philosophy*, in *British Journal of Sociology*, VIII (1957), 378.

[19] The most delightful treatment of this notion is La Mettrie's. For a learned discussion of his work and the suggestion that computers and servomechanism theory may render this intractable machine more predictable, see Aram Var-

Hegel on his feet, the marginalists stood Epicurus on his head. I mean by this that the principle of the diminishing marginal utility, which is quite epicurean in spirit, was, for the sake of rendering aggregate demand infinitely elastic, joined to the idea of the insatiability of wants, which is not epicurean. The reconciliation of these two principles has subsequently been seen to be no simple feat. But the fundamental difference between Epicurus and Benthamite (or marginalist) would seem to lie in the separation of economic behavior from total behavior. Vaihinger held that such erroneous fictions are useful if the known error can be corrected for when the fiction is put to use. Thus, Marshall believed that the maximizing homunculus maximized not pleasure as measured in utils or money returns but rather what he calls "net advantage." But this makes any qualification just that much more difficult.[20] In any case, it is this abstracting of one department of human affairs from all others that enables many economists today to criticize utilitarianism as a superficial and even contemptible philosophy, then diligently turn to using it under the guise of rational *homo œconomicus*.

Once born into a society, men, for Plato, are able to specialize in that form of labor for which they are best suited. They are thus bound together by common dependence, although the society they form is stratified. So long as appetites are held in

---

tanian, *La Mettrie's L'Homme Machine* (Princeton, N.J.: Princeton University Press, 1960).

[20] But, "no one who was acquainted with recent value theory could honestly continue to argue that it has any essential connection with psychological hedonism. . . . So far as we are concerned, our economic subjects can be pure egoists, pure altruists, pure ascetics, pure sensualists or—what is much more likely—mixed bundles of all these impulses." Lionel Robbins, *An Essay on the Nature and Significance of Economic Science* (2d ed., London: Macmillan, 1952), pp. 85, 95.

check by reason, there need be no obstacle to the peaceable co-existence of many such stationary societies. Substantially the same views were held by the Schoolmen. One worshiped God from the station to which it had pleased God to call one. The Scholastic concern with distributive and commutative justice thus took account of the medieval social order, and the just price seems to have included an element of return, permitting the seller to enjoy that level of living to which his status entitled him. The debate as to whether the Mercantilists were essentially Scholastic in their outlook or rather the midwives of liberalism can be resolved conceivably by an examination of whether the outlook of the particular writer was, in context, based on the static, zero-sum economy concept or rather, in the face of quickening economic development, an appeal to the belief in the gains of trade being shared by both parties. One of the most appealingly sensible contributions to the controversy largely precipitated by Heckscher puts it so:

He [Hecksher] stressed the importance of the static conception of economic life, of economic resources and activity so evident at that time; he emphasized that this provided one reason for the many commercial wars; implicit in the "tragedy of mercantilism" was the belief that what was one man's or country's gain was another's loss. Yet, vital as this is, as he himself says, to an understanding of the attitude of the time, he nowhere asks why men should have believed it to be true.

But is it in fact a surprising notion in the pre-industrial economy? It was, after all, a world in which population remained static; in which trade and production usually grew only gradually; in which the limits of the known world were expanded slowly and with great difficulty; in which economic horizons were narrowly limited; and in which man approximated more closely than today to Hobbes' vision of his natural state: for most men most of the time, life *was* "poor, nasty, brutish and short." [21]

[21] D. C. Coleman, "Eli Heckscher and the Idea of Mercantilism," *Scandinavian Economic History Review*, V (1957), 18–19.

But this is, of course, subject to the following qualification:

At the same time as certain characteristics of economic life remained the same during these centuries, so also were forces of change gradually making themselves felt. Two main channels through which they were making themselves felt were the great expansion of trade, to the East, to Africa and above all to the New World; and the growth of industry in many nations of Europe. As the economic implications of these new developments gradually became apparent, the old idea of fixity and limited horizons became intolerable.[22]

Even by 1691 we find in North "the magnificent conception of all nations forming a community of trade" and the "clear realization that in the sense in which former writers had assumed it, harmful branches of trade did not exist." [23] However much it may have scandalized or titillated the public, the social vision of Mandeville in "The Grumbling Hive" and the *Fable of the Bees* clearly adumbrates, as early as 1714, the economic liberalism, both in the organic nature of society and in the laissez-faire doctrine, associated usually with the Physiocrats and Adam Smith.[24] But these were latecomers, and by and large it is probably correct to say that the Mercantilists viewed mankind as fragmented into nation states and disposed hierarchically within these states. Internationally they were belligerent, although on occasion they appealed to the brotherhood of man and advocated freedom of (usually some particular) trade among nations that had received different endowments from God to the advantage of all. Thus,

[22] *Ibid.*, p. 20.
[23] Joseph A. Schumpeter, *Economic Doctrine and Method* (New York: Oxford University Press, 1954), pp. 28–29.
[24] For a discussion of Mandeville's intellectual inheritance and bequest, see the brilliant and elegant commentary by F. B. Kaye in Bernard Mandeville, *The Fable of the Bees* (London: Clarendon Press, 1925), and compare Nathan Rosenberg, "Mandeville and Laissez-Faire," *Journal of the History of Ideas*, XXIV (1963), No. 2.

In the ancient Greek and Roman Classics is to be found the doctrine that differences in natural conditions in different countries made trade between these countries mutually profitable. The early Christian philosophers took over this doctrine and gave it a theological flavor. God had endowed different regions with limited but varied products in order to give mankind an incentive to trade, so that through a world economy they would become united in a world society, and as children of one God they would learn to love one another. . . . This doctrine was taken over to some extent by lay writers on commercial matters, but they managed ingeniously to adapt the intent of Providence to their own particular views.[25]

The violence of the Civil Wars in England turned the thoughts of two subsequently influential thinkers to the question of social order and its theory. These were Hobbes and Locke. Each using an *histoire raisonée* asked into the nature of man in his "natural," or prepolitical, condition. Hobbes could visualize such a world only as a *bellum omnium contra omnes*, while Locke imagined a somewhat more peaceful scene, but both reasoned that natural men are rational. Less cautious followers were inclined to believe in the state of nature as a reality rather than as a fiction and used such discoveries as the *fille sauvage* to "prove" their own psychological, political, or religious doctrines.[26] Such credulity was bound to suffer under the expanding knowledge of the diversity of social orders in the world. In the battle of the Ancients and the Moderns we see to what an extent the eyes of the explorers and travelers were increasingly being lifted from the pages of Pliny and directed toward the real world. Men became interested in the savages

[25] Jacob Viner, *Studies in the Theory of International Trade* (New York: Harper and Row, 1937), pp. 100–01. But compare Edmond Silberner, *La guerre dans la pensée économique du XVIe au XVIIIe siècles* (Paris: Librairie du Recueil Sirey, 1939), who cites evidence of the bellicosity and xenophobia of Mercantilist writers. See especially pp. 109ff.

[26] Vratanian, *La Mettrie's L'Homme Machine*, pp. 222ff.

and strange animals that were actually discovered, rather than those described by classical authors. Caliban comes from Montaigne, and Montaigne's cannibals come from travelers. "The anthropophagi and men whose heads do grow beneath their shoulders" had been seen by Othello, not derived from antiquity.[27] Yet the credulity of the age can be illustrated by the fact that in 1703 the Bishop of London entrusted the translation of the Catechism into Formosan to the hands of one Psalmanazar, who it later turned out when he was sent to study theology at Oxford was not a Formosan nor had ever been there but did have the ingenuity to invent an alphabet and a country.[28] All ages are, of course, credulous. As late as 1898 the popular mind was thrilled to read of the experiences of Rougement, who had lived as an adopted king of the cannibals. His mention of the flight of some wombats in his kingdom introduced a note of skepticism among scholars.[29]

As an example of something both real and exotic, the Chinese kingdom had a vogue in Europe during the Enlightenment. Although Russell claims that Hegel's knowledge of China was confined to the fact that "it was," this is contradicted, at least to the non-Sinologist, by the section in Hegel's *Theory of History* on that same subject.[30] Diderot had written of China in the *Encyclopédie*. Turgot had written a "principles text" for two very real Chinese students and must have learned something from them. Quesnay had attacked Montesquieu for calling China barbarous and had discussed it glowingly as a "model

[27] Bertrand Russell, *A History of Western Philosophy* (New York: Simon and Schuster, 1945), p. 516.
[28] See Edmund Blunden, "Psalmanazar," in *Today's Japan* (Tokyo: Cross Continent Company, 1960), Vol. V, No. 1, p. 29.
[29] Edith Sitwell, *English Eccentrics* (New York: Vanguard Press, 1957), Chap. 9.
[30] Russell, *History of Western Philosophy*, p. 516.

for Europe." His admiration was not only for the wealth of
China but for its government by a divinely constituted and
benevolent despot and most of all for its stability. The correct-
ness of the European belief in the stability of China is attested to
by a contemporary scholar: "China in the 18th century witnessed one of the most flourishing periods in her uninterrupted
history of over 4,000 years. . . . Diderot's view of China seems
sound and correct." [31] This is of a piece with the Physiocratic
vision that any economy is organically interconnected and will,
if left alone, flourish—if a thing can both be stationary and
flourishing. At first I took it as paradoxical that the Physiocrats
could seem to believe in the infant as *tabula rasa* and at the same
time in a rigid social hierarchy, but if the infant is to know
nothing else, then where could it get the impulse towards vertical social mobility? The Physiocratic Heavenly City is
Thomist, whereupon arising everyone would chant,

> O let us love our occupations,
> Bless the squire and his relations,
> Live upon our daily rations,
> And always know our proper stations.[32]

It is, of course, true that one can distinguish with difficulty
whether Quesnay really was taking China as a model for Europe
or only as a foil with which to expose European shortcomings
without committing the crime of lese majesty. The view that
the Physiocrats were revolutionary and its opposite both have
respectable proponents, but I imagine that they would have
taken as inconceivable that "a threat to the stability of any
society is introduced by the permanent invasion of new born

---

[31] Takeo Kuwabara, "The Encyclopédie (1751–1780), a Corporate Study,"
in *Silver Jubilee Volume of the Zinbun-Kagaku-Kenkusyo* (Tokyo: Iwanami
Syoten, 1954), pp. 554ff.
[32] Charles Dickens, *The Chimes*.

barbarians ignorant and careless about social demands." [33] Mirabeau spoke of his awareness of other cultures:

Nos vaisseaux plus prompts que le messager de Dieu fondent l'air et les eaux, portent et reportent avec une célérité incroyable nos volontés et nos ordres d'une extrémité de la terre à une autre. Les glaces du Nord, les chaleurs brulantes de la ligne ne les arrêtent pas dans leur course. Le Japon et le Chinois nous sont presque voisins.[34]

And how could the world have seemed large in either space or time to that proficient writer on astronomy, Adam Smith? He draws examples from Bengal, Goa, China, Japan, and the West Indies, not to mention ancient Athens and Babylon. As much as Mirabeau was Smith sensitive to the fact that the world was growing smaller. Political economists as well as scientists and philosophers were increasingly aware that if the task of aesthetics and science, natural or social, were to detect uniformity amidst variety, variety seemed to be increasing at a more rapid pace than uniformity. The problem was twofold: First, what has the true-born Scot in common with cannibals and "men whose heads do grow beneath their shoulders"? Second, if all men are appetitive, how are their appetites har-

[33] Kaare Svalastoga, *Prestige, Class and Social Mobility* (Copenhagen: Glydendal, 1959), p. 362. Quesnay's critique of Montesquieu is in his *Despotism in China*, translated by and included in Lewis A. Maverick, *China, a Model for Europe* (San Antonio: Paul Anderson, 1946). As to the reactionary versus revolutionary "activism" of the Physiocrats, the classic references are Henry Higgs, *The Physiocrats* (New York: Langland Press, 1952, first published in 1897); Max Beer, *An Inquiry into Physiocracy* (London: Allen and Unwin, 1939); and for a more recent discussion, which surveys the intervening discussion, Warren J. Samuels, "The Physiocratic Theory of Property and State," *Quarterly Journal of Economics*, LXXV (1961), No. 1, and "The Physiocratic Theory of Economic Policy," *Quarterly Journal of Economics*, LXXVI (1962), No. 1.

[34] An account of Turgot's idea of progress can be found in Howard Becker and Harry Elmer Barnes, *Social Thought from Lore to Science* (New York: Dover, 1961), II, 470. The quotation from Mirabeau is in Ernst Oberfohren, *Die Idee der Universaloekonomie* (Jena: Gustav Fischer, 1915), p. 149, n. 1.

monized within a social framework? To the first question Smith
gave what I have called the Lockean answer, the "sameness of
human endowment." In the *Wealth of Nations*, the answer to
the second was the invisible hand. As suggested above, some
scholars feel that it was, as well, altruism or sympathy analyzed
by Smith as a motive in the *Theory of Moral Sentiments*. This
would be more satisfactory than a *deus ex machina*. The problem is that where there are conflicting desires in the individual,
the degree to which one holds the other in check cannot be referred to the "disinterested spectator," since through his interaction with the observed event any spectator loses his quality of
disinterestedness. To call it a matter of conscience is either to
refer it to divine revelation or to social sanction—which is what
we desire to explain.

One's knowledge of Smith is enhanced by knowing the
Theory of Moral Sentiments. What none of those who has
undertaken it has succeeded (at least to my satisfaction) in
doing is to present a consistent self-contained system made by
combining the *Wealth of Nations* with the *Theory of Moral
Sentiments*, in which conflicting interests in the individual are
resolved and to which there is a social analogue. Any solution
may, of course, be the philosopher's stone of the social sciences.[35] Smith's intellectual genealogy has been variously traced.
On the one hand, we read from Plato to the Cambridge
Platonists, from the Cambridge Platonists to Shaftesbury, from
Shaftesbury to Hutcheson.[36] On the other, we find not Plato

[35] But compare the attempts by those who take the opposed position, for
example, Becker and Barnes, *Social Thought*, II, 537ff.; Joseph Cropsey, *Polity
and Economy* (The Hague: Martinus Nijhoff, 1957); Overton H. Taylor, *A
History of Economic Thought* (New York: McGraw-Hill, 1960), Chap.
I–IV; see also Bryson, *Man and Society*, and A. W. Coats, "Adam Smith: The
Modern Reappraisal," *Renaissance and Modern Studies*, VI (1962), 41ff.
[36] See Taylor, *History of Economic Thought*. The phrase "uniformity
amidst variety" is Hutcheson's.

and Epicurus but rather their glossators—Cicero, Marcus Aurelius, Seneca, and Epictetus, as well as later writers, Grotius, Puffendorf, and Hutcheson. This is the tradition which, according to Macfie, was borne along by Smith, "but in a Scottish dress. It is optimistic, tolerant, always eager for social benefits between as well as within nations. . . . They [Hutcheson, Smith, Hume] were citizens of the world, and they behaved as such." [37] But Smith was of his time and under the Newtonian influence was clearly aware, along with Saint-Simon, Comte, and Fourier (if the anachronism be forgiven), that "the sciences search for basic units and entities which are not divisible in themselves," [38] which, once found, might be found to be subject to that "universal gravitation [which] began to play an even greater role than 'evolution' did seventy-five or a hundred years later." [39] Smith found the basic unit in the "sameness of human endowment," the social glue in the increasing returns to the division of labor, and the optimality in the harmonization, through no intention of their own, of voracious and conflicting appetites. His technique, at least in Book I, is also Newtonian, what is presently called that of static equilibrium. In accepting the hypothesis relating to the sameness of human endowment, Smith need not have accepted for all peoples any sameness of the natural resource endowment, and recognition of this is made explicitly by his followers, for example, Ricardo's doctrines of comparative advantage and his distinction between value and riches. But in accepting the fundamental sameness of men, Smith was necessarily compelled to find variety not only in resource endowment but in institutions. Thus, in prescribing

[37] A. L. Macfie, "The Scottish Tradition in Economic Thought," *Scottish Journal of Political Economy*, II (1955), 87.

[38] See Weisskopf, *Psychology of Economics.*

[39] Vladimir G. Simkhovitch, "Approaches to History: I," *Political Science Quarterly*, XLIV (1929), 505.

the removal of monopolies and barriers to international trade to Bengal and China, he must implicitly have regarded both the Chinese and Bengalese as capable of economic progress as were Scots and Englishmen.

Certainly the cosmopolitical liberalism that found its fountainhead in the *Wealth of Nations*, once the Malthusian bogey had been laid, was based on a belief in some fundamental identity amongst all men, at least in the economic sphere. Ample evidence for this is provided by Silberner from the writings of McCulloch, Senior, Cobden, Say, Bastiat, Rossi, and Chevalier, among others. Just as an example, from, of all people, that dour Scot, McCulloch:

It is to Political Economy that we owe an incontrovertible demonstration of these truths;—truths that are destined to exercise the most salutary influence on humanity—to convince mankind that it is for their interest to live in peace, to deal with each other on fair and liberal principles, and not to become the dupes of their own short-sighted avarice, or the willing instruments of the blind ambition or petty animosities of their ruler.[40]

But all these truths, be they in McCulloch or in Bastiat, were ultimately derived from the achieving of harmony through the free play of self-seeking by egoists, the irreducible social element, and by the equilibrium analogy with Newtonian mechanics.

Reason from strong cases and you are likely to have an argument, perhaps with a poet or a political economist. First, the poet, William Blake:

[40] Quoted by Edmund Silberner, *The Problem of War in Nineteenth Century Economic Thought*, trans. by Alexander H. Krappe (Princeton, N.J.: Princeton University Press, 1946), p. 59. This aspect of economic liberalism has been treated intensively. See, for example, in addition to the foregoing, Michael A. Heilperin, *Studies in Economic Nationalism* (Geneva: Droz, 1960), and Dean Russell, *Frédéric Bastiat* (Geneva: Kundig, 1959).

. . . how is this thing, this Newtonian Phantasm,
This Voltaire and Rousseau, this Hume and Gibbon and Boling-
broke,
This Natural Religion, this impossible absurdity.[41]

And again,

I turn my eyes to the Schools and Universities of Europe
And there behold the Loom of Locke, whose Woof rages dire,
Wash'd by the Water-wheels of Newton: black the cloth
In heavy wreathes folds over every Nation: cruel Works
Of many Wheels I view, wheel without wheel, with cogs tyrannic
Moving by compulsion each other . . .[42]

Among political economists who rejected the atomization and identification of all men as a basis for using the principle of universal gravitation in the mechanical analogy may be found such men as Bagehot and Ingram in England and, earlier in Germany, List, the historical school, and later Spann. Bagehot reasonably said: "Travellers fresh from the sight, and historians fresh from the study, of peculiar and various states of society, look with dislike and disbelief on a single set of abstract propositions which claim . . . to be applicable to all such societies." [43] And Silberner calls List "the most determined adversary of this cosmopolitan concept of economic liberalism." [44] Thus, List's emphasis on the national unit and on the need for restraint of trade in the form of protectionism might be taken as a denial of any universal concept of man and as an espousal of particularism. Yet this seems not the case. "Et la patrie et l'humanité" is List's motto. His own system of economy, List thinks, is des-

[41] "Milton," *Poetry and Prose of William Blake*, Geoffrey Keynes, ed. (London: Nonesuch Press, 1939), p. 429.

[42] "Jerusalem: I," *ibid.*, p. 449.

[43] Walker Bagehot, *Economic Studies* (London: Longmans, Green, 1880), p. 16.

[44] Silberner, *Problem of War*, p. 141.

tined to "conciliate the interests of the nation with those of mankind,"[45] whereas he felt that the liberalism of Smith and Quesnay, "with an exclusively cosmopolitan orientation . . . considers only mankind as a whole, the welfare of the entire species and nowhere the nation and its welfare."[46]

The bellettrists are not known for their economic rigor, but their cries of indignation at the evils wrought under the economic system of their time gave their writings a great popular importance. Among them might be mentioned Coleridge, who longed for what he felt had been the medieval hierarchy of responsibility, Carlyle, Ruskin, Kingsley, and Dickens. Each one of them was deeply worried about what they considered an apologetic for that evil to which all others may be reduced, "the failure to check that something in man which is reaching out for more and ever for more."[47] This, not theory but Manchester, Liverpool, and Birmingham.

We may say that Jevons and the Austrians were concerned with the question of historical and geographical variety in man as opposed to universal uniformity in the celebrated *Methodenstreit* with the German historical school. Jevons and the Austrians asserted that there are some economic decisions, for example, the allocation of one's time between labor and leisure, which have to be made by all men and they queried how such decisions ought to be made *logically*, to the point, for example, where the pain of an additional hour of labor was exactly equal to the gain obtained through that hour of labor. The latter were more concerned with the question of not how logically, but rather how historically men have in fact reached decisions of this nature.

[45] *Ibid.*, p. 143.   [46] *Ibid.*

[47] Irving Babbit, *Rousseau and Romanticism* (New York: Meridian Books, 1957, first published 1919), p. 157.

Surely the classical statement of the anti–Newton-cum-Locke position in economics is to be found in the writings of Othmar Spann, who uses the word "universalism" to describe his approach. In his preface to the sixteenth edition of *The History of Economics*, he traces his pedigree:

A red thread runs through economic teaching from Adam Mueller to the new historical school; . . . the names of Adam Mueller, Fichte, Baader, Baron vom Stein, List, Thuenen, Roscher, Hildebrand, Knies, Bernhardi, Schmoller—and even those of Carlyle, Ruskin, and Carey—form, as it were, a single line of descent; . . . they incarnate a universalist-organic and idealistic doctrine contrasting with the atomist-individualist and materialist doctrine of Smith, Ricardo, Say, Rau, Menger, and Jevons.[48]

The crux of the contention as to the meaning of the Fichte-List-Spann position is probably clearer not in their ideas about the internal reticulation of the nation, the appropriate economic unit, but rather in the geographical delineation of that "natural unit." I daresay List's argument awoke anxieties among the citizens of Holland, Denmark, Switzerland, and non-German middle Europe, since he felt that Germany's natural boundaries included all those countries. List may not have been guilty of demanding the more and ever for more, but he did ask what his neighbors would have thought far too much.

Marx, regarding the individual as the product of the mode of production in any economic structure, saw men's behavior as tropistically determined as did any utilitarian. They gravitated

---

[48] Immediately before, however, he had accused the Schmollerian school of falling away towards positivism. Othmar Spann, *The History of Economics* (New York: Norton, 1930, first German edition about 1911). For a wittily unsympathetic treatment of Fichte, see Alexander Gray, *The Socialist Tradition* (London: Longmans, Green, 1947), Chap. IV (e). A brief account of Mueller's work is contained in Eric Roll, *A History of Economic Thought* (Englewood Cliffs, N.J.: Prentice-Hall, 1956), pp. 212ff.

universally, the capitalist impelled by the desire to exploit, the proletariat impelled by hunger to be exploited. Marx was perhaps the first economist to show rigorously the equilibrium condition for the stationary state and then oppose to it the force, desire for accumulation, which dynamically disturbs it. It is all too frequently misunderstood that, perhaps because of his sarcastic invective and indignation, at bottom Marx viewed all men as doing what they had to do. This is generally regarded as the essence of the Marxian view of man in society.

In the social production which men carry on they enter into definite relations that are indispensable and independent of their will; these relations of production correspond to a definite stage of development of their material powers of production. The sum total of these relations of production constitute the economic structure of society—the real foundation, on which rise legal and political superstructures and to which correspond definite forms of social consciousness. The mode of production in material life determines the general character of the social, political, and spiritual processes of life. It is not the consciousness of men that determines their existence, but, on the contrary, their social existence determines their consciousness. . . . The bourgeois relations of production are the last antagonistic form of the social process of production—antagonistic not in the sense of individual antagonism, but of one arising from conditions surrounding the life of individuals in society; at the same time the production forces developing in the womb of bourgeois society create the material conditions for the solution of that antagonism. This social formation constitutes therefore, the closing chapter of the prehistoric stage of human society.[49]

Hence, Marx was mechanistic in a way but did not believe in a universally uniform human nature subject to universally experienced laws analogous to the laws of natural science. Even where he felt there could be enunciated "constant drives," such

[49] Karl Marx, *A Contribution to the Critique of Political Economy* (Chicago: Kerr, 1904), pp. 11–13.

as hunger and the desire to reproduce (which do not differentiate the human from the nonhuman animal), they are modified as to form and direction by the economic institutions within which they must manifest themselves.[50]

Smith had felt that there is a universal harmony which reveals itself through the operation of competition or conflict. Marx, too, emphasized the conflict which characterizes precommunistic societies, and man's fate is the necessity of resolving these social antagonisms. This is the essential problem of the following section:

"But if you wish to see a state at fever heat . . . then we must enlarge our borders . . . and we shall want more. . . . And so we shall go to war, Glaucon. Shall we not?" [51] Thus did Socrates see man when appetite outweighs reason. Plato was much too balanced to regard the history of man as being really explosive. It rather traced a sine curve—democracy leading to tyranny and tyranny in turn to oligarchy, which degenerated into democracy once more. But the driving force for Plato was economic, the urge for more. As suggested, among the Scholastics the conception of social process was one of adjustment to a divinely ordained and unchanging natural order.[52] One can

---

[50] Studies of the Marx-Engels view of man in relation to nature and to society are Vernon Venable, *Human Nature: The Marxian View* (London: Dobson, 1946), and Erich Fromm, *Marx's Concept of Man* (New York: Ungar, 1961). The first draws heavily on the work of Engels. The second leans more on Marx and particularly on his *Economic and Philosophical Manuscripts*. In an unpublished paper, "Karl Marx on Secular Economic and Social Development: A Study in the Sociology of Nineteenth Century Social Science," Bert F. Hoselitz uses the same manuscripts to indicate that Marx has a generic concept of man, which underlay the distortions produced because of the contradictions of capitalism, at least nineteenth-century capitalism.

[51] Plato, "The Republic," *Dialogues of Plato*, trans. by Benjamin Jowett (New York: Pocket Books, 1951), pp. 247-48.

[52] Compare Schumpeter, *History of Economic Analysis*, p. 112.

only infer that this society, Christendom, would expand to world hegemony and then exist homeostatically until the millennium. Hopefully, the expansion would be by peaceful proselytization. If not, although canon law placed some limitations on violence, "killing, as well as dying for Christ, and killing in most terrible ways were accepted instruments of Church policy, sanctioned by the Papacy in the Crusades." [53]

The doctrines enunciated by the Mercantilists imply setting the national household in order, that is, autarchically, and then the achieving of increasing geographical domination. I think this generalization need not conflict with the comment that

Portuguese mercantilism in the sixteenth century was focused on the spice trade, while Spanish mercantilism from 1550 to 1650 centered in American bullion; and Dutch mercantilism in the seventeenth century was built around the carrying trade, while English mercantilism after 1660 was based on colonial commerce. . . . Perhaps what we have been calling mercantilism is merely economic nationalism.[54]

The liberal element grew stronger in mercantilism as the advantages of trade became more obvious or at least could be demonstrated. I add the proviso, since what *ought* to have required demonstration was the reason it was not. "Economic exchanges present so many advantages that even when political considerations might interfere, ways of perpetuating the exchanges are often developed." The anthropologist who made this observation points to the "peace of the market place as it has been practiced by American Indians, Islamic countries, and in pagan Africa, not to mention Europe in the middle ages." [55]

[53] Nef, *Cultural Foundations*, p. 72.
[54] Charles W. Cole, "The Heavy Hand of Hegel," in E. H. Earle, ed., *Nationalism and Internationalism* (New York: Columbia University Press, 1950), pp. 76, 78.
[55] Ralph Linton, "An Anthropological View of Economics," in A. Dudley

Smith has been criticized for regarding the propensity to barter and truck as natural or innate in man, yet archaeologists believe it "suggests commerce" that obsidian tools and decorative shells have been found in Iranian villages which were occupied some ten thousand years ago and to which these objects must have been brought from a considerable distance.[56] Yet Smith's "proof" that the division of labor is limited by the extent of the market was required as the rallying point for his liberal followers who sought to expand the market by all means and who frequently spoke of the peace-bringing implications of an expanding economic network. The logic of the matter lay, to repeat, in the sameness of human endowment and the universality of rational economic behavior. The *deus ex machina*, though invisible, was very much there.

In his still provocative *Physics and Politics* Bagehot marvels not at what interrupts progress but rather that it ever takes place. Thinkers of the Enlightenment too had to pose the question of why, with the same natural endowments, some cultures had advanced beyond others. Thus, Turgot, in an early discourse "On the Successive Advances of the Human Mind," put it:

Is not nature, then, everywhere the same? And if she guides all men to the same truths, if even their mistakes are akin, why do they not all advance at an equal pace along the path which is marked out for them? Doubtless the human mind contains everywhere the principle of the same progress; but nature, impartial in her gifts, has endowed certain minds with an abundance of talents which she has

---

Ward, ed., *Goals of Economic Life* (New York: Harper and Row, 1953), p. 328.

[56] Compare Robert J. Braidwood, "The Agricultural Revolution," *Scientific American*, CCIII, No. 3 (September, 1960), p. 144. Braidwood also suggests that the presence there of great number of fertility figurines hint at the "growing non-utilitarian dimensions of life." *Ibid.*, p. 143.

refused to others; circumstances develop these talents or leave them buried in obscurity; and to the infinite variety of these circumstances is due the inequality in the progress of nations.[57]

Turgot introduces differences in supposedly innate talents and because of "circumstances." Voltaire is less guarded:

It is clear that everything that belongs intimately to human nature is the same from one end of the universe to the other; that everything that depends on custom is different, and it is accidental if it remains the same. The empire of custom is much more vast than that of nature; it extends over manners and all usages, it sheds variety on the scene of the universe; nature sheds unity there; she establishes everywhere a small number of invariable principles.[58]

And Hume, in England: "Mankind are so much the same, in all times and places, that history informs us of nothing new or strange in this particular. Its chief use is only to discover the constant and universal principles of human nature."[59]

These cheerful and illuminated utterances are cited for having characterized the climate that produced systematic economics—Physiocracy in France and both Smith and, less systematic, Godwin in England. For it was into this optimism that economists, the Physiocrats and Smith, injected a note of caution that was to swell into a cry of alarm in Malthus' first *Essay on Population*—the realization that man's infinite capacity to increase his numbers could not continue indefinitely in a finite and bounded universe. But humanitarianism overcame logic in Smith, who was a comparatively early advocate of high or rising wages for the laboring class and looked to the following of liberal principles to improve the condition of man through-

---

[57] Quoted in Becker and Barnes, *Social Thought*, p. 471.
[58] Quoted in Ernst Cassirer, *The Philosophy of the Enlightenment* (Boston: Beacon Press, 1951), p. 219.
[59] Quoted in Carl L. Becker, *The Heavenly City of the Eighteenth-Century Philosophers* (New Haven: Yale University Press, 1932), p. 95.

out the world. Malthus, on the other hand, argued equally inconsistently against Ricardo that in backward countries an increase in wages would lead to a reduction in hours worked rather than to increased output.[60]

Not the least interesting aspect of economic thought in its aspiration to be scientific, its ability, that is, to generate propositions that are conceivably falsifiable, is how, when it has produced some such assertion as, "All swans are white," it has dealt with the discovery of black swans in Australia.[61] More precisely, how did economists handle universal propositions such as the Malthusian theory of population or the principle of diminishing marginal returns when circumstances, as in the New World, seemed to falsify them? Just as the logician, appalled by the black swan, could modify his generalization to, "All swans are either black or white," or to, "All swans are white except Australian swans," so could economists faced by the sight of relatively stable populations or the failure of the "law" of diminishing marginal returns. It is the modification that has usually been resorted to. Thus, Ricardo and Marshall, impatient with a Malthus for pointing to a Mexican Indian as a patent exception to or falsifier of their theories, retreated to such phrases as "in an old country," or "civilized," still implied in any static analysis, which abstracts from the very elements through which growth, that is, life, takes place. If there is any justification for

[60] For an account of the change for the better in the attitude toward the laboring class, see A. W. Coats, "Changing Attitudes to Labour in the Mid-Eighteenth Century," *Economic History Review*, Second Series, XI (1958), 35. He sees the change as owed to the "influence of the Enlightenment in the growth of sympathy for the oppressed classes, religion—particularly the decline of the Puritan conception of the shamefulness of poverty and the rise of Methodism, and literature—the emergence of romanticism and sentimentalism." *Ibid.*, p. 36.

[61] I paraphrase T. W. Hutchison, *The Significance and Basic Postulates of Economic Theory* (London: Macmillan, 1938), p. 25.

the belief that Malthus was looking for a set of principles more nearly universal than those of Ricardo, it is a pity that the exception from South America he adduces was not by Ricardo "shewn to be consistent with the principles that it was brought forward to overturn," rather than dismissed as "so little applicable to countries with a dense population abounding in capital, skill, commerce, and manufacturing industry, and with taste for every enjoyment that nature, art, or science will procure, that it does not require a serious examination." [62]

Believing either more or less in these principles of population and marginal returns, most of the English classical school believed that sooner or later every country would reach its resource limits and life could then proceed in dreary stationariness. The optimistic element lay in their belief that for any country the day of judgment could be indefinitely postponed by increasing trade with other countries, since this permitted further international division of labor and a corresponding increase in the world's wealth. Ultimately, one imagines, the entire globe would reach its resource limit, and each country, specializing in the production to which it was best suited, would then become stationary. The world, at all events, would have achieved the *maximum maximorum* of wealth. It does not, of course, necessarily follow that it would have achieved the same summit of happiness. This would imply at the very minimum the international equalization of factor rewards.[63]

The Listians advocated free trade, but only when the nations among which trade took place had each attained a certain level of economic development. List would seem to have been willing to settle for something under maximum world output for the

---

[62] David Ricardo, *The Works and Correspondence of David Ricardo,* ed. by Piero Sraffa (London: Cambridge University Press, 1951), II, 340–41.
[63] Compare the essay in this volume by David Felix.

sake of modifying its distribution. Both the Mills departed from classical liberalism in regarding the stationary state not as something to be dreaded as dull and as "shallows and misery," but as something to be desired—James Mill, because he felt that in the progress of civilization men's wants would change from the material, as these were modestly satisfied, to the intellectual or esthetic; John Stuart Mill, because he hoped that measures would be taken suddenly to increase the standard of living so much as to cause men to stop the increase in population while it was still small relative to its resource base. He further, somewhat illogically, seems to have felt that innovation in the production of wealth could continue in the stationary state. The younger Mill had an unshakable belief in progress, and far from feeling complacent about what light economic theory could shed on this problem, hoped for the development of a real science of civilization, or ethology.[64] At least one ethological law was stated by Mill, "that power passes more and more from individuals, and small knots of individuals, to masses; that the importance of the masses becomes constantly greater, that of individuals less." [65]

The German historical school were similarly evolutionary in their vision of the progress of civilization in their very conception of stages through which civilizations progress. They were not greatly successful, however, in producing any theory of just what happened within each stage to produce the next.[66] Marx, too, held a stage theory of progress, the stages being the

---

[64] Compare Joseph J. Spengler, "John Stuart Mill on Economic Development," in Bert F. Hoselitz, ed., *Theories of Economic Growth* (New York: Free Press of Glencoe, 1960), p. 115.

[65] Quoted in Oskar Alfred Kubitz, "Development of John Stuart Mill's System of Logic," *Illinois Studies in the Social Sciences*, XVIII (1932), 214.

[66] Compare Bert F. Hoselitz, "Theories of Stages of Economic Growth," in Hoselitz, *Theories of Economic Growth*, p. 238.

Asiatic, ancient, feudal, and bourgeois. He concerned himself almost wholly with the last, finding like the classical school the motivating force to be the insatiable desire of the capitalist for accumulation. But whereas the classical stationary state continued ceaselessly to churn away within the legal, political, and other institutions familiar to its architects, there is no such possibility in Marx's doctrines. Mankind will take up the problem of the solution of the contradictions of material life—the antagonism—and thus end the class struggle characteristic of the bourgeois society when the productive forces have been adequately developed and come in conflict with the existing relations of production. The change of the economic foundation brings forth the social revolution, and the collapse of all institutions with the superstructure coming tumbling down. One surmises, however, that he thought the conflict would cease and a communistic bliss succeed the dictatorship of the proletariat, under whose direction the state would wither away. Hence, paradoxically enough, if happiness for mankind is the absence of struggle, the Marxian tale has the same kind of ending as that of the utopian socialists.[67]

If the classicists, utopians, and scientific socialists reasoned that forces were at work that would bring the world to a halt, the marginal revolution succeeded in halting the world. This was necessary in order to isolate the economic forces that would in a timeless world establish an equilibrium set of prices and outputs. Such a theory of Robinson Crusoe choice is essentially a theory of individual psychology and not, as one critic said, even a social science. For unfortunately, "the object as a whole disappears in this process: it will no longer be recog-

[67] I have referred previously to a modification of, if not dissent from, this view. (See unpublished paper by Bert F. Hoselitz, "Karl Marx on Secular Economic and Social Development.")

nizable from the elements brought to light in the analysis." It would seem that economics from the end of the nineteenth century has become, in Mannheim's terminology "analytic" and is no longer "articulant," since the "latter while it also seeks to discover simple components of a complex whole, never loses sight of the way in which the parts combine to make a whole. The complex object always remains in sight during the process." [68] As in any art, much of contemporary theorizing that "looks like progress from the point of view of the mastery of a medium can also be viewed as decline into empty virtuosity." [69] To be sure, Keynes made one valiant effort to transcend the confines of the mechanical analogy, to write, as he said, a non-Euclidean economics, but he was quickly reinterpreted back into the fold. Further, the charge leveled by Boulding seems all too much justified that "the moral philosophers have argued too much as if we were already in a stationary state, and as if the problem of economic justice were mainly one of distributing a fixed product, rather than encouraging an increasing product." [70]

Keynes' explicit acknowledgment of his indebtedness to Malthus has been discussed by commentators without reference to the fundamental issue of the rejection of the Newtonian equilibrium analogy. Yet Darwin too found an inspiration in another aspect of Malthus, and there is little stationariness or equilibrium in Darwin. Perhaps the distinction should be drawn between the mechanical and the evolutionary analogues rather than, as some have done, between the mechanical and the

[68] Karl Mannheim, *Essays in the Sociology of Culture* (New York: Oxford University Press, 1956), p. 186.
[69] E. H. Gombrich, *Art and Illusion* (New York: Pantheon Books, 1960), p. 10.
[70] Kenneth Boulding, "Economic Progress as a Goal of Economic Life," in Ward, *Goals of Economic Life*, p. 60.

biological-ecological. There would, I fear, be little to add. The intellectual ferment occasioned by the popularization of Darwinism left little impression on economics. Although Marshall acknowledges the influence of Spencer, it remains pretty much in the preface; and it is the other principle, that of Newtonian continuity, which pervades the unbelievably influential *Principles of Economics*. Wedded as he was to the mechanical analogy, the principle of universal gravitation, Marshall found Leibniz' motto, *Natura non facit saltum*, far too congenial to risk a flirtation with Darwinian sports. Peirce, the first American pragmatist, accepts without demur the Darwinian and Lamarckian theories and the cataclysmic evolutionary theory of Clarence King.[71] The intellectual forebears of American Institutionalism or holistic economics have been listed as Spencer, Darwin, Marx, and Hegel in Europe and Dewey, James, and Peirce in the United States. [72] But, however one may dislike the methodological stance of Robbins, it is probably true that at the time he wrote in 1932, the "great multiplication of this sort of thing under the name of Institutionalism, 'Quantitative Economics,' 'Dynamic Economics,' and what not . . . have been doomed to futility from the outset and might just as well never have been undertaken." [73]

Plato examined the origin and nature of the state as a part of his inquiry into the meaning of justice. He disliked equally democracy and commercial activity because they both made it difficult to apprehend the divine equilibrium of universals— democracy as the seedbed of tyranny and the businessmen in

[71] For example, *Values in a Universe of Chance* (New York: Doubleday Anchor Books, 1958), pp. 148ff.

[72] Allen Gruchy, *Modern Economic Thought* (Englewood Cliffs, N.J.: Prentice-Hall, 1947), p. 15.

[73] Robbins, *Essay on Economic Science*, p. 112.

their conscious excitation of the public appetite for more and ever for more.[74] The Schoolmen, too, were concerned with justice within an ordered and essentially stationary society. The Mercantilists, at least to the extent to which the earlier ones correctly apprehended the stagnancy of the European economy, were probably right in their feeling that "the more there is for me, the less there is for you." But the expansion of the European economy permitted the development of the idea that there might be more for everybody. With the development of the natural sciences an attempt was made to look for permanencies in human as well as nonhuman nature, and it seemed perfectly natural to utilize the techniques that had been so successful in the natural sciences. But Smith and his followers, being primarily interested in the increase of wealth, seem to have believed that they had first to solve the problem of evaluation, that is, pricing, which was, in fact, incidental to the more important inquiry. But in England, Austria, and the United States it nudged out entirely the problem for whose solution it was meant to be only an instrument. Up to now we have no satisfactory theory of relative prices in a disequilibrium economy, be it growing or declining. Perhaps we do not need one. However useful the static marginal analysis might be in providing categories for analyzing those economies whose characteristics or whose institutions correspond within reasonable limits to its assumptions, its poverty in helping us to think about the development of economies which have not developed in the West

[74] Compare Overton H. Taylor, "Philosophies and Economic Theories in Modern Occidental Culture," in F. S. C. Northrop, ed., *Ideological Differences and World Order* (New Haven: Yale University Press, 1949), pp. 147–49. For a brilliant analysis of Plato's fears as they were borne out in Petronian Rome, see Erich Auerbach, *Mimesis* (New York: Doubleday Anchor Books, 1957), Chap. 2.

European industrial tradition has become distressingly apparent, especially since the end of World War II and the emergence of nation after nation as political entities that desire growth.

Indications are there that economists of this time are, in fact, groping for some theory of uniformity amidst variety in the matter of economic development. Samuelson lists six categories of economic inquiry, the static and stationary, the static and historical, the dynamic and causal (nonhistorical), the dynamic and historical, the stochastical and nonhistorical, and the stochastical and historical; [75] and Haavelmo has cautiously set out a theory of economic evolution sufficiently general to embrace the growth or decline of virtually any economy that is exposed to the civilized world. He incorporates what he calls the interregional contagion of education and know-how as well as the effects of strategies of "grabbing," protection, and cooperation, not to mention the incalculable number of chance events that could never be accounted for one by one. As he is the first to say, such a theory contains many as yet unsolved problems of measurement. It is still a valiant attempt to find some uniformity amid the variety that characterizes the economic condition of mankind that he observes in his opening sentence.[76]

Is it possible, even at the risk of compounding generalizations all equally suspect, to draw any conclusions about the concept of mankind in the history of economic thought? Several might be ventured.

While the Physiocrats may seldom have raised their eyes

---

[75] Paul Anthony Samuelson, *Foundations of Economic Analysis* (Cambridge, Mass.: Harvard University Press, 1953), pp. 315–16.

[76] T. Haavelmo, *A Study in the Theory of Economic Evolution* (Amsterdam: North-Holland, 1954).

beyond the boundaries of France, they and, as I have shown, their philosopher contemporaries knew that the world was there and more especially that an increasing application of the rapidly developing natural sciences was making it smaller and smaller. They recognized the fact as well of increasing international communication and, in particular, trade. In their efforts to reason about Frenchmen in the eighteenth century in a scientific manner, in order to detect permanencies in human nature, they had necessarily to emerge with some conclusions about all men; this turns out to have been the hypothesis that all men are basically the same and can be educated to follow the dictates of reason and to progress materially, emotionally, and intellectually. This is true also of Smith.[77] When he said that "equal quantities of labour, at all times and places, may be said to be of equal value to the labourer," I believe he meant just that. Somewhat acidly a commentator observed, "Presumably he means that an aching back to Adam, after his expulsion from the garden of Eden, is equivalent to the aching back of a navvy taking up Regent Street." [78] And why not? The pleasure-pain calculus is one way of expressing the fact that all men are alike in at least one set of responses to their environments.

Most economists today would deny the possibility of making interpersonal comparisons of utility. We make such comparisons all the time. We are also given to looking down on utilitarianism as a philosophy, yet scratch an economist and find a Benthamite. And this is not so bad. Utilitarianism, even if re-

[77] I have profited considerably from an article by Rudolph C. Blitz, "Some Classical Economists and Their Views on Education," published in Spanish in *Economía* (Quarterly Journal of the Faculty of Economic Sciences of the University of Chile), No. 72–73 (1961), and privately circulated in English translation.
[78] Alexander Gray, *The Development of Economic Doctrine* (London: Longmans, Green, 1931), p. 130.

garded as a Sorelian myth, was not ineffective. Auden is speaking of deist theologians, but it is equally applicable to economists and utilitarians of the Enlightenment and early nineteenth century, when he says

It is difficult for us to be quite fair . . . unless we remember the actual horrors of persecution, witch-hunting, and provincial superstition from which they were trying to deliver mankind. Further, reaction of the Romantics against them is a proof that up to a point they had succeeded. If the final result of their labors was a desert, they had at least drained some very putrid marshes.[79]

From the point of view of all mankind, the Enlightenment produced an equally hopeful theory of social evolution, be it in Smith or, much more importantly, in the German historical school, the various-stage theories of economic and social development. Thus, if one society has been able to move from savage to pastoral, from pastoral to agricultural, and from agricultural to agricultural and manufacturing, might not any society be equally expected to evolve? Even the capitalists and proletariat of Marx, bound in *Inferno* like Paolo and Francesca, are yet destined to emerge into *Paradiso*.

I am by no means insensible of the fact that the humanitarian and essentially sanguine ideas outlined above are unacceptable to those who consider economics as a theodicy and the whole Enlightenment, a *Weltanschauung* I have stressed in the belief that its ideas still pervade economic theory if nothing else, as a period of

exploded values . . . [of] uncritical faith in the virtues of formal

---

[79] He continues: "A transcendent God of Nature of the Newtonian type can be related to the human reason by his intelligibility, and to matter by his power to command exact obedience; the trouble begins when the question is raised of his relation to the human heart, which can and does suffer, and to the human will, which can and does disobey." W. H. Auden, *The Enchafèd Flood* (New York: Random House, 1950), pp. 51–52.

education . . . [of] fallacious belief that democracy is the antithesis of autocracy, rather than its seed-bed . . . [of] rationalist conviction that human passions and social antagonisms can be harmonized by neat philosophic or political formulae.[80]

It is further denigrated as the "cult of a leisurely moneyed middle class" [81] and that economic theory which is a part of or at least heir to the Enlightenment as, in fact, "an apologetic of a certain social order." [82] Economics is then a rationalization of how it is that this is the best of all possible worlds.

Of course, this is not the best of all possible worlds. No economist in his right mind would claim that it is. Nor would many economists feel that anyone had succeeded in showing that "human passions and antagonisms can be harmonized by neat philosophic or political formulae." The cupola on allocation theory is called welfare economics, of which it has quite wittily been said,

If Hobson's welfare economics left the scientific economics out, the form of theory which now bears the name can without real unfairness be described as welfare economics with the welfare left out, in a remarkably resolute attempt to meet the real or supposed requirements of economic science.[83]

Having admitted that one cannot justifiably speak of the "advance of philosophy from Plato to Hegel" or "of the advance of poetry from Homer to Shakespeare," Hutchison still feels that one can speak of the "advance of biology from Aristotle to Mendel or even of economics from Petty to Mar-

[80] Geoffrey Barraclough, *History in a Changing World* (Oxford: Basil Blackwell, 1955), p. 165.

[81] *Ibid.*, p. 163.

[82] Maurice Dobb, *An Introduction to Economics* (London: Gollancz, 1932), p. 138.

[83] John Maurice Clark, "Aims of Economic Life as Seen by Economists," in Ward, *Goals of Economic Life,* p. 40.

shall." [84] While it is true that Petty reasoned from an organismic analogy and Marshall from the mechanical, I detect little progress in the detection of uniformity amid variety in any global aspect.[85]

To end on a somewhat more hopeful note, economists, except for the most bellicose of the Mercantilists, like most sensible men, have realized that in an "increasing system" trade is likely to be more binding than divisive to men trading. And this is true both of internal and external economic relations. It was a river nymph who bore Phoroneus, who according to Greek myth not only was the first to use the fire Prometheus had stolen from heaven but also founded the first market town.

[84] Hutchison, *Significance of Economic Theory*, pp. 6–7.
[85] My colleague, J. G. Cummins, thinks this comment applies less to Marshall himself than to his codifiers. I agree.

II

KENNETH E. BOULDING

The Concept of World Interest

ONE OF THE CONSEQUENCES of the Space Age is that earth itself has begun to look like a spaceship, even in the popular imagination. In the scientific imagination, of course, this happened many centuries ago with the final realization of the global nature of the earth. We think of the earth easily, therefore, as a succession of spheres—a lithosphere, an atmosphere, a troposphere, a biosphere, and so on. It is a simple extension of this notion to think of the "econosphere" as the whole web of economic relations extending over the globe. This is pretty thin in Antarctica, though it now exists there, and very dense in New York; but there is now hardly any point at which it does not exist. The elements of the econosphere are the persons of the human population of the earth in their economic aspects, connected by an intricate web of exchange, payments, transfers, and organizational roles and communications. The notion of the econosphere is essential to the concept of mankind, although it does not encompass all the relationships of what might be called the "homosphere," the sphere of mankind in all its relationships.

When we look at the econosphere as a whole, one of the first questions which comes to mind is whether there is any concept of the "world interest" to correspond to the national interest in the case of the national economy. The economist uses the term "national interest" in a somewhat different sense from that of the political scientist. The political scientist thinks of the national interest in strictly relative terms—in terms, that is, of security or of the military or political strength of one country relative to that of another. In the political science sense, therefore, the concept of national interest cannot be generalized to a world political interest unless we define it in terms of the stability of some future world government and its ability to cope with world problems. The economic concept of the national interest, however, is easily generalizable to the world as a whole. It is in fact, a concept of "group interest," or "public interest," which is contrasted with "private interest" but which is not closely connected with the organizational boundaries of the nation-state. Thus, we can take any arbitrary collection of people, say, all the people named Smith, and contrast two different states of their economic condition, A and B. A particular X. Y. Smith might be better off in A than in B, but Smiths as a whole might be better off in B than in A; there would then be a conflict between the "private interest" of X. Y. Smith and the "public interest" of Smiths as a whole. This conflict only becomes visible and operational, of course, when the group is organized to take action. The economic conflict, however, between older and younger members of a trade union over seniority is not essentially different from that between doctors and patients under a national medical plan or between farmers and nonfarmers under a national agricultural policy. The concept, therefore, of the public or group interest as opposed to the private or personal interest is easily generalizable to the world economy. We can easily postulate two states of the world economy, A and B, in which one person, or one group is better off in A than in B, whereas the world as a whole is better off in B than in A.

It must be admitted, however, that there are a great many conceptual difficulties in the definition and measurement of the national interest that also apply to the concept of the world economic interest. For either the world or a national economy we can define a "state" of the economy, S_1, as consisting of all the relevant economic variables and magnitudes existing in a moment of time; similarly, S_2 is the state of the economy at a subsequent moment. These states are multidimensional and consist, indeed, of a very large number of different quantities, such as prices, incomes, and capital stocks. The measurement of the world economic interest depends on our ability to find some index of linear scale by an operation on the innumerable magnitudes of S_1 and S_2, so that we can say, with some degree of certainty, that S_2 is larger or smaller than S_1 along the line that measures the world interest. The most obvious candidate for this measure is, of course, the world per capita income in real terms. If this is increasing steadily, we have some confidence that the world as a whole is getting better off. If it is decreasing the world is getting worse off. The calculation of per capita real income, however, whether for the world as a whole or for any segment of it, presents substantial conceptional and statistical difficulties. An unequivocal measure of real income, for instance, is impossible if there are changes in relative prices—as, indeed, there always are. In a very heterogeneous economy, as a world economy undoubtedly is, an additional difficulty arises that prices which are relevant in one part of the economy may not be relevant in another part. Hence, even if we have figures for the consumption by households of all commodities, it is impossible to reduce this heterogeneous aggregate to a single number, for example, a value in constant dollars, without a good many arbitrary assumptions. In practice we may have to content ourselves with a figure that is significant for substantial changes but not significant for small changes. There is hardly any aggregate statistic or index, even in the most developed economy, that attempts to measure some quantity in real terms, that is, in monetary units of constant purchasing power, in which, say, a 1 percent change in the index can assure us even of the direction of the change in the quantity we are trying to measure. If, however, we have a 10 percent change in the index, we are pretty sure that something has happened in the direction which the index indicates.

Even if the statistical difficulties involved in the computation of an index of world per capita real income could be overcome, there are other conceptual defects in this measure which indicate that it should be used only with the greatest of caution. It might well be, for example, that world per capita real income would be increasing at a time when the distribution of this income is growing more and more unequal. Some parts of the world might actually be getting somewhat poorer, while other parts of the world are getting much richer. This, indeed, is what may be happening today. Under these circumstances we might have some doubts that the world economic interest is being advanced. I know of no statistical measure that takes account of this possibility, although I see no reason why one should not be devised. Inequality itself is a multidimensional concept and is hard to reduce to a single scalar magnitude without many arbitrary assumptions. There are, however, statistical measures— such as, for example, the area between the Lorenz curve of cumulative distribution and the 45-degree line of equal distribution—that are generally recognized. An index that consisted of per capita income divided by some index of inequality, suitably weighted, would at least be an interesting measure. The main difficulty seems to be that there are no logical reasons to employ one set of weights rather than another. That is, we could weight inequality either lightly or heavily, depending on our attitude toward it, and the measure might well turn out different, depending on which way we did it. This, however, is not a mere statistical difficulty; it is a recognition of the fact that the very concept of the world economic interest itself of necessity involves some kind of value system, and it is these value systems that will determine the weights in the index. It is perfectly possible, therefore, for exactly the same set of circumstances to result in a rise in the index of the world economic interest under one set of values and weights and a fall under another set of values and weights. We might, for instance, have a situation in which per capita real income rose but inequality increased somewhat. If we weight inequality lightly, the index of the world economic interest will show a rise; if we weight it heavily, it will show a fall, and there is no way in sheer logic of resolving this dilemma.

The dependence of the measurement of the world economic interest on the value systems employed shows up also in consideration of the commodity structure of real income. If our measure of the world per capita real income increased, but the increase consisted mostly of alcohol, drugs, prostitution, and armaments, we might again feel dubious about the accuracy of per capita real income as a measure of the world economic interest. The economic statistician himself tries to be neutral in regard to the nature of the commodity mix; anything that people want and are prepared to pay a price for is all right with him. A moralist, however, might feel different and might want to give another set of price weights. The price weights tend to be arbitrary enough anyway, especially on a world scale, so that a moralist's claim to construct his own index cannot simply be dismissed. In the last analysis the statistician is almost forced to say, "Choose your weights, and I will calculate your index."

These difficulties of measurement reflect an even more fundamental conceptual difficulty that is involved in the structural aspect of the world economic interest. In the case of a single, well-integrated nation such as the United States, if per capita real income is increasing, we have some confidence that this is an aspect and a measure of a growing structure towards which all the parts make some contribution, although even in this case we may have doubts about the sharecropper and the hillbilly. Suppose now, to take an extreme case on the other side, the world was divided into two parts that had no intercourse of any kind with one another, and per capita real income in the one was increasing, while in the other it remained stationary. A statistical measure would then give us an increase in the world per capita real income that would mean very little, since it would not represent any general increase in the total structure. This is a structural aspect of the statistical difficulty encountered previously regarding the modification of the index by some measure of the distribution of income. If, indeed, we had two halves of the world that had no economic connection between them, then we would not have an econosphere, and the concept of world economic interest would be quite inapplicable. Any measure of the world economic interest would then be a mere empty statistic, since it would not correspond to any structural reality.

The actual state of the world is somewhere between the two extremes of an integrated econosphere, on the one hand, and a world of independent and unrelated segments on the other. The world is divided into two economic halves, the socialist camp on the one side and the "free world" on the other. These two halves are by no means completely isolated, and there are a good many economic and other relationships between them, but the relationships between them are much less significant than the internal relationships within each half; and in some degree it may be said that each half of the economic world is pursuing a line of development that is largely separated from that of the other half. Even within each half of the world economy there are important divisions. Within the socialist camp, for example, the Russian economy is a fairly well-integrated structure, but it is not integrated with the Chinese economy at all and is only partially integrated with the national economies of the socialist countries of Eastern Europe. Even before the present split, trade between Russia and China was marginal though not insignificant; aid was negligible, as was foreign investment. Quantitatively, the Russian contribution to the Chinese economy has amounted to about 1 cent per Chinese per ten years, and even the qualitative contributions in terms of technical personnel have now largely ceased. The course of the Chinese economy, therefore, can be considered as relatively independent of the course of the Russian economy, even though the two countries are within the same ideological camp. The nonsocialist world is not quite so sharply divided, but even here the economies of the developed countries are pretty well integrated, whereas in the poor countries of the tropical belt a large majority of the population still continue to live in a subsistence or traditional economy that is not closely related to the developed world economy.

At the moment, therefore, the econosphere is not a closely integrated network. It consists of a number of different networks, somewhat tenuously connected; and it is, therefore, at least arguable that the fragmented structure of the world economy does not yet permit a valid concept of a world economic interest. I would argue strongly, however, against this position. Even where the direct economic connections and relationships may be somewhat tenuous, the indirect relationships as expressed through the world communications structure and the structure of political power are of great importance. Two thousand years ago we might well have argued that what happened in Mexico was totally irrelevant to what happened in the Roman Empire, for these two centers of civilization pursued completely independent courses, and neither of them could affect the other in the slightest. It was almost as if they existed on different planets. Today, however, in spite of the tenuous nature of the actual economic relations between, say, China and the rest of the world, what happens to the Chinese economy is of profound importance to the rest of the world, even though the actual trade relations may be small. The future economic system, indeed, of a large part of the world may depend on the success or failure of the present Chinese economy. In this sense, the Chinese economy is very much a part of the world economic interest. An economic decline in China would certainly have an effect on the world per capita real income, and it would also have a marked effect on its distribution. A decline in the index of the world economic interest, which might follow from an economic collapse in China, would therefore certainly represent a world reality. If we wish to refine our index of the world economic interest, we might wish to weight different parts of the world according to their participation in world trade. A change in an isolated part of the world would not then be weighted heavily in the total index. Trade, however, is an inadequate measure of the total connectedness of one part of the world with another, especially in this age of rapid communications, and a refinement that rested solely on the volume of trade might do more harm than good.

The question may be raised at this point as to whether the concept of a world economic interest implies ideological homogeneity. Can we have a world economy that is half socialist and half capitalist and still retain a meaningful concept of the world interest? This is, of course, merely an aspect of the problem of homogeneity we have discussed above. In so far as the ideological differences insulate one part of the world from another, then, as we have seen, they may have some impact on the validity of the concept of a world economic interest. I would argue, however, that the ideological difference itself is not particularly relevant to this concept. The measure of per capita real income, weighted by some value system, is valid as a measure of the world economic interest no matter whether the world as a whole or in part is socialist or capitalist. People are better off if they have more to eat and to wear, better houses to live in, more channels of information, and more opportunity for variety of experience, no matter whether they live in a socialist or a capitalist economy. We may, of course, wish to introduce a discounting factor for certain intangible values, depending on our own value system. In a free democratic society we will want to subtract something from the per capita income of people in socialist countries to represent the loss of political freedom and the burden of an arbitrary price system. People in the socialist camp might well wish to make similar discountings for those of us who have put up with television commercials and a venal and vulgar press, for one man's freedom is another man's license. These modifications, however, do not destroy the basic concept, and one suspects that quantitatively they are likely to be small. No matter whether we use a "Western" or an "Eastern" system of weights, the Chinese and the Indians will measure as "poor" compared with either the Russians or the Americans, and the system that they live under is largely irrelevant to this proposition.

Another fact of great importance in assessing the validity of the concept of a world economic interest lies in the diverse nature of economic relationships in themselves. The network of economic relationships that encompasses the globe and that constitutes the econosphere is in large measure made up of two different kinds of "string"; that is, between any two individuals or organizations there are two possible kinds of economic relationship. One is the exchange relationship, which is a two-way relationship in which some exchangeable goes from A to B and another exchangeable in return from B to A. The "price," or exchange ratio, is, of course, the ratio of the quantities of the two things exchanged. A very large number of economic relationships fall into this category, such as the ordinary purchase and sale of commodities, the purchase and sale of labor for a wage or salary, and even, in the long run, the exchange of present money for future money in financial markets and the exchange of one currency for another in the foreign exchange market.

The exchange relationship, however, even though it is the main subject of economic science, does not exhaust the economic relationship. The second type is the transfer, or "grants," relationship, the one-way relationship in which something goes, let us say, from A to B but nothing goes from B to A. The unsolicited and unrequited gift is the best example of a transfer. Taxes and subsidies are also frequently regarded as transfers, even though in the case of taxes there may be a quasi-exchange in the sense that the tax authority provides certain services in return for the taxes collected. Even exchanges in financial markets, such as loans and the sale or purchase of stocks, look something like transfers in the short run, since it is only in the long run that the exchange is consummated. Interest payments likewise look something like transfers, since there is no obvious physical commodity or service that the owners of interest-bearing investments give for the interest received. In the national accounts, indeed, interest is regarded as a transfer payment, even though in the long run it should clearly be regarded as part of the exchange economy. This distinction between exchanges and transfers, therefore, is not always clear; nevertheless, it is extremely important, and indeed the nature of the economic system cannot be understood without it.

We can, then, roughly divide the relationships of the econosphere into what might be called the "exchange economy" and the "grants economy." From the point of view of the world economic interest, questions arise in both these sections. Even within the confines of the exchange economy it is legitimate to ask whether there may be conflict between the private or the sectional economic interest and the world economic interest. We can, for example, ask ourselves whether the exchange network results in "exploitation," in the sense that some people have terms of trade that are too good—that is, they get too much for what they give out—and others have terms of trade that are too poor—that is, they get too little for what they give out. Classical or neoclassical price theory would argue with a good deal of cogency that in an economy which is technologically relatively stationary and in which there is a competitive market for most commodities and no artificial hindrances to the mobility of capital and labor, whatever exploitation may result from the price system and the exchange network is, in fact, self-correcting. If the price system gives some people too small a return for what they are producing, they will simply stop producing it and transfer their resources to some more profitable occupation. This will automatically raise the prices that are too low and lower the prices that are too high. We can reasonably assume, therefore, that in long-run equilibrium the exchange system will not result in any exploitation, even though it may still result in poverty for some and relative affluence for others, depending on their natural endowments. In a highly dynamic economy, however, these conclusions of equilibrium theory are less secure. In a dynamic economy, which is advancing technologically, the structure of the economy—that is, the proportion of resources devoted to different occupations—constantly changes, usually in one direction.

Thus, in the course of the last two hundred years in the developed part of the world the proportion of resources devoted to agriculture and to most raw material production or extraction has continually declined, whereas the proportion devoted to manufacturing and to services has increased. With the advent of automation, indeed, it is likely that the proportion devoted to manufacturing is now going to suffer a rapid decline. Under these circumstances, those people or those areas which are committed to the declining industries are likely to find themselves constantly depressed by unfavorable terms of trade unless they are unusually mobile; and it is a peculiar irony that it is the very virtue (in the form of rapid technological advance) of these occupations that contributes to the unfavorable terms on which they must sell their products.

The only exception to this would be where the resources of a declining industry anticipated its decline and got out of it before unfavorable terms of trade set in. This, however, is most unusual and requires a degree of foresight that is almost unattainable. Normally it takes an actual squeeze before people will leave a declining industry, and it is almost impossible to force resources out of a declining industry fast enough to prevent a worsening of its terms of trade. A possible exception is where a continued slow squeeze suddenly results in a "fashion" for quitting the industry, and a very sudden outward movement of resources may take place that may even go too far and lead to an industry so small that its terms of trade turn unusually favorable. I cannot think, however, of a single example of this happening with the dubious exception of the "hog cycle." The declining state is, as Smith said, miserable.

A good case can be made, therefore, that the dynamics of the price system operate to create a certain injustice, although the problem of how to correct this injustice without preventing the necessary readjustment in the proportion of resources engaged in different occupations presents one of the most difficult problems in economic policy. Even though, therefore, objective criteria in regard to exploitation and the price system are extremely hard to come by, the problem cannot be dismissed out of hand, and one hopes that it is not intrinsically insoluble. Just as in the national economy, therefore, we find attempts made to adjust the exchange relationships and the terms of trade, of agriculture, for example, it is likely that we would find similar attempts to manipulate the price system in favor of politically important disadvantaged groups and regions if we had a politically integrated world.

Whereas the concept of a world economic interest might be expected to modify the exchange economy, it would dominate the grants economy, for the grants economy cannot be explained at all without some concept of community of interest. If *A* gives *B* something without expecting anything in return, the inference must be drawn that *B* is "part" of *A* or that *A* and *B* together are both parts of a larger system of interests and organizations. In the family, for instance, the parent sacrifices for the children because he identifies with the child and because the family is an intimate community that transcends the interests of the individuals within it. It is true, of course, that there are important elements of exchange in the family relationship.

The parent, for instance, may support the child in infancy in the hope or expectation that the child will support the parent in the parent's old age. The support of the child then becomes simply the first part of a deferred exchange. It is impossible, however, to explain family relationships solely on these grounds; and in so far as a grants economy exists distinguishable from the exchange economy, we must postulate some sense of community or identity as between the grantor and the grantee. In the case of philanthropy, even though there may here also be a hidden exchange in the sense that the donor may receive moral gratification or even social approval in return for his gift, there always seems to be a residuum that has to be explained by a sense of community between the donor and the recipient. This may be no more than pity, which arises out of empathy—"Your misery makes me feel miserable; therefore, I must relieve your misery in order to relieve my own"—or it may be empathy with the achievements of the recipient, as in the case of research grants or the relation of the patron to the artist.

This sense of community is formalized and institutionalized in the domestic economic policy of the national state. All developed national states set up some level of poverty below which they do not allow their citizens to fall. Here again some things that look like transfers may, in fact, be exchanges, like social security or even veterans' benefits, which may be thought of as deferred payments for services rendered in the past; but here again there is a residuum of "support" that is not part of the exchange economy and can be explained only by the sense of community which all citizens of one nation have with one another.[1]

This sense of community is now slowly being extended from

---

[1] In the language of technical economic theory, what this means is that the utility or economic welfare index of one person is a function not only of his own economic condition but of the economic condition of others.

the national to the world arena. This begins, as it did also in the national state, with the appeal to pity or to patronage. The sensitive burgher of Europe or America responded to the appeals for the relief of famine in China or for the salvation of the heathen long before there was even the remotest organization of the world economic community—as, indeed, in the Middle Ages the relief of all the poor depended on private charity. We are now in an intermediate stage, where the responsibility of the rich countries for the development of the poor is rather generally acknowledged and where modest and wholly inadequate sums are granted for this purpose in foreign aid. An interesting case is that of the relationship of an imperial country to its colonies or its former colonies and dependencies or of a great power to its satellites or those countries which it regards as peculiarly in its sphere of interest. British grants for colonial development, the similar and even more extensive grants of the French to their colonial dependencies, and the American Alliance for Progress with the Latin American countries are cases in point of what might be called a regional economic interest. All these rest on some sense of historic community. These efforts, however, are sporadic and incomplete, and at the moment there is really no world grants economy organized on a world interest. It is at this point that the development of a sense of world community, especially as institutionalized in world political institutions, would make the greatest impact on the world economy. A world grants system organized on a world interest would look very different from a grants system organized on a national interest, and it would be likely to involve a much larger volume of grants than now obtains from the rich countries to the poor. The change to a genuinely world interest economy would be much more dramatic, therefore, in the grants system than it would be in the exchange system.

When we look at the total dynamics of the world economy,

a number of other points arise also at which there may be a considerable difference in a world economy organized along the lines of world interest. An interesting problem in this connection, for instance, is that of population control and the control of migration. Does the world interest, for instance, require unrestricted migration among all parts of the world? A case can easily be made out in dynamic terms that it does not, even under conditions of a strong sense of world community. A region that does not control its own population has no right to export poverty to other regions by exporting its population continuously to them. In the static model we might agree that world population should be distributed in such a way that nobody has a special advantage from his location. Thus, we would expect a movement towards some kind of long-run equilibrium in which the world population would be distributed among the various geographic regions in such a way that no region was either over- or underpopulated relative to the resources that it enjoyed. Unrestricted migration, however, for the reason suggested above, may not be the best way of achieving this ideal in the absence of any general population control. When we look at the broader problems of cultural and political integration, however, we may feel that unrestricted migration is necessary. Certainly the establishment of a national state has almost universally resulted in eventual freedom of migration within it. In the United States, for instance, the rural South and the Appalachian backwoods have to some extent been allowed to export part of their poverty to the northern cities.

A difficult problem arises here because of the qualitative differences in migration. A poor and disorganized part of a country often loses its better and more able people to the richer parts. Consequently, once a community or region gets poor and disorganized, the people who might lift it out of this condition often leave, and the poverty and disorganization become self-perpetuating. This is a problem which is very far from solved even within national economies, and it would unquestionably be intensified in the world economy. Even now there is considerable evidence that the poorer countries are actually contributing substantially in terms of educated personnel to the United States simply because many of the abler and more educated people of these countries are attracted to the United States by the greater rewards there. We should point out, however, that even though these problems might be intensified in the world economy, they are not peculiar to it, for all of them are found within the larger national economies.

A rather similar question is whether a world economy and a world economic interest require unrestricted trade. Here again, national economies have generally promoted free trade within the national boundary, and it might likewise be expected that a world economy would require free trade on a world scale. On the other hand, it is also argued that the interest of certain regions requires some interference with the free course of trade and that universal free trade would produce too much specialization for the cultural, social, and long-run economic health of particular regions. A region that is highly specialized in a one-crop economy is not only dangerously exposed to fluctuations in its terms of trade, but its development may also be slowed down by the lack of that vivacity of spirit and those external economies that frequently are the accompaniments of a diversified industry. Here again these are problems which we fail to solve at the level of the national economy, even though the present attempt of the United States to deal with its internal depressed areas is perhaps a foretaste of things to come on a world scale. It may be, indeed, that this problem can be solved through an extension of the grants economy rather than through any attempt to interfere with the exchange economy and that this will be just as true on a world scale as it is within the nation. These problems are by no means unique to the world economy, but they would unquestionably be intensified if we looked at things from the point of view of world interest rather than from the point of view of national interest. When we look at the cultural diversity of the world, the difficulty of applying intelligently a unified system of grants becomes very great. One wonders, therefore, whether a certain amount of economic nationalism and even political nationalism would not be consistent with the general concept of a world economy, even though the constant tendency of nationalism to get out of hand should make us chary of this solution.

The problem here is visible even at the national level in terms of states' rights, voluntary versus compulsory insurance, decentralization of education, and so on, but it becomes intensified as we begin to apply this system to a unified world. It is the problem essentially of developing a proper hierarchy in the "grants economy" with proper functions allocated to the family, the neighborhood, the voluntary group, the church, the city, the state, the nation, and the world. This is an important and largely unexplored field for research. We do not want—at least I do not want—a world government so centralized that the whole grants economy of the world is administered from the world capital. Neither do I want a world where the family is the only organizer of the grants economy nor one where there is no organized grants economy beyond the national state. Exactly how these various tasks should be apportioned in different stages of society and different modes of culture is, however, as yet an unanswered question.

Finally, one must emphasize again that any concept of the world economic interest implies an ethical system of some sort.

There is no way of avoiding this, and there may need to be as many concepts of the world economic interest as there are ethical systems. Whatever our concept of the economic system, the ethical system implied should be spelled out in detail. In welfare economics, for example, we have the concept of the Paretian optimum. According to this we would define an improvement in the world economic interest as taking place as long as one person were better off and nobody else worse off. Even a criterion as technical as this, however, cannot be divorced from ethical implications. There is in the Paretian optimum an implication that there is no malevolence. A malevolent person—and there are plenty of them—might prefer a situation in which his enemy was worse off, and he might even be prepared to buy this by being a little worse off himself. The economics of the arms race, indeed, suggests that this is a very important motive in the relations of national states. We all make ourselves worse off in the hope that our enemies will be still worse off. Even the concept of benevolence can cause difficulty for the Paretian optimum. I may, if I am benevolent, not wish to be better off unless somebody else is better off too. We may perhaps rescue the Paretian optimum technically by making each person's welfare a function of the economic states of others as well as of his own state; this, however, eliminates most of the conclusions which have been drawn from the theory. An even more difficult problem is posed by the fact that in many ethical systems the act of exchange itself has a value, positive or negative, quite apart from what is exchanged. Thus, in highly honorific, military, ceremonious, and feudal societies, exchange is regarded as something degrading and low-class in itself, and the merchant and the moneylender are often despised members of an outcaste group. At the other extreme there are small subcultures around organized markets where exchange is valued very highly and the good trader valued above the practitioners of arts and ceremonies. All this merely illustrates the conclusion that technical economics alone cannot provide an unequivocal definition of the world economic interest, although it can help in relating whatever definition is arrived at to the ethical system that is implied by it.

We can, perhaps, go beyond the bounds of formal economics in searching for reasonably simple criteria by which ethical systems can be evaluated. It may be possible, for instance, to generalize the concept of economic development, which is widely accepted today as at least a qualitative goal of economic institutions, into concepts of social, political, even ethical development, although here the difficulties of measurement are very great, often, indeed, seemingly insuperable. It might be possible, however, to measure political development by per capita violence, social development by the extent and depth of the grants economy, and so on.

Another possible line of attack is to look at human history as a genetic, evolutionary process with *degree of organization* as its main "value," progress then being defined very roughly as a movement from chaos to order. We then look for those interpersonal relations which are capable of creating social organization. I have distinguished three broad systems of such relationship. The threat system orders people into a role structure by the threat of injury or disutility; both king and priest historically have been originators of threat systems. Second, the exchange system consists in reciprocated benefits and mutual promises. The conditions under which it can be established are not immediately obvious, since it requires a certain degree of trust and confidence that promises will be fulfilled; the more the exchange extends into the future, the more important this element of confidence becomes. Third, the integrative system is the whole complex of relationships that involve love, affection, respect, trust, dignity, and status.

The econosphere is mainly concerned with the exchange system; an exchange system cannot exist by itself, however, in the absence of integrative or even coercive relationships. In the present day the focus of both the coercive and the integrative systems lie in the national state; the world coercive system, represented by the United Nations, exists, but on a very small scale. The world integrative system is even weaker; there are a few world-wide churches, scientific associations, and so on that develop a nascent sense of world community. Compared with the intensity of the sense of community within the nation, however, the world community is very weak. It may be, therefore, that the formation of a genuinely integrated world economy must wait on the development of a world community.

On the other hand, the existence of an econosphere, thin and patchy in places as it may be, is itself a strong force making for world community. In the history of the building of nations from local communities a complex interaction can be traced in which the webs of trade, law, police, and loyalties constantly grow by reinforcing one another. We can now reasonably expect this process to be repeated on the world scale. It is by no means an automatic process, especially as the web of trade itself is highly flexible and can be shifted around drastically, following political changes, without great loss, as demonstrated by the experience of Japan and of Poland after 1946. Each of the various systems has a degree of independence as well as interdependence, and a failure of one can arise from its own inner dynamics and yet impinge sharply on the others. Thus, the breakdown in the exchange system represented by the great depression of the 1930s, although it originated mainly within the exchange system itself, had profound repercussions on political, military, ethical, and ideological systems and played an important role in producing World War II.

It is clear, then, that the problem of the world economic interest is not a trivial one, even though conceptually it may be little more than an extension of the concept of the national economic interest or public interest. It is a problem that deserves much further study, especially from the point of view of the relationship between the econosphere and the world political and integrative structures. The whole question of the relationship between developed and undeveloped areas needs a great deal of attention at the present stage of world development, now that colonialism is discredited but the questions to which it was the wrong answer still remain unanswered. The problem of the interaction of economic, political, and integrative systems needs to be studied from the point of view of the dynamic process by which the psychological foundations and the institutional superstructure of world community can be built. Finally, the world economic interest is worth study as an economic problem in its own right. We need to study the problem of a completely closed economy with no outside trade not merely as a stepping-stone to the study of open national economies, but as the econosphere itself, which, pending interplanetary or interstellar trade, at least, is the one perfect example of a closed economic system.

III

BERT F. HOSELITZ

Unity and Diversity in Economic Structure

A STUDY of the economic structures of different societies, whether undertaken historically or on a comparative contemporary basis, will show profound differences. Certain societies display economic orders with high levels of productivity, others with low productivity. In some societies the most important economic decisions are made by persons unrelated to political organizations. In other societies persons with political power or involved in political action also make fundamental economic decisions. It appears that with the passing of time the differences both in the level of output and productivity and in decision-making structures have become greater. The discrepancies in economic welfare or per capita income have become wider, so that some might argue that unification and the formation of a mankind-wide economy are more difficult and are confronted with possibly more insoluble problems today than at any time before. Moreover, it may be said that the tendencies which have led in the past several decades to the differences mentioned, that is, to variabilities in the distribution of decision-making functions and the growing divergence in productivity and per capita output, are likely to continue in the future. Therefore, the possibility of combining the countries of the world into an economically more highly unified system may become even more difficult as time progresses.

I shall attempt to discuss these problems in somewhat greater detail and to examine conditions under which, in spite of the profound structural differences in the economic systems of different societies and in spite of pressures in the direction of enlarging these differences, considerable unification of the economy of mankind might be produced and some basic conditions for this unification could be elaborated. I shall be concerned not so much with alterations in the rules or conditions affecting international exchange or with problems of capital movements or the migration of persons from one society or nation to another. These matters are treated in other essays in this volume. My concern will be primarily to examine whether and in what form different economic decision-making systems may be brought into closer contact and in what way conditions of economic growth in different countries may bring about results which may make possible a closer approach among the various parts of mankind.

Rather than approaching this problem directly, I shall show first that economic unification, or rather the spread of some very fundamental economic conditions over time, may take place, even though political and social conditions vary greatly. I shall select a rather remote historical example to illustrate this process in general outline.

Let us take a case of technological and associated economic and productive change that affected all or almost all mankind. Let us consider first the development of technological processes during the early period of human history, mainly because the low level of output per capita, which appears to have been characteristic of all societies until the past few decades, was one of the main determinants of economic structures and apparently also was related to social conditions.

It has often been asserted that the dominant feature of socio-historical development has been the almost unilinear improvement of technology, but this simplifies the history of technology and science too much. There have been long periods of extremely slow technological progress during which, in spite of major social and cultural changes, little basic improvement took place in productive technology and economic organization and structure. The two most important steps in the development of human technology, as applied to economic structure as well as to processes, were the invention of agriculture and the invention of modern industry. The first took place in the fifth millenium B.C. in the region of the Fertile Crescent in Asia and the second in the eighteenth century A.D. in northwestern Europe. Each of these inventions was the product of the work and thought of many men. Each turned into a movement gradually affecting all mankind. The practice of agriculture spread during the first two millenia after its introduction; the spread of the Industrial Revolution is still with us. Let us examine these two processes in somewhat greater detail.

We shall start with agriculture. In the Fertile Crescent a gradual selection of plant and animal varieties subject to domestication took place. Some men who had been hunters and gatherers, and hence wanderers, became stable and permanently sedentary cultivators.[1] In the course of this process of the invention of agriculture, a village culture emerged. This culture exhibited the new feature that the food requirements of a given

---

[1] An extensive and most instructive discussion of this matter may be found in Robert J. Braidwood, *The Near East and the Foundations of Civilization* (Eugene: University of Oregon Press, 1952), pp. 9ff.

group of people could be significantly augmented or that the needs for food of a larger group could be met by the labor of a smaller group.

During the following 1,000 to 2,000 years, there was an explosive wave of technological, intellectual, and social inventions and change. Starting with the advantage of a more ample and storable food supply, most of the fundamental discoveries were made that until quite recently formed the technological backbone of human productive efforts. The villages were succeeded by cities with large buildings of brick and stone and arched construction. The basic techniques of metallurgy and metal-forming were applied to copper, bronze, and the precious metals, and finally to iron. Animals and the wheel were adapted for transportation, and the wheel was employed in ceramic arts. Textile fibers and textile arts were developed. Alcoholic beverages, perfumes, and perhaps even cleansing materials, such as soap, were invented.

The intellectual creations of this restless period were no less impressive. Probably the major step forward in this field was the fact that a genuine written language was devised. An interest in measurement developed into a mathematics of definitely abstract form. Both of these inventions are signs of the development of an ability to manipulate and use symbols in abstract ways, which is central to all later intellectual achievements. In addition, astronomy as an empirical science was developed to a point where quite precise predictions of celestial events could be made.

All these developments, which had a profound effect upon productivity, were contingent upon socio-cultural attainments that we also associate with the historical period following the introduction of agriculture. Perhaps the main socio-cultural basis for the process of economic and technological progress during this age was the development of systems of government by which large numbers of people could be moved to accept and enforce common rules of behavior and could become directed to common purposes. The creation of organized political societies under a common government was the fundamental change in social arrangements that made possible technological and intellectual progress leading to higher productivity.

The great expansion in resources, especially food resources, available to men produced a virtual population explosion in that period. In the four millenia between 10,000 and 6,000 years ago, it is estimated that the numbers of mankind increased from 5 million to 86 million, and the population density more than twentyfold from one person in 10 square miles to 2.6 persons in 1 square mile.

We now come to a fact of striking importance. For about 5,000 years after the great changes introduced by the invention of planned food production and the development of the first organized, stable, and permanently sedentary human societies, mankind experienced a virtual technological standstill. There were continuing and important modifications and improvements of the earlier discoveries, but very little that was fundamentally new or that opened up production and consumption possibilities previously unavailable. Productivity increased, but the pace was slow. Average human living standards probably also increased gradually, not so much because of new discoveries, but because of gradual dissemination and wider use of technologies already developed. There were only a few basic new inventions and all of these came rather at the end of the five millenia: the horse-collar, the windmill, the water wheel, and finally gunpowder and movable type.

The description presented in the preceding paragraphs is based primarily on technological developments in Europe and the adjoining regions of western Asia. The progress of technology in China—and also in India—was similar, although some new inventions were attained there earlier than in Europe. It is commonly known that the inventions of gunpowder, of movable type, and of porcelain in China preceded and probably even influenced some of these steps of technical progress in Europe. What is not quite so well known is that the Chinese also made significant technical inventions in the use of coal, the smelting of iron, other processes of metal production, and fabrication of metal objects long before corresponding developments occurred in Europe. But all these steps also took place near the end of the five millennia since the "invention" of agriculture.

Can we identify the main reasons that a technology grounded upon the exploitation of the uses of mechanical energy and going on to more fundamental discoveries did not develop some 3,000 or 4,000 years earlier? We know that this did not happen, but it may not be entirely idle to speculate about the reasons. Toynbee suggests that civilizations develop in response to a challenge. It may be that a period of great change does not appear to the people taking part in it as a continuing challenge or that the challenge loses force and begins to affect others who have not initially participated in it or in the benefits accruing from the changes produced. But these explanations are quite speculative, and a much more reasonable explanation may be found in fundamental socio-cultural factors.

It is a fact that, in spite of manifold apparent differences, the basic scope and form of human social organization changed very little until the later Middle Ages in western Europe. Societies continued to exhibit the over-all pattern that had grown to reality in the early empires of Mesopotamia. Society was composed of two almost completely separate layers: the ruler and the ruled, or the masters and the slaves. The first group monopolized all the wealth, education, and political power; the second were only a short step removed from beasts. Whether we look at Greek democracy, the Roman Republic, the Byzantine Empire, the Frankish state in the "Dark Ages," the realms of Asoka, or the Han dynasty, we find basically very similar forms of social organization. A new revolution in productivity and economic organization would most likely come about only if the fundamental pattern of the old society could be destroyed and replaced by one in which greater social mobility, greater access to power by the members of the previous lower social orders, wider spread of education, and a new distribution of status in society were attained; but this happened only in the two or three centuries preceding the second great technological innovation, the Industrial Revolution.

What this discussion points up is that before the onset of industrial development as a rapid process, the economies of the various parts of the world, though exhibiting some significant differences, nevertheless showed levels of income and performance that were not profoundly different. It is true that in the early period, following the introduction of agricultural productive methods, the contrasts between different economies and societies were extensive. It is also true that at that stage of development the importance of socio-cultural conditions in different societies played a very important role, a role they never completely lost. It may be argued strongly, however, that by the end of the period, that is, the twelfth to the fifteenth centuries A.D., the economies of the major states in the world were not very different and that, if political processes had been developed by means of which greater unification between the various parts of the world could have been brought about, or if communications between the various political entities had been broadened, closer economic approaches would have become possible, with the result of more equal and more closely related new developments in economic performance.

It must be pointed out, however, that these developments, though perhaps not absolutely impossible, would have been very unlikely, for in the fifteenth century all parts of the world were predominantly agricultural, and many peasants in all countries were to a considerable extent self-subsistent. Hence, unification would not have led to economic advantages, and hardly any initiatives existed in the economies of the various parts of the world to bring about much larger market or productive entities. It should also be remembered that in the fifteenth century transportation and communication technologies were still quite underdeveloped. Only in the subsequent two or three centuries did the growth of shipping, the development of better roads, the foundation of postal services, and other transportation and communications facilities support the potential integration of economic action in various parts of the world. Hence, an effective world economic integration or even a close approach of the different parts of the world before the nineteenth century would have been extremely difficult and subject to serious technological shortcomings.

Another conclusion that may be drawn from this discussion is the fact that economic divergence and differing conditions of productive activity in different parts of the world are relatively recent phenomena; that is, they cover only the past five centuries of the history of the world. It has been in these five centuries that different levels of economic growth have been reached in different continents, that per capita income levels have tended to grow farther apart in different countries, and that the major fundamental economic policies influencing productive activities in different parts of the world have become more sharply elaborated. Today, as has often been pointed out, the two main differences in the economic structure of various countries are the differences between economically developed and economically underdeveloped countries, that is, between countries with relatively high and others with quite low per capita incomes, and the differences between free enterprise and planning as the major socio-political condition influencing economic activity, especially investment and the allocation and use of income. We may now turn to these two differences in order to see how they influence the possible unification of mankind's economy and in what way they cause mankind to move economically further apart.

Let us begin by examining in somewhat greater detail the differences and possibilities of developing more similarities between planned and nonplanned economies. In the popular mind, and even among quite a few economists, this difference is considered rather profound. In many textbooks on differences between economic systems, planned economies are treated as quite separate entities, and in many universities and colleges special courses on economic planning or planned economies are presented. In brief, economic planning is considered as a special system of economic structure, whereas a free enterprise economy is usually set up as the basic contrast to economic planning. This contrast has become even firmer since planned and partly or allegedly nonplanned economies became divided after World War II into two political camps between which serious and strong tensions developed. We shall not consider the political problems in this context but shall concern ourselves exclusively with economic ones. It may be granted that even the economic unification of mankind may depend primarily upon the political rapprochement of the countries on the two sides of the Iron Curtain, but in this essay political developments will be considered only as consequences rather than as determinants of economic change.

Let us first ask some questions on the historical development of economic planning and of free enterprise systems. Although quite a few specialized accounts on this subject are found in the economic history literature, I consider the discussion of these subjects in Eucken's *Foundations of Economics* a very helpful piece of writing.[2] I shall, therefore, attempt to apply his discussion of these points to our problem. I need not go into his statement that an "immense, almost unlimited, variety of economic systems have arisen and disappeared." Eucken stresses this fact when he points out that at various times in the past and in different parts of the world quite distinct forms of economic organization, kinds of choices, and forms of cooperation existed; but he agrees that with the growth of new patterns of economic performance, especially as a consequence of the application on an increasing scale of industrial, technically advanced, and scientifically supported patterns of production, certain greater basic uniformities in economic systems developed. In particular he concludes that

History can show only a few cases where an economic system was constructed on the basis of certain general, rationally thought-out constitutional principles calculated to render it efficient. The great re-shaping of the economic system which took place at the turn of the eighteenth and nineteenth centuries and in the first half of the nineteenth century is a relevant example. Private property and freedom of contract and competition were the governing principles by which the economic system was to be shaped. Out of the understanding of the interdependence of the whole of everyday

[2] Walter Eucken, *Foundations of Economics: History and Theory in the Analysis of Economic Reality*, trans. by T. W. Hutchison (Chicago: University of Chicago Press, 1951), especially pp. 17–104.

economic life, and from the discovery that competition is a highly effective regulating mechanism, the classical economists developed their governing principles, and proposed great reforms in order to realize these principles in practice.[3]

In other words, we see here that a system of liberal free enterprise was introduced partly as the result of the reasoning of philosophers and economists but mainly as a consequence of new developments in legal and productive conditions. It was found in practice that the suggestion of economists to let competition rule tended to support patterns of economic growth in the more advanced countries. Extensive freedom in the establishment and control of new enterprises tended to enhance the rate of economic advancement and the introduction of the most "efficient" means of production, efficiency being measured in terms of profitability, the meeting of existing or increasing demand, and technological effectiveness in productive processes.

Of course, a free enterprise economy, even as it was described by the classical economists or by Alfred Marshall and his followers, did not emerge in perfection anywhere. What the economists described was an ideal type of economy. In practice there developed monopolies and cartels through the establishment of special rights—privileges or contracts among business leaders, on the one hand, and various forms of governmental regulations of enterprises on the other. In other words, in the various European countries that adopted, in principle, the economic systems outlined by the classical writers and their followers, the practical detailed patterns of economic relations diverged from the way they were described as "ideal systems" in the treatises. An observer concerned with the details would have encountered a number of very differently styled economic systems.

[3] *Ibid.,* pp. 82–83.

This means that economic systems which, on a more theoretical level, can be described as identical, or almost so, still show substantial differences on the concrete level. But these differences apparently are due only to a small extent to variations in economic decision-making patterns and are much more basically the result of differences in legal, political, or sociocultural conditions.

Consider, for example, the frequency and development of monopolies in what is commonly interpreted as a free enterprise economy. A comparison of two actual economic systems, both founded basically on free enterprise decision-making patterns, may exhibit quite different "quantities" of monopolies and cartels. If we investigate why these differences actually came into existence, we shall normally find that they were not due to differences in investment decisions or responses by entrepreneurs to demand changes but primarily to differences in the legal order, in political interests and the power objectives of entrepreneurs, and perhaps in social behavior, patterns of social association, and other socio-cultural factors.

Such an observation is of great importance for the study of the problem of whether an economic system, or a set of systems compatible with the economic unification of all mankind, can evolve, for the question may be asked whether relatively closely related and unified economies based on modern technologies can develop, even though cultural and social differences of rather wide divergence continue to exist. In other words, the major question that must be answered, whether a greater and ultimately perhaps complete system of economic unity of all mankind may develop, consists in trying to determine whether differences in non-economic social, political, and cultural conditions would destroy an economically uniform system and, if so, why and under what conditions.

It appears that, although social, cultural, and political differences may continue and, in fact, may remain permanent, greater economic unification may be compatible with these differentiations in the non-economic area. The main support for this view is supplied by observations in a number of developing countries in which a fair degree of economic interdependence has come into existence, even though different enterprises and different workers operate on levels of productivity and technological sophistication far removed from one another. In fact, some of these developing countries, particularly those with "mixed" economies, show that a fair degree of economic unification can be reached not only when economic processes of quite different degrees of productivity are coordinated in the same economic system but also when one economy is made up of several planned and unplanned sectors. In other words, we have socioeconomic systems in which quite different subsectors of the economy do coexist effectively even though each subsector, if examined in detail, represents a very different set of economic structures from the others. Concrete examples of such socioeconomic systems, in which widely differentiated subsectors coexist reasonably effectively, may be found in a number of developing countries of Asia or Latin America. In the major urban areas modern industries, commercial systems, transportation and communication sectors, and other forms of services are provided, whereas in the surrounding rural areas many types of handicrafts, technologically underdeveloped agriculture, and traditionally influenced services are common. These contrasts in productive efficiency and types of output are not only based on differences in technology, but are also associated with substantial differences in social and cultural conditions. Yet in many developing countries, a relatively high degree of adjustment, integration, and mutual dependence among rural and urban social entities has been achieved to constitute a relatively high and fairly smoothly functioning unified socio-economic system.

The problem that forms the central core of this essay must then be restated in the following terms: The major contrasts and conflicts in the economic systems in reality today show the previously mentioned two major distinctions, planning versus free enterprise and high versus low per capita output. Can we discern tendencies that will bring these systems closer together or take them farther apart, and can we indicate the consequences for the possibility of developing a mankind-wide economic system if either of these two consequences follows?

As concerns the relationship between planned and free enterprise economies, several points have already been made. Within free enterprise systems, basic similarities may exist in the fundamental economic decision-making processes, even though different free enterprise economies may be based on different cultural, social, and political systems or different degrees of monopolization or cartelization or even governmental regulation of economic action may prevail. Such economies are rather highly developed; that is, per capita incomes are relatively high. The decision-making processes in private firms similarly modern and economically productive in poorer countries are not too different, although these poorer countries usually contain large economic sectors that are still highly underdeveloped and in which productive performances may be subject to somewhat different objectives from those of the plants and enterprises constituting modern domestic or foreign-induced investments. As a concrete example, let us take India, where we find that privately owned modern firms employing up-to-date machinery and being run with the objective of profit maximization perform in a very similar manner to firms in more highly developed countries, although the large modern Indian firms may differ greatly from the small rural handicrafts and cottage industries still widely spread over the country.

This means that modern plants, particularly in secondary and tertiary industrial fields but also in those areas of primary production where modern techniques have been adopted, exhibit very similar kinds of economic behavior and economic objectives regardless of the political entity in which they are located. This means further that the general modernization of the economies in less well-developed countries would probably lead to patterns of economic objectives and decision-making that are not only compatible on a mankind-wide scale but also would potentially lead to much closer patterns of economic action in quite different countries. Some of the evidence for this process is presented by the economic changes in western and central Europe in the last 150 years. In Germany economic unification, strongly supported by the formation of the Zollverein, anticipated political unification during the nineteenth century; and in the Common Market area of Europe in the last decade various steps of economic integration and unification have taken place, although political unification has progressed much less rapidly. It is, of course, true that some setbacks and even interruptions of the formation of an ever-widening Common Market have taken place. France's recent opposition to the inclusion of Britain is a case in point. But if we consider a longer period of time, several decades instead of a few years, it may be reasonable to predict that various patterns of attraction for those western and central European countries still outside the Common Market group can be developed which may eventually make possible the economic integration of all western and central Europe. We have a case here in which the higher level of economic unity precedes political measures, and it appears that the main reason for this possibility of economic unification is the relatively high rate of economic performance in the countries forming the economic union. In more concrete terms, the formation of larger markets, the better distribution of products, the development of more specialized productive entities, and various other general developments characteristic of a large unified economic system become possible once the various parts of such a system have reached a relatively high level of economic performance.

These reflections tend to indicate that the major obstacle toward greater economic unification of the various parts of mankind appears to be primarily the great differentiation in productivity and in per capita incomes in different countries, a gap that, as already pointed out, appears to have become wider rather than narrower during the last few decades. But before we consider the contrast between economically highly developed and underdeveloped countries more closely, we must turn to the problem of planning and its potentially different impact.

Eucken in his *Foundations of Economics* discusses economic planning as a result of a centrally directed economy and distinguishes several types of centrally directed economies, depending upon the degree of freedom of consumers' choices. What matters to him is the fact that investment and resource allocation decisions are made by one central authority, although this organization may under certain conditions be willing to provide substantial freedom to persons as concerns their choices of consumption.[4] From the standpoint of purely theoretical considerations, the decision of resource allocation and levels of investment may be analyzed in a very similar fashion to those applicable to modern free enterprise economy. The objectives of the individual firm may vary greatly from those of the

[4] *Ibid.*, pp. 186ff.

central authority. Whereas the firm normally is assumed to make choices with the objective of maximizing income, the central authority may have other objectives, some of them politically determined and others related to issues of economic growth. That is, its major objective at a certain period may be the desire to attain a maximum economic growth rate, most effective military security, or possibly even the greatest differentiation and augmentation of consumer goods. But once given the objective of the central authority, the investment and resource allocation decisions can be examined and analyzed in a fashion very similar to that applied to the critical examination of related decisions by profit-oriented private enterprises.

What matters to us, however, is not the question of whether or not theoretical economic propositions of a similar kind are applicable to planned and nonplanned economies, but whether modern planning develops into a direction in which its over-all economic functions can be related more closely to those of non-planned economies so as to bring about a closer form of interaction between different countries and to determine whether some form of economic unification of different parts of mankind can be approached even though basically planned and free enterprise economic systems continue to exist.

In order to come closer to an evaluation of this question, it may be useful to examine the problem of planned economies from a slightly different point of view from that expounded by Eucken. In examining the different conditions under which economic growth takes place, I have in an earlier study made a distinction between autonomous and induced growth.[5] The former was described as a pattern of growth in which all decisions affecting economic advancement were made by in-

---

[5] See Bert F. Hoselitz, "Patterns of Economic Growth," *Canadian Journal of Economics and Political Science*, XXI (1955), 416ff.

dividuals other than those holding political power, that is, in countries presenting an entirely liberal state in which the system of political checks and balances within the government is supplemented by a system of checks and balances in the distribution of social tasks. The other extreme type, that of induced growth, was described as one in which economic decisions leading to the advancement of the economy are made by a politically controlled or influenced central planning authority. Now, induced patterns of growth are not necessarily modern, that is, are not characteristic of policies exercised only during the past few decades in countries in which economic planning was the generally accepted economic policy. Strong induced features were characteristic also of the economic policies in some Western countries during the mercantilist period, although at that time the stress of government was much less strong than in some currently centrally planned societies. To distinguish mercantilist and modern planning, one may consider the differences between the policies in the two situations, the former of which may be referred to as planning in breadth and the latter as planning in depth.

Planning in breadth designates an economic policy under which regulatory activity embraces a mass of specific rules for many minute transactions and forms of economic behavior. A good example may be an economic plan that makes detailed provisions for the output of various industries and plants, sets up an extensive system of priorities and allocations of materials, and minutely prescribes prices and conditions of exchange. The early plans of the Soviet Union and other centrally planned states adjoining it approximate this type of planning. Another example is the characteristic policy of a mercantilist society, which often minutely prescribed conditions of production, import and export, consumption, and exchange. Tolls, sumptuary laws, guild regulations, rules for state enterprises, premiums, prohibitions, staples, patent rights, monopoly privileges, and many other regulatory features characterize this system. The usual outcome of such a plan is that it is overdetermined and contains contradictions and that a working economy is possible only when certain regulations are disobeyed or when the system is allowed to break down at certain points.

Planning in depth is an economic policy under which regulatory activity is concentrated in a limited number of spots that are crucial for a wide range of economic decision-making. Examples of such vertical planning are the system of functional finance proposed by Lerner and the social planning of a "market economy" type proposed by Lange.[6] In general, policies of price control and direct allocation are typical of planning in breadth, and monetary and fiscal policies of planning in depth. Many governmental regulatory systems, even in the economically most advanced countries, that rely on planning in depth often include elements typical of planning in breadth, while in some economic systems characterized still by planning in breadth, certain characteristic measures of planning in depth are encountered.

In general, it is not unreasonable to assume that with economic progress the significance of planning in depth increases on the whole and that minute prescriptions characteristic of planning in breadth lose in significance. In fact, an examination of the various forms of economic policies in countries that consider themselves as not having planned economies shows that various policies and economic measures in these countries exhibit quite

---

[6] See A. P. Lerner, *Economics of Control: Principles of Welfare Economics* (New York: Macmillan, 1944), pp. 302ff.; and Oskar Lange and Fred M. Taylor, *On the Economic Theory of Socialism* (Vol. II of B. E. Lippincott, ed., *Government Control of the Economic Order;* Minneapolis: University of Minnesota Press, 1938), pp. 72ff.

different characteristics. Some economic policies appear to be far removed from and others very close to measures typical of planned economies. Robert A. Dahl and Charles E. Lindblom have presented a number of tables in *Politics, Economics and Welfare*, in which they have shown how close some policies employed in the United States are to direct controls, compulsory impositions of economic action by government, prescriptive rules by public agencies, and relatively direct, as contrasted with highly indirect, controls by publicly appointed or publicly controlled agencies.[7] It is not my point in this paper to discuss these matters in detail, but the result of the reflections presented by Dahl and Lindblom is that even in a relatively free, unplanned, modern economy, quite a few measures of economic policy that are extremely similar to typical policies customary in centrally planned economies are being used and apparently widely accepted.

This means, however, that planning in depth may become a characteristic procedure associated with economically growing societies. In many of the planned economies of eastern Europe, strong tendencies of planning in breadth still prevail; but I believe that this is largely a consequence of the low level of economic advancement characterizing these economies and that it is not an extreme assumption that with progressive economic advancement the actual basic conditions of planning will gradually lead to greater emphasis on planning in depth and a reduction of planning policies in breadth. For example, although the level of economic performance in Poland is not yet high enough to induce the government of the country to give up planning in breadth, some Polish economists have discussed

---

[7] See Robert A. Dahl and Charles E. Lindblom, *Politics, Economics and Welfare: Planning and Politico-Economic Systems Resolved into Basic Social Processes* (New York: Harper, 1953), pp. 10–18.

quite openly the question of how planning in their country could be developed to provide the government with a few crucial areas in which its decisions are to be imposed, while at the same time the highest degree of consumer sovereignty, the freest choice of professions, and similar widely exercised private decisions can be made.

I believe that this discussion leads to the conclusion that planning in some countries and its absence in others are not aspects of economic decision-making that would strongly prevent a greater unification of the economy of mankind. Economies that have grown within a planned system as well as economies that have maintained strong liberal and free enterprise conditions have with the progress of economic advancement, with the development of greater concern of the importance of public welfare, and with the growth of more modern concepts about and more advanced skills in the application of economic policies, arrived at a point where gradually relatively similar patterns of planning in depth have come to predominate. Although the actual policies in different societies may differ greatly, measures to influence economic behavior leading to maximum satisfaction of consumers' needs, to a generally acceptable rate of growth, and to the maintenance of economic security are likely to produce a set of economic policies that come to resemble one another rather strongly. Once economies advance in terms of per capita income above a certain level and once relatively wide consumer choices on a mass basis become possible, the distinctions in economic policies tend to lose their importance, and various forms of economic approach between these economies through common markets, customs unions, economic unification, or other economic kinds of association can be achieved.

This leads to the conclusion that the major obstacle to greater economic unity of mankind is probably not the distinction between planned and unplanned economies but the growing separation in levels of economic advancement of different nations and societies during the last few decades. I should like to turn briefly to this problem and examine its significance.

There has been a long debate on what are the characteristics of economically advanced and underdeveloped countries, what are the principal differences between the two, and what variables are the major determinants of the two situations. The determination of what is an underdeveloped society has fluctuated; some people have said that all underdeveloped societies have low per capita incomes—of less than 200 dollars, for example—others have used some different characteristics, and one distinguished UN specialist has said that, although it is difficult to define what an underdeveloped country is, it is easily recognizable if one lives in one for a short time. Perhaps it may not be out of order to list a number of related economic aspects that together make up the economic characteristics of an underdeveloped country and to add to them some socio-cultural factors, which together will provide a fairly well-rounded description of these societies.

The economic features of an underdeveloped country may be listed as follows:

1. Low per capita income.

2. A low level of domestic savings and consequently little investment from internal sources.

3. A low level of technological achievement and technological complexity compared with related levels elsewhere.

4. Dominance of the primary production sector in the economy and a narrow range of output, especially of exportable products. The bulk of the country's income is earned in agriculture, and its major exports consist primarily of agricultural

products, sometimes even the output of limited "monoculture," and sometimes other raw materials, such as minerals.

5. The subsistence sector, that is, the group of persons who concentrate on production for their own subsistence or local exchange, often of a nonmonetary kind, is relatively large.

6. With these features and in part as a result of the large portion of the labor force devoted to relatively simple patterns of agriculture, there is associated a relative shortage of labor skills and of entrepreneurial and management capacity.

7. In many underdeveloped countries there may be found a relatively large amount of disguised unemployment, much of it in the agricultural sector; and some workers, even though nominally employed, actually contribute very little to total output.

8. International trade of an underdeveloped country consists primarily of exchanges with economically more advanced countries rather than with other underdeveloped countries, and total foreign trade among advanced countries is proportionally and absolutely larger than underdeveloped countries.

9. As a consequence of the relatively heavy concentration on primary production, the bulk of individuals economically active in an underdeveloped country work in the countryside or in small towns. Although all these countries do have large cities, many of the economic and even administrative institutions of large urban centers are weak, occupational structure often embraces few skilled and many unskilled workers, and as a consequence of excessive rural-urban migration, extensive slums are found in urban areas.

These features describe most of the specific economic characteristics that can be encountered at the present in the underdeveloped regions in Asia, Africa, and Latin America. Actual levels of per capita income, the pattern of exports, the degree of concentration in certain rural areas, and the ratio of rural and urban populations as well as ratios of occupational differences may vary; but these variations in the economies are of relatively minor importance, and the great and genuinely important gap is that which exists between economically developed and under-developed countries. Moreover, as already pointed out earlier in this essay, the gap between most underdeveloped countries and most developed countries has become larger. There are a few nations that have tended to fill this gap by passing gradually out of the state of underdevelopment into one in which development becomes a likely prospect in the next few years or decades; but most of these countries are relatively small, and a comparison of the entire area of south and southeast Asia, the Middle East (except possibly Turkey and Israel), and most of Africa (except South Africa), as well as a large portion of Latin America—especially Central America and a range of countries along the Pacific coastline of South America—have fallen behind relatively because of the recent high rates of economic advancement of western Europe, North America, and Oceania. The Soviet Union and perhaps even China—though Chinese data are quite difficult to evaluate and are seriously under-explored as yet on a fully objective level—have grown as fast and perhaps faster than the highly advanced countries, and so has Japan.

These reflections suggest that on the purely economic level, in terms of average output, productivity, and economic structure, we are presently witnessing a development that is perhaps unique in the history of mankind. Different parts of the world that—with few exceptions of very primitive traditionally oriented peoples in Australia and the removed regions in certain parts of America, Asia, and Africa—were always economically rather closely related in terms of productivity up to the sixteenth century have been drawing more and more apart since that time. In the postwar decade, in spite of foreign aid and the establishment of international agencies in the political and economic spheres, the general trend of greater differentiation became worse as the advanced countries grew faster than the underdeveloped regions of the world; and the gap is likely to increase or at least to become much more difficult to be narrowed.

All this means that we are now in a situation in which the economic coordination of the different parts of the world is likely to be more difficult than ever before and will probably, if the difference in the rates of growth continues, become even worse. As a consequence, the occupational patterns and the over-all economic structures in different countries will be more widely apart from what they have been in the past. In an earlier part of this essay I have shown how under the impact of the invention of agriculture, a series of economies developed over the entire world, which, in spite of the scarcity of communications between them and the persistence of profound differences in local customs and cultural conditions, developed economic structures of relatively great similarity. On the basis of this examination, one might conclude that similar results may be attained if the second great socio-economic invention, the Industrial Revolution, comes to penetrate all areas of the globe and to become a form of socio-economic behavior of all mankind. But before we enter into a discussion of this point, it may be necessary to list, as I have done on some of the main descriptive economic aspects, the principal socio-cultural features exhibited by an underdeveloped society. This task is in many ways much more complex than the listing of economic features, mainly because differences are considerably greater and because cultural and social traits of various underdeveloped countries are, or at least appear to be, much more varied than economic features. It may be possible, however, to list at least some of the most relevant and most often observed characteristics in social organizations and structures of underdeveloped societies. The following appear to be the ones most widely found:

1. Absence of a highly centralized authority or at least the existence side by side with a central authority of strongly marked sectors of the community, each with its own set of loyalties and solidarity.

2. A status system in which the position of an individual tends to be ascribed, that is, to be due to his family or kinship relations, and in which, therefore, social mobility beyond a person's family relationships is relatively slow and difficult.

3. Economic as well as social relationship are strongly influenced by a personalized order; that is, they are based upon the strong emphasis of a person's status in the society rather than on his capacity to perform certain tasks or even his education and training. This characteristic is associated with a related point, that is, the close relationship between a person's economic role and his role in other fields of social action. This matter may perhaps be explained by pointing out that in a highly developed industrialized society, a person's economic role is often regarded as a completely distinct role unrelated to his family, political, or religious functions. In many underdeveloped societies this relationship is different, since many individuals are subject to what has been called by some British anthropologists a "multiplex social position," that is, a position in which there are close relationships among economic, kinship, political, and even religious behavior.

4. Values about the social and moral significance of work are such that occupations tend to be status-linked, on the one hand, and restricted, on the other, to certain limited social categories.

5. A system of distribution is regulated by traditional claims. In some cases, while the more vulnerable social categories were protected economically, they and the majority of workers received incomes usually not greatly above the minimum subsistence level. In other cases distribution was and is more egalitarian, but in either case the rewards gained by an individual were and are group-oriented rather than individually oriented.

6. The consequence of these features tends to be that in little-developed societies there are still strong traditional customs applying to the economic as well as to the intergroup or social relationship. Moreover, social mobility is low, and the dependence of each individual to other members of his subgroup is close. Although there is a good deal of personal motivation to pursue higher earnings, the rational inclination towards profit maximization in many enterprises is little developed, and often new economic departures are not entered into because of uncertainties and the disinclination to experiment.

All these socio-cultural features are strong impediments to the adoption of many new and modern forms of economic activity. It is likely that these non-economic features of poor societies are more strongly opposed to their adopting rapid industrial and other forms of economically forward-pushing development than their poverty and low levels of average income. These considerations have led to the assumption by many students of economic growth that unless underdeveloped societies adopt the major cultural and social conditions prevailing in economically advanced countries, they will be unable effectively to transform their economies, except possibly in those instances in which strong centralized governments engage in strictly planned economic policies as, for example, in China. Although the Soviet Union, which followed this pattern, has experienced quite rapid economic growth, it is not certain whether and at what rate China will be able to match this performance. At the same time, we have witnessed rapid economic growth in Japan, even though it did not adopt a planned economy. At the early stage of its economic advancement, however, governmental influence was relatively widespread and certainly played an important role in the economic transformation of Japan.

Let us now dwell at some greater length on the culture of industrialism, for the capacity to adopt this culture is said by some to be one of the major propelling forces affecting the spread of modern industrial production. On the level of social organization, industrialism requires a "great" society, the parts of which are closely integrated and which function in harmony. In a society disrupted by tribal distinctions and conflicts, by caste or ethnic disharmony, a smoothly functioning industrial complex cannot be developed. On the level of the productive unit, industrialism requires organizations that allow and, in fact, necessitate the cooperation of individuals for a common productive purpose. As long as such western European organizations as mercantile companies, banks, corporations, and other private or semipublic bodies exhibiting the capacity for mutual collaboration are absent, industrial development lacks an important ingredient. It is not necessary to imitate the organizations specifically developed in western Europe for the mobilization of resources on a scale too large for any one individual to control. In fact, in place of such organizations in the field of private enterprise many newly industrializing countries may charge the public authorities with the formation of large industrial plants and other related public enterprises. But a society in which family business predominates and in which manifold patterns of social discrimination exist and continue to influence the admission of persons to participate in economic enterprise, industrial development on a sizable scale cannot take place.

The predominant pattern of allocating economic roles in nonindustrial societies is, as already pointed out, due to passing them on in families. The system that exhibits this pattern in the purest form is the idealized caste system, in which the sons step into the business of their fathers. But even in a pre-industrial society in which caste does not exist, a merchant passes on his business to his son and a manufacturer his enterprise to his son. If they have no sons, they leave it to some other relative, usually a close relative. Partners in a business are often brothers or other blood relatives, and a merger of two businesses is often reinforced by marriage. The circle of trust is limited to persons who are related to one another, not on the basis of impersonal contractual relations, but by some close bond of social unity, such as family ties, joint membership in a religious or ethnic community, or provenance from a common place of origin.

New industrial civilizations have overcome these highly personal and rigorously ascriptive ties that nonindustrial cultures maintain. In modern advanced societies the major form of economic interaction is based on contract. When Henry Sumner Maine argued that human societies show a tendency to progress from the predominance of status relations to contractual relations, he was expressing the gradual development of one chief characteristic of an industrial society. When contemporary writers, discussing the conditions for successful industrial development, stress the importance of law and order, they merely repeat in other terms what Maine said. For law and order are important precisely because cold, impersonal contractual relations are the rule. In a society in which persons consider their associations primarily on the basis of family, religion, or other ascriptive and particularistic ties, the maintenance of law and order is of less importance, for the cohesion of the group is guaranteed by close interpersonal, rather than contractual, interactions. This change in the form of social organization from the predominance of status to that of contract is, therefore, an important concomitant of the growth of industrial culture and rising productivity.

The question may be raised whether industrialism could thrive without these concomitant changes in the legal system. In considering an answer to this, one must remember that the transition from status to contract is not merely a change in the legal system but a change in social organization. It makes possible the development of entirely new enterprises on a scale that are not possible without this change. The bank, the large corporation, the big national trade union are examples of this development. It makes possible the more rational distribution of tasks and the close association of a given task with a given remuneration. It allows the smoother functioning of markets and analogous processes of resource allocation, all of which are important contributing aspects of high productivity resulting from the spread of industrial culture.

These considerations lead to a study of personal relationships. We have seen that industrialism and the high productivity it implies are associated with new forms of organization on the level of the society as a whole, on that of groups within the society; and it would be strange if this had no repercussions on the personal level. In other words, industrial civilizations tend to produce individuals with new motivations and a new outlook. This is a difficult and as yet little explored field. Can we say that there is such an individual as an "industrial man," and if so, what are his characteristics?

Some scholars assert that it is possible to identify a number of traits by which industrial man is distinguished from persons in preindustrial societies.[8] His sense of time, his sense of duty, and

---

[8] For an interesting discussion of these issues, see, for example, Melville J. Herskovitz, "The Problem of Adapting Societies to New Tasks," in Bert F.

his sense of discipline change. He regards his job not as a pre-ordained station in life, but as a means to the end of earning an income that he can spend as he sees fit. In view of the pre-dominance of contracts in an industrial society—and this pre-dominance is characteristic not only of industrial capitalism but also of industrial societies with extensive economic plans—a person will often be motivated by a high need for achievement. In other words, he will consider his professional and sometimes his personal career as implying a challenge to meet new tasks and to overcome various obstacles.

These aspects of the personality of individuals in an industrial culture have sometimes been summarized under the heading of "commitment to industrialization." Once industrial urban ex-istence and the rules of achievement and successful perform-ance are accepted as the main criteria for an economic function or a job, once a person is at home in the anonymous world of contractual relations and maintains close personal ties with only a small number of friends and near relatives, once we have a clear predominance of the small nuclear family, then we have a man committed to modern industrialism and modern high-level productivity.

The points mentioned in the preceding paragraphs tend to indicate that apparently one of the primary conditions for in-creasing industrial development on a world-wide scale, particu-larly in the economically less advanced countries, is the change in certain social and consequently general psychological con-ditions still standing in the way of more rapid and effective industrial development. Although some assistance on the tech-nological and even basically economic level can be given by the

Hoselitz, ed., *The Progress of Underdeveloped Areas* (Chicago: University of Chicago Press, 1952), pp. 89–112.

more advanced countries, by the United Nations, and by other international agencies, the major need for development is the cultural and socio-psychological conditions prevailing in the poorer countries themselves. This does not mean that they must adopt wholesale the cultural and social patterns of the economically more advanced countries; but, as was outlined in the preceding paragraphs, there appear to be a number of necessary, or at least desirable, steps leading to industrial achievement, which if adopted will facilitate the general pattern of industrialization and with it greater economic advancement. It appears, however, that only if modern industrial and tertiary occupations become widely introduced into the countries with less advanced levels of economic performance, greater economic unification of mankind will be attained; this unity in turn will make possible a more intimate degree of economic interrelations and a more likely and more favorable pattern of economic integration of mankind.

As was mentioned earlier in this essay, when reference was made to such developments as the Common Market in Europe, economic integration on some level does not require fully equal cultural and social conditions in the various countries establishing closer economic relations. Neither does it require a complete level of political integration of mankind. But the general approach of levels of economic performance in different countries appears to be the main developmental pattern on a world scale which may more closely unify mankind economically. This development is due partly to investment, distribution of international loans and grants, and levels of international transfers of capital but primarily to greater approximation of some of the basic socio-cultural and psychological attitudes in various countries, especially in those which still make up the bulk of the underdeveloped regions of the world.

It is extremely difficult to suggest how these changes can be brought about. To some extent closer economic relations between advanced countries and less advanced ones may produce these effects. To some extent perhaps, the increase of people educated in modern knowledge may be another push to lead to this result. To some extent political modernization in the poor countries may lead to these effects. Our knowledge of these problems is still so limited that we cannot accurately predict which policies and which measures would be most likely to bring about the more or less complete socio-cultural transformation of underdeveloped countries to a situation in which their economies could approximate those of the economically advanced portions of the world.

It is futile, in my opinion, to believe that economic aid as such is the only or even the main measure that will produce this result. In his scheme of patterns of social action, Parsons has divided actions systems into four major areas, of which the so-called "adaptive," or economic, sector is only one.[9] The others are the sectors of cultural, social, and political action; and, of course, action attributed to these sectors interrelates with economic activity. Integration on a reasonable level among different political and social entities have economic sectors that are relatively similar, at least in the levels of competence and productivity. But these levels of productivity in each social entity or each nation are attained as much, and perhaps even more, by changes in the cultural, social, and to some extent political action systems as in the economic action system alone. This means that a greater unification of the economy of mankind is likely if these other patterns of interaction change; and anyone interested in bringing about greater unification of the economy

[9] See Talcott Parsons, *Working Papers in the Theory of Action* (New York: Free Press of Glencoe, 1953), pp. 89ff.

of mankind must be as much concerned with cultural, social, and political changes as with economic changes alone.

The problem before us, therefore, is one of devoting attention not merely to economic aid, to the questions of international economic assistance by the more advanced to the underdeveloped countries but to over-all alteration of cultural and social systems in the world as a whole. If this can be achieved, the possibility of a more uniform and more highly interrelated economic system of mankind as a whole may become a possible solution.

IV

DAVID FELIX

International Factor Migration and World Economic Welfare

THE MAINSTREAM of economic thought over the past century and a half has been self-professedly liberal and cosmopolitan in its outlook. It has generally looked longingly toward free trade as a desirable ideal and viewed with distaste "beggar-my-neighbor" policies between nations as leading to a reduction in world economic welfare.

Yet economic orthodoxy has been also quite ambivalent as to the practical importance of factor movements in advancing world economic welfare. Within closed models of perfectly competitive economies, the mobility of factors, their freedom to move from lower to higher rates of return, is a necessary condition for attaining optimal economic efficiency. When these models are then related, in the casual manner of economic theorists, to imperfect national economies, the orthodox policy prescription has usually been to remove internal barriers to geographic and occupational mobility in order to increase economic efficiency. By simple analogy, the argument should surely be extended to the world economy. The widest international factor mobility should also be encouraged as a necessary condition for maximizing world economic welfare. Economists have, however, been generally reluctant to stress the necessity for such a policy, particularly as it relates to labor mobility. Indeed, throughout the nineteenth century, the heyday of international migration and international capital movements, the main body of international trade theory operated with the explicit assumption that, while productive factors were fully mobile within each nation, they were immobile between nations.[1] Moreover, although trade was assumed to have no generally predictable effect on inequalities of labor and capital remuneration among the trading countries, free trade would still, it was contended, maximize world economic welfare. The implication was not drawn that this was a sub-optimal welfare position, since a higher aggregate output might be obtained by shifting factors internationally in order to equalize world factor prices.

Paradoxically, it was after World War I, when barriers to trade and immigration were already being progressively raised by national policies and the great nineteenth-century wave of international private capital movements was ebbing, that international trade theory took a new tack and began to emphasize the welfare significance of international factor price equalization. The Swedish economist and historian, Heckscher, was the first to elaborate this train of thought, which rapidly transformed the older orthodoxy.[2] It was, however, a revolution in

[1] The existence of international capital movements was explicitly recognized only in the monetary-balance of payments section of international trade theory, where the problem of how such movements affect the price levels, terms of trade, and balance of payments of the borrowing and lending countries was analyzed. The effect of such movements on aggregate output and on domestic income distribution was, however, generally ignored.

[2] Eli Heckscher, "The Effect of Foreign Trade on the Distribution of Income," *Economisk Tidskrift*, XXI (1919), 497–512, trans. from the Swedish by Sven Laursen and reprinted in H. S. Ellis and L. A. Metzler, eds., *Readings*

thought rather than policy. Heckscher did point out that international factor movements could reduce differences in the remuneration of factors internationally, but this was not always necessary in order to equalize factor prices. Free trade, by altering national productive structures, might do it alone. The older orthodoxy was wrong, not so much in slighting the importance of factor movements as in underestimating the optimizing effect of free trade on world economic welfare.

The doctrinal cohesiveness of economists on international economic policy has weakened greatly in recent years. But even among those still devoted to the libertarian tradition, ambivalence on the importance to economic welfare of free labor migration, if not of private capital movements, persists.[3] Economists with planning proclivities tend to be skeptical of both.

This tradition of minimizing the importance of international factor movements in fact and in policy is due, I believe, to an attempt to accommodate to two major world phenomena, nationalism as an economic force and what has come to be called the international "north-south" problem—the great and widening gap in income and productivity between the rich and poor nations. For those in the liberal tradition, the accommodation is largely evident in their asides and in lacunae in their analysis. Those not in this tradition, on the other hand, have probed these

---

in the Theory of International Trade (Philadelphia: Blakiston, 1949), pp. 272–300.

[3] This is true of even the most passionate and articulate spokesmen for extreme economic liberalism. For example, Milton Friedman, in his *Capitalism and Freedom* (Chicago: University of Chicago Press, 1962), boldly denounces a wide array of U.S. government interferences with the market without concern for political feasibility, but does not mention U.S. immigration policy, although it is one of the more restrictive and politically and racially illiberal policies followed by rich countries today.

lacunae in order, among other things, to disprove the liberal analysis.

The spirit of nationalism has often lurked beneath the cosmopolitan façade of liberal free trade economists. This was a standard accusation of the nineteenth-century German historical school against *smithianismus*. But we need not rely merely on the complaints of hostile critics that the English free traders were primarily interested in advancing England's rather than the world's economic welfare. A sympathetic historian of liberal economic thought, Lord Robbins, writes,

It must be realized that this consumption which was regarded as the end of economic activity was the consumption of a limited community, the members of the nation-state. To the extent to which they repudiated former maxims of economic warfare and assumed mutual advantage in international exchange, it is true that the outlook of the Classical Economists seems, and indeed is, more spacious and pacific than that of their antagonists. But there is little evidence that they often went beyond the test of national advantage as a criterion of policy, still less that they were prepared to contemplate the dissolution of national bonds. If you examine the ground on which they recommended free trade, you will find that it is always in terms of a more productive use of national resources. . . . I find no trace anywhere in their writings of the vague cosmopolitanism with which they are often credited by continental writers. I do not claim this as a virtue—or a deficiency; the question of the extent to which, at this stage of history, it was incumbent on political thinkers to transcend the ideas and the criteria of the nation-state is a matter of great difficulty. All that I contend is that we get our picture wrong if we suppose that the English Classical Economists would have recommended, because it was good for the world at large, a measure which they thought harmful to their own community. It was the consumption of the national economy which they regarded as the end of economic activity.[4]

Whether liberal economists were personally imbued with

[4] Lionel Robbins, *The Theory of Economic Policy* (London: Macmillan, 1952), pp. 9–11.

the animus of nationalism is less important than is Lord Robbins' suggestion that had they chosen truly cosmopolitan criteria of welfare, they might only have condemned themselves to irrelevance. Nations were not prepared to find satisfaction in an increase in world output in which they did not share. Free trade and factor movements could thus be justified in terms of economic welfare only if each participating nation gained materially. A distributional norm was vaguely implicit in the classical notion of world welfare.

Would free trade and factor movements always implement such a norm? And might not some nations gain more by other policies? "Yes, but" was the answer given in both cases, although the "but" was much more pronounced for the second question. While English classical economists had no explicit theory of institutional change,[5] they did have a sketchy cultural theory of economic development, consisting largely of observations on the importance of differences in national character and institutions in explaining international differences in economic efficiency. Variations in productivity among nations, relating to these differences as well as to natural resource differences, made mutually profitable trade possible. Moreover, although the converse influence of trade and international factor movements on production functions was held, generally, to be too unpredictable to permit generalization,[6] the theoretical va-

[5] There are elements of such theorizing in Adam Smith. The Reverend Richard Jones, who was outside the main classical tradition, also attempted to develop a theory of economic development incorporating institutional change. See Richard Jones, *Essay on the Distribution of Wealth* (London, 1831). Jones had some influence on J. S. Mill as well as on Marx. Marshall was, of course, a keen student of economic history, but his formal theorizing was done with reference to an exogenously given institutional framework and technology.

[6] Richard E. Caves, *Trade and Economic Structure* (Cambridge, Mass.: Harvard University Press, 1960), pp. 125–26.

Adam Smith was a partial exception. His "vent for surplus" argument for

lidity of the "infant industry" argument was admitted. The ingredients were thus present for the conception that nationalism could be a major force for economic development, for through a sustained national effort to reform institutions and aptitudes the "lesser breeds without the law" might aspire to the levels of productivity and standards of living of the economically advanced countries. This in turn should have raised as a central issue for investigation, whether such efforts could be made consistent with simultaneous adherence to a policy of freedom of trade and of factor movements. The issue, however, was not really faced. Orthodox theory disposed of the infant industry question by pointing up the rapacity of protectionist interests and the difficulty of identifying increasing-returns industries. It dealt with the broader question of the distribution of the gains from trade by showing that *if* there was no unfavorable feedback from trade on other determinants of economic growth, then free trade would increase the economic efficiency of all trading nations and hence world economic welfare. The question virtually answered itself by the way it was formulated. What was omitted was a systematic analysis of when the *if* was justified and when it was not.

Thomas has recently pointed out that nineteenth-century

---

international trade implied (1) that a country's exports may use inputs which could not be transferred to other profitable uses and (2) that by widening markets international trade increased the scope for division of labor, that is, increased productivity. International trade thus could affect the degree of utilization of productive factors, their productivity, and could effect irreversible changes in a country's productive structure.

Mill expressed nineteenth-century orthodoxy in rejecting the first proposition as "a surviving relic of mercantilist theory" and in accepting the second proposition without exploring the effect on international trade theory and policy of its implications of increasing returns and irreversibility. See John Stuart Mill, *Principles of Political Economy* (5th ed., New York, 1904), Vol. II, Chap. 17.

English economists did not really intend the assumption of the international immobility of factors to apply to relations between Great Britain and the newly settled overseas areas. If so, the exclusion was a major one, for, as these relations expanded rapidly, there came to be formed what Thomas loosely calls the "Atlantic economy," with labor and capital flowing in waves from Europe to North America and in wavelets to parts of Latin America and the Antipodes.[7] Labor and capital served also as vehicles for the easy transmission of European technology and aptitudes to the newly settled regions, where the institutional obstacles to the absorption of new techniques were even weaker than in the European countries emitting the technology. Within the Atlantic economy the "rich nations club" was fully formed by the end of the nineteenth century, drawing rapidly away in productivity and income from the rest of the world and establishing the broad outlines of the present worldwide north-south problem.

Of these three major modes of economic influence among nations—the transfer of goods, of factors, and of technique—the classical economists thus chose to emphasize the sufficiency of the first and to relegate treatment of the other two to more casual asides. Yet even though the general assumptions of classical trade theory—international factor immobility, major differences in factor efficiency, and the like—best fitted economic relations between "north" and "south" countries, it was the economic growth of the Atlantic economy countries, where such assumptions were least applicable, that was usually held up as factual proof of the mutual gains to world economic welfare from relatively free trade. Nor did the succeeding orthodoxy, the Heckscher-Ohlin line of analysis, acknowledge that the

[7] Brinley Thomas, *Migration and Economic Growth* (London: Cambridge University Press, 1954), Chap. I–III.

gains may have been the consequence of a particularly favorable conjuncture of all three modes of influence in a limited part of the world.[8] If anything, by discarding the assumption of classical economists that there were institutional and technological determinants of intercountry differences in productivity and by its obsession with showing that trade was a substitute for factor movements, the newer orthodoxy provided an even poorer set of spectacles for viewing nineteenth-century trade and development and for recognizing the outlines of the north-south problem.

Today the normative and positive issues posed by nationalism and the north-south problem can no longer be passed over so lightly. Despite shrinking distances, nuclear bombs, and common markets, there is little reason to assume that the nation-state will shortly fade away, when in fact its numbers have been increasing. Nor is there evidence that international income differences are not continuing to widen. Whether a truly cosmopolitan set of economic policies capable in a world of nation-states of overcoming the worsening north-south problem is politically possible is no doubt a moot question; but the question cannot even be assessed until one specifies the distribu-

---

[8] Bertil Ohlin, *Interregional and International Trade* (Cambridge, Mass.: Harvard University Press, 1933), presents the fullest elaboration of the Heckscher approach; hence, we shall follow custom by referring to the "Heckscher-Ohlin theory."

Ohlin shows that formally the theory deals with the trade and factor movement interaction of two Walrasian general equilibrium economies, each with different initial ratios of productive factors but with common productive techniques. However, as Ohlin attempts to accommodate diverse real world situations within the theory's basic building blocks, the concepts of a productive factor and of common production functions become increasingly emptied of meaning. The emptiness is perhaps a bit less obvious when in the Heckscher-Ohlin cryptography countries A and B are deciphered as America and Britain than when they are assumed to refer to Argentina and Bolivia or Albania and Belgium.

tional norms implied by such a set of policies and examines why the mechanisms for the transfer of goods, factors, and techniques among nations have thus far had such widely different consequences for the rich and the poor nations.

National and International Distributive Norms

That each nation values its economic welfare over that of the rest of the world is not of itself sufficient to deny the operational importance of a mankind interest. Individuals, families, and other subgroups in a nation are also biased in favor of their own economic welfare, yet it is usually meaningful to speak of a nation's economic welfare. It is meaningful not merely because of economic interdependence among subnational units, but because in at least the advanced capitalistic countries as well as in socialist countries, individual and group egoism is tempered by broadly shared norms of social welfare and of income distribution and by mechanisms for making these norms operational. Of course, economic exchange between subunits already implies some community of interest or market "rules of the game," although the welfare significance of this would be trivial if exchange took place under drawn pistols. Physical coercion may be the last resort in a society, but it cannot intrude visibly in all transactions if the notion of social welfare is to accommodate at all to individual egoism. Similarly, if economic exchange is minimal or if distributive norms are not broadly shared and made operational by the market or other social mechanisms, the notion of national economic welfare also becomes trivial. National income as a measure of economic welfare takes on more meaning the greater the economic interdependence and the more broadly held and operational are a nation's distributive norms. For this reason national accounts are less meaningful measures of economic welfare in Nigeria, Brazil, or China than in Great Britain, the United States, or the Soviet Union. For the same reason world output is a less meaningful index of economic welfare than is national output.

Of course, such national norms are not very precise. Indeed, Arrow has shown that it is not generally possible to derive a social welfare function fully consistent with the purely ordinal utility function of each of the members of a society. It must be imposed by some higher authority.[9] Arrow's possibility theorem lends itself to more than one interpretation, including the identification of the higher authority with a political dictator; but surely the simplest deduction is that a stable society of untrammeled egoists is not possible. Each society constrains the egoism of its members by imposing on them rules of the game as well as by indoctrinating them with standards of right conduct and compassion justifying the rules, neither of which can be derived merely from the individual calculus of gain and loss.[10] This is true whether we are concerned with market contracting or political bargaining. In each case the individual is confronted with a received set of rules and normative standards that he is not free to alter at will. But because the legal constraints permit some freedom of choice—indeed, egoism prefers that the scope of freedom be wide—one dimension of the moral question arises. Conscience is not merely the small still voice that tells us someone may be watching.

The moral question takes on still another dimension because in a broader sense social norms always deviate from the actual conduct of a society. Utopia is ever before us. Do such deviations exist because social changes—improvements in technol-

---

[9] Kenneth J. Arrow, *Social Choice and Individual Values* (New York: Wiley, 1951). Alternatively, the distribution norms are internalized; that is, utility functions are cardinal, rather than merely ordinal.

[10] For an incisive and delightfully caustic development of this view, see Joan Robinson, *Economic Philosophy* (London: C. A. Watts, 1962).

ogy, for example—create novel situations which existing norms and their exegesis had not anticipated or because the exegetic process creates novel moral perspectives toward existing social practices? There is no generally accepted answer to this question. Victor Hugo's cryptic aphorism, "Nothing is more powerful than an idea whose time has come," exemplifies the ambiguity surrounding the subject. Which is the prime mover, the idea or the material changes that make people receptive to the idea? Marshall thought that material conditions gave rise to the idea of nationalism, that it was the product of more trade and industry and the spread of literacy and communications within territorial states. Accordingly, he suggests that European nation-states first came on the scene in the seventeenth and eighteenth centuries.[11] Many historians would push the date back, perhaps to the Hundred Years' War, during which the English and French discovered their respective national identities by learning to hate each other.[12]

The point is of more than pedantic importance. The external enemy has always been a powerful force for group and national solidarity. Defense before opulence was the one justification for interfering with free trade that classical economists did not try to sweep under the rug. Appeals to the Deity to smite the enemy and confound his knavish tricks are predictable contributions of the religious establishment to the national effort. It would, however, be grossly unfair to Marshall to imply that he was unaware of the importance of spiritual forces in shaping national attitudes.

[11] Alfred Marshall, *Money Credit and Commerce* (London: Macmillan, 1923), pp. 1–11.
[12] Even so, material interests were not unimportant. During the fifteenth century London merchants favored an anti-French pro-Burgundian foreign policy because this was more likely to protect the wool and cloth trade with Flanders.

The idea of nationalism, however it came upon its time, has in turn gradually put the ruling classes of each nation at an ideological disadvantage. Their slogans have tended to be taken over and turned against them by the lower orders. If citizen Atkins was to risk his life for the nation, he seemed entitled to a say-so in its politics and a fair shake from its economy. The notion of economic freedom underwent a dialectic transformation. From a fighting slogan of the bourgeoisie directed against state controls and monopolies, it was taken over by the lower orders to justify the reimposition of controls on the market economy. Freedom of opportunity came to mean the removal of social and economic barriers to social mobility rather than the mere elimination of legal obstructions to entry. The power to tax is the power to destroy but so, it could also be argued, is the denial of education or employment. "The destruction of the poor," Marshall wrote at the dawning of the welfare state, "is their poverty. . . . The study of the cause of poverty is the study of the causes of the degradation of a large part of mankind." [13] Social Darwinism and *harmonielehre* notwithstanding, the power to tax began to be used to redress the balance between rich and poor.

Egalitarianism has been largely kept in check by growth-manship, but even the latter is being partly converted into an additional justification for interfering with the market and for egalitarian measures. The classical economic defense of inequality has always been what may be called the horse-and-sparrow theorem. Feed the horse well and the sparrows eat; feed the horse badly and the sparrows starve. Income inequality is needed to provide incentives to save and take risks; hence,

[13] Alfred Marshall, *Principles of Economics* (8th ed., London: Macmillan, 1920), p. 3.

egalitarianism weakens the mainsprings of economic growth. Rather than share poverty, it is better to increase total output so that everyone can be absolutely, if not relatively, better off. The rich should always be with us so that the poor may fatten and prosper. Keynes, however, exposed the weakness of one of the implicit premises of the theorem, that market forces suffice to keep labor and capital continually fully employed. With unemployment and excess capacity, increased investment or a reduced willingness to save may instead be needed; and greater income equality is one means of promoting either of these. More recently a second implicit premise of the theorem, that capital and labor markets are sufficiently fluid to adjust smoothly to technological change, is being questioned. The increasingly rapid pace of technological change in advanced countries is tending, it is argued, to leave a widening trail of technological unemployment and economically depressed regions in its wake. Another rationalization is thus created for measures, often egalitarian, to improve mass education, retrain the unemployed, and direct public and private investment to depressed regions. Finally, the spread of socialist ideas and improvements in fiscal and planning technology have broadened possibilities of accumulating capital without relying on capitalist horses. The last has a special attraction in backward economies, whose capitalist horses may eat well but suffer from colonic blockage. Thus, egalitarianism and growthmanship have been forming intermittent alliances. Individual and family egoism may still provide a basic economic rationale for a weakened horse-and-sparrow theorem, but the theorem is no longer the invincible champion of inequality.

There has in sum been a general movement toward what Myrdal calls "national integration . . . the abolition of social and economic barriers and the gradual realization of greater equality of opportunity.[14] To be sure, this has been carried furthest in economically advanced capitalist and socialist economies, while in nations where feudal and tribal influences predominate, it is only the spread of the idea rather than the reality that is visible. Political action in the first group of nations has created various mechanisms for achieving "national integration," while in the second group the great gap between norm and reality is as yet manifesting itself only in heightening political tension and social unrest. Still, it is mainly from a nation's politics and its pattern of economic policy that we derive clues about its distributive norms. The politician is, after all, the main instrument through which the elusive social welfare function of the nation finds expression. Twentieth-century patterns and trends suggest as a safe welfare rule of thumb that for increases in national income to be accepted as genuine improvements of economic welfare in most nations today, they must not occur at the cost of increased inequality.[15]

---

[14] Gunnar Myrdal, *An International Economy: Problems and Prospects* (London: Routledge and Kegan Paul, 1956), pp. 22–23.

[15] In welfare capitalistic nations struggling to reconcile full employment, economic growth, and egalitarianism with price stability, the emergence of an "incomes policy" should provide additional evidence on national distributive norms. Characteristically, "incomes policy," which began as an euphemism for government measures to slow the increase in money wages in order to halt inflation, seems in Great Britain and other Western European countries to be evolving toward broader measures linking wage with profit restraints.

To be sure, there is no unanimity in any society about its distributive norms; but neither, except in the frictionless world of perfect competition, do all individuals prefer all changes in economic efficiency that might raise their measurable income. Since the welfare economics which has been erected on the basis of the latter premise alone has proved to be as useful as a one-legged stool, perhaps the addition of explicit distributional premises will provide a less elegant but more serviceable structure.

For some recent efforts in this direction, see I. M. D. Little, *A Critique of*

Suppose we also accept this as a feasible normative rule for the distribution of increments of world output among nations. Today, after all, pronouncements by politicians and publicists of rich nations that imply acceptance of the rule are easier to find than statements hostile to it. Spokesmen for poor nations tend, of course, to be even more boldly egalitarian, prodding the rich nations to assume responsibility for narrowing the income gap between rich and poor countries, however inoperative such egalitarianism may be within the latter. This significant change in attitude from even a generation ago, when such issues hardly merited concern in either group of countries, is no doubt due in large part to increased unrest in poor countries and to the fear that political upheavals might upset the balance of power in the Cold War. But the fact that normative changes may follow rather than initiate real changes does not in itself suffice to denigrate the normative changes. The basic problem is rather how to make even the weaker of these newly articulated norms operative. Moreover, such distributive norms concern only one aspect of economic welfare. The horse-and-sparrow theorem still lurks in the background. International distribution that lowers the rate of growth of world output would undoubtedly be unacceptable to the rich nations, which are usually able to generate high rates of growth of national output. The problem is, therefore, to develop international economic mechanisms that can reconcile national and international egalitarianism with the continued desire of rich nations to enjoy rapid economic growth. Clearly this involves much more than the comfortable prescription that rich nations should main-

---

Welfare Economics (London: Clarendon Press, 1950); J. D. V. Graff, "On Making a Recommendation in a Democracy," *Economic Journal* LXXII (1962), 293–98; and Harvey Leibenstein, "Notes on Welfare Economics and the Theory of Democracy," *Economic Journal*, LXXII (1962), 299–319.

tain full employment and a high rate of growth so that the poor nations may prosper.

Factor Movements and Trade in Historic Perspective

Economists have tended, we have indicated, to regard international factor movements as a subordinate mechanism for advancing economic welfare—subordinate to international trade or to national efforts to accumulate capital and skills. Generalizations based on experience under one set of institutions and attitudes need not, of course, remain valid if the attitudes and institutions change. Nevertheless, the fact that from differing perspectives economists have managed to arrive at something like a common conclusion is a sufficiently rare occurrence to merit respect.

Unfortunately, the consensus does not extend to the reasons for the conclusion nor to views about what should be done about it; nor, as we try to show in the following survey, is the conclusion entirely valid. Migration was a crucial component of the nineteenth-century institutional structure within which the rich nations of the world developed. Far from trade being an effective substitute for factor movements, as the Heckscher-Ohlin theory would have it, the relationship was strongly complementary in the period when both international commodity and factor markets were freest and the rate of expansion of international trade was highest. Nor, despite the views of Marxist theorists, if not of Marx himself, was colonialism of more than peripheral importance in accounting for the pre-World War I capital movements. It was predominantly freely working markets, reflecting a special constellation of background conditions, that determined the main lines of international trade and factor movements with their widely divergent effects on the economic welfare of different regions. Accumulating market restrictions have been the proximate cause of the progressive decline of international factor movements since World War I; but the restrictions should in turn be understood as national policy reactions to the unevenness with which free market forces had affected the welfare of different regions and classes and to crucial changes in technology and other background conditions. Finally, factor migration of a larger scope and a different order than that attainable under either free market forces or existing allocative mechanisms may well be needed if international welfare norms are to be implemented.

CAPITAL AND LABOR MIGRATION: 1840–1914

The broad statistics on the international migration of labor and capital of this period are well known, as are some of the institutional factors that guided the flow. The data show that around the middle of the nineteenth century there was an explosive increase in migration from Europe to sparsely settled overseas areas in the northern and southern temperate zones, the outflow from Europe reaching a peak just before World War I but diminishing sharply after the War. This explosion of free migration, totaling nearly 60 million in the century preceding World War I, was a historically unique event.[16] In the previous three centuries free migration, mainly to British and Iberian colonies in the Western Hemisphere, had totaled perhaps 2 million, being far outnumbered by the 20 million estimated to have been exported from Africa as slaves in the same period.[17]

---

[16] Fifty million migrated in the period of 1846–1914. Return movements however, were substantial; an estimated 30 percent of U.S. immigrants and 47 percent of Argentine immigrants subsequently returned home. Julius Isaacs, *The Economics of Migration* (London: Routledge and Kegan Paul, 1947), pp. 60–63.

[17] Alexander Carr-Saunders, *World Population* (London: Clarendon Press, 1936), pp. 47–48. "The movement of Africans relative to their numbers in the

Following World War I, free migration, now closely controlled by the countries of immigration, has been a trickle by contrast to the nineteenth-century flood. Instead, war and political and religious persecution have been the main motive forces for such outbursts of migration as have occurred during this period.[18]

Labor migration of the pre-World War I decades was accompanied by an outflow of private capital from Europe that was also historically unique in size relative to the value of international trade or to the gross domestic investment of the capital lending countries. Total British holdings abroad are estimated to have been about 20 billion dollars in 1914 and those of the next largest capital exporters, France and Germany, about 13 billion dollars.[19] British long-term foreign investment during the 1870–1914 period averaged 38 percent of gross and 48 percent of net domestic investment in Great Britain, while French

---

eighteenth century was on a larger scale than the movement of Europeans relative to their numbers in the nineteenth century." *Ibid.*, p. 48.

[18] The outbursts were of massive proportions during and immediately after World War II. Following the partition of India in 1947 some 16 million people were transferred between India and Pakistan. The single largest post-World War II European transfer was the expulsion of 13 million Germans from central Europe. See P. R. Brahmananda, "The Impact on India of Population Transfers in 1947 and After," in International Economic Association, *The Economics of International Migration* (London: Macmillan, 1958), p. 283; and Joseph B. Schechtman, *Post-War Population Transfers in Europe, 1945–55* (Philadelphia: University of Pennsylvania Press, 1962), p. 363.

International migration exclusive of forced transfers totaled around 8 million between 1946 and 1954. This figure, however, includes a large proportion of displaced persons and political refugees relocating from their initial place of refuge and admitted by the receiving countries under special waiver of normal immigration restrictions. See W. D. Borrie, "Concepts and Practices," in *The Cultural Integration of Immigrants* (Paris: UNESCO, 1959), Chap. I.

[19] *International Capital Movements during the Inter-War Period* (New York: United Nations, 1949), pp. 1–2. The three countries together held about three-fourths of total long-term overseas assets in 1913–14.

foreign investment averaged about 44 percent of net domestic savings.[20] Some two-thirds of British investments were in overseas areas that were also the focus of European labor migration: the United States, Canada, Australasia, South Africa, Argentina, and Brazil. Although the proportion of total French and German investment that flowed to these areas was considerably smaller, over 50 percent of the combined overseas investment of the three major European capital exporters paralleled the outflow of European labor.[21] After World War I the outflow of foreign capital declined greatly in relative importance. Long-term investment of the United States, which after World War I succeeded Great Britain as the leading foreign investor, has averaged less than 5 percent of U.S. gross private domestic investment.[22] It has in some cases—notably petroleum investment in Venezuela and in the Middle East—stimulated a moderate inflow of migrants to these areas, but there has been nothing like the close relationship between capital and labor migration that existed in the nineteenth century.

Why the outburst of private capital and free labor migration and its subsequent diminution? Most international trade economists seem now to accept what economic historians, less encumbered by the deadening weight of static international trade theory, had come to recognize earlier: that the outflow was

[20] Simon Kuznets, "International Differences in Capital Formation and Financing," in National Bureau of Economic Research, *Capital Formation and Economic Growth* (Princeton, N.J.: Princeton University Press, 1955), pp. 70–72, Table II-4.

[21] *Ibid.*, Table II-5.

[22] In current dollars U.S. private long-term investment now exceeds the 1914 total of European foreign investment, totaling 45 billion dollars by 1961. However, because of rising prices and the growth in the real value of world trade and domestic investment since 1914, U.S. private foreign investment has been much less significant for the world economy than was European foreign investment in the pre-World War I decades.

the result of an historically unique conjuncture of circumstances. But while there is probably general agreement on the cataloguing of these circumstances, their relative importance and precise mode of interaction is still shrouded in controversy. It must not be assumed, therefore, that the following implications drawn from this cataloguing represents any general consensus; no such consensus exists.

The pre-World War I flow of capital and labor occurred during the heyday of relative free trade and unrestricted migration between Europe and the countries of immigration, on the one hand, [23] and the European colonies on the other. Colonialism, however, has been vastly overrated as a stimulant to foreign investment. Colonial investment was indeed privileged investment, for in various open and subtle ways colonial powers sought to reserve colonial investment opportunities for their nationals and to protect them against risk. But the interesting fact is that, despite this, foreign investment in what has become the core of today's underdeveloped world was a small fraction of the foreign investment of each of the major colonial powers.[24] "The main flow of capital . . . was not to the needi-

[23] It is a minor qualification that some of the immigration areas were within the British Empire. They had all become virtually autonomous politically prior to World War I. Similarly, while it is true that free trade was not prevalent in the United States and continental Europe, trade barriers of various types were much more moderate in the pre-World War I decades than in those following the War.

[24] Writing of British investment in India, H. J. Habbakuk comments that "The greater part of the guaranteed interest on Indian railway loans was paid out of colonial taxation." "Free Trade and Commercial Expansion, 1853–1870," *Cambridge History of the British Empire* (London: Cambridge University Press, 1940), II, 764. Yet investment in India and Ceylon made up only 10 percent of total British overseas investment in 1914. The French and German governments were fairly successful in directing foreign loans and investment to European political allies and hoped-for allies, but a small fraction of their foreign investment went to their respective colonies. On this see Herbert Feis, *Europe, the World's Banker, 1870–1914* (New Haven: Yale University Press, 1933).

est countries with their 'teeming millions,' but to the sparsely peopled areas where conditions for rapid progress along familiar western lines were exceptionally favorable." [25] The newly established Asian and African nations are not likely, therefore, to find the provision of a favorable legal and ideological climate for foreign investment to be the key to sustained economic growth. Such investment was modest enough when investors enjoyed a much more favorable climate under colonialism.

It is by now also recognized that the pre-World War I migrations were stimulated by special demographic, geographic, and technological circumstances. The general influence of these factors, if not the precise manner of their interaction, is fairly clear.

Demographic forces in the nineteenth century were generating increases in population growth rates of a size and duration unique in European history at a time when industrialization and improvements of labor productivity in agriculture were also undermining the labor-absorptive capacity of agriculture and traditional handicrafts. Industrialization and urbanization were, moreover, increasing the demand for food and industrial raw materials at rates that pressed against the growth of agricultural and raw materials supplies. So conscious were nineteenth-century economists of this last interrelation that some apotheosized it into an inexorable economic law of the falling rate of profit. Industry operated under increasing returns—that is, historically falling real unit costs—while agriculture and raw materials operated under diminishing returns—historically rising unit costs—because of the fixity of natural endowment. Industrial expansion was, therefore, continually threatened and in

[25] Ragnar Nurkse, "The Problem of International Investment Today in the Light of Nineteenth Century Experience," *Economic Journal*, LXIV (1954), 750.

the long run could be brought to a halt by adverse terms of trade between industrial and primary products.[26] We know now through hindsight that the "law" was an historically bounded generalization, rendered plausible by the special characteristics of nineteenth-century technology and economic organization. Today, the "law" still emphasizes critical obstacles for backward economies attempting to industrialize. It may even retain plausibility for the prophetic-minded as a threat for the ultra-long run, when the exhaustion of energy, fresh water, or parking space may force interplanetary migration. But the premises on which it is based seem largely irrelevant as intermediate long-term relationships for at least the economically advanced part of the world, where accelerating advances in chemical and energy technology are progressively freeing economic growth from dependence on specific natural resources. Technology is increasingly capable of "creating" the natural resources it needs.

This was not so for nineteenth-century economic growth, which was almost as vitally dependent on coal, iron, timber, and agricultural land at the end of the century as it was at the beginning. The critical technological feature of the period was the advance in transportation: the railroad, the iron-hulled sailing ship, and the ocean-going steamship. With these Europe largely overcame the threat to its economic growth from natural resource limitations. Cheap transportation facilitated the migration of labor, the export of European industrial goods, and the return shipment of foodstuffs and raw materials from the newly settled areas. The opportunity to invest in overseas trans-

---

[26] W. S. Jevons, *The Coal Question: An Inquiry Concerning the Progress of the Nation and the Probable Exhaustion of Our Coal-Mines* (London: Macmillan, 1865), was a dramatic effort to extend the "law" to industrial energy supply.

port facilities was also by far the most important stimulus to European foreign investment. According to one recent estimate, about 60 percent of British foreign investment in the period 1865–94 was in railroads alone.[27] However, capital moved much more slowly and European labor in only a trickle to the heavily populated backward regions, whether colonial or nominally independent, where plantation agriculture and the mining of secondary minerals were the main stimuli. To obtain labor for such activities, the indentured labor system and similar forced labor devices were often applied to the native population. Until outlawed by reformist colonial administrations, the limited nineteenth-century migration of Asiatics to Africa, to other parts of Asia, and to Latin America was largely of indentured labor. The distinction between rich and poor regions was already notable in the nineteenth century, and in the poor regions private acquisitiveness tended then as now to pick the more accessible fruit from the weedy jungle of backwardness rather than systematically to cultivate the terrain.

European social organization and laissez-faire ideology also played an important role in stimulating emigration; and, in turn, both were protected by it. In a market economy the broad sharing of economic gains from advancing technology depends on the ease of internal factor mobility, not merely within a given class but among classes. But nineteenth-century Europe was hardly a society in which economically displaced peasants and agricultural workers could readily become commercial farmers or technologically obsolete craftsmen, factory owners. Nor did social policies exist to divert some of the income gains of those benefiting from technological advances to compensate the losers. Emigration eased the burden for the losers and thus

---

[27] Harvey H. Siegel and Matthew Simon, "British Foreign Capital Issues 1865–1894," *Journal of Economic History*, XXII (1961), 576.

also the pressure on European society for radical remedies. In one European country after another, emigration reached a peak in those decades in which the country was undergoing intense demographic pressures or severe tensions in agriculture or handicrafts associated wth industrialization or free trade. Then, as the population pressures eased and the occupational structure gradually adjusted, emigration fell off. Thus, Irish emigration reached a peak in the decade after 1846 and then gradually diminished. The British peak decades were the 1870s and 1890s, the Scandinavian were the 1880s and 1890s, the German was the 1880s. By 1900 the major outflow was from southern and eastern Europe—but here World War I and postwar immigration restrictions checked the inflow at its flood, and migration ceased to be a major safety valve.

It was sheer good fortune for the stability of the laissez-faire rules of the game that resource-rich overseas areas were available to absorb the relatively unskilled hordes of European immigrants in agriculture, construction, mining, and even industry. There is, in fact, no general agreement on how the economic push of population growth and occupation displacement in Europe interacted with the pull of cheap land and higher wages overseas. More immigrants, for example, came to the United States in its prosperous years than in its depressed years.[28] But Thomas also found migration related to the twenty-year building cycle in the United States and in Great Britain in an intricate pattern that suggests that "push" factors dominated in a number of critical periods.[29] What is evident is that a return

[28] Harry Jerome, *Migration and Business Cycles* (New York: National Bureau of Economic Research, 1926).

[29] Brinley Thomas, *Migration and Economic Growth*, Chap. VI–XI. The alternating of British troughs and U.S. peaks of their respective twenty-year building cycles, and the association of higher rates of emigration and capital export from Great Britain with troughs in the British building cycle is the basic pulsating mechanism linking the Atlantic economy. Leads and lags be-

to laissez-faire rules of the game now, even if politically possible, would not suffice to make labor migration as effective an alleviator for today's newly industrializing nations. Modern industrial and agricultural technology has less and less use for the ill-tutored and unskilled. It is questionable whether the market for unskilled labor in advanced countries could easily absorb immigration of nineteenth-century proportions. Moreover, the new industrializing nations are obviously incapable of exporting capital to higher income nations in the nineteenth-century pattern so as to facilitate the absorption of the immigrants. The rich receiving nations could certainly bear the capital cost of integrating large volumes of immigrants, but this would be more an act of international solidarity than of national self-interest. If the balance of social benefit and cost from mass immigration was favorable to the resource-rich underpopulated nations of the nineteenth century, it has shifted the other way in the twentieth century.[30]

---

tween the peaking of immigration and the peaking of the building cycle in the United States are the indicators Thomas uses to identify whether "push" or "pull" forces dominated a particular cycle. Thomas' Atlantic economy mechanism is an imaginative construction which, however, becomes less convincing when extended to include other European countries than Great Britain, and other overseas areas than the United States. Even the validity of the mechanisms for these two countries has been questioned recently by H. J. Habbakuk, "Fluctuations in House-Building in Britain and the United States in the Nineteenth Century," *Journal of Economic History*, XXIII (1962), 198–230. The questioning, however, consists primarily in suggesting other plausible explanations for the apparently inverse relation between the U.S. and the British twenty-year building cycles rather than in outrightly rejecting the Atlantic economy mechanism.

[30] It is perhaps conceivable that technology might have taken a different course if twentieth-century immigration barriers had not altered the supply of labor in advanced countries. The proposition, however, should not commend itself to free traders; for it suggests that a nation may be able to elevate its technology by making labor relatively scarce, which can be done by restricting immigration or by protecting labor-intensive industries against competing imports.

In short, within the institutional and ideological constraints on economic policy in the nineteenth century, factor migration did play a vital role in facilitating the great expansion of free trade and in promoting the economic development of western Europe and the overseas areas which received the labor and capital inflows. It is arguable, and indeed many economic historians and economists have recently made the point, that Great Britain and France might have been better off to have diverted some of their capital exports to home investment. But whether true or not, factor migration and the great expansion of international trade worked well enough to ease pressures to change domestic laissez-faire policies. It is strange that nineteenth-century economic orthodoxy should have failed to appreciate the extent to which the expansion of trade was interrelated to capital and labor migration. Thomas suggests plausibly that this "strange air of isolationism" was due to an unwillingness to popularize the notion that free trade in a society of "non-competing groups" (strong obstacles to interclass mobility) could harm some groups and force some of their members to emigrate.[31] What is even less comprehensible is why the Heckscher-Ohlin school of economists, writing from the vantage of historic hindsight and with a model that emphasizes the domestic occupational shifts resulting from free trade, should have devoted so much ink to showing how trade can substitute for factor movements and so little to the broad complemen-

---

[31] There was awareness among some late-nineteenth-century English economists that free trade could force emigration. The point, however, tended to be made as a doctrinal aside in the international trade literature. Indeed, Charles Bastable went so far as to deny its logical validity. See Thomas, *Migration*, Chap. II. Jevons, a notable *enfant terrible*, predicted that coal exhaustion would accelerate British emigration and the industrial development of overseas countries. As a patriotic Englishman, however, he could only view this prospect with alarm. See Jevons, *The Coal Question*, Chap. XV.

tarity that existed between the two in the period of history in which trade and factor movements was freest.[32]

CAPITAL AND LABOR MIGRATION SINCE WORLD WAR I

After World War I the interlocking chain was broken at various points, with the result that international migration of labor and capital has become a less significant force in the past half-century. Again it is easier to list the changed conditions that brought this about than to establish precise causal connections between these conditions and factor migration.

Xenophobia clearly played a role in the gradual raising of immigration restrictions in the twentieth century by the United States and other major recipients of the pre-World War I emigrants. Even at the height of this inflow, measures were adopted by the United States, Canada, Australia, New Zealand, and South Africa to halt Oriental immigration.[33] The "new" immigration from southern and eastern Europe after 1890 aroused more widespread hostility in the United States than the "old" immigration from northwest Europe. The immigration quotas established by the U.S. Immigration Act of 1924 were explicitly designed to discriminate against the "new" immigration, a policy that with some modification still prevails.[34]

Nevertheless, the picture is seriously incomplete if we concentrate only on racial and cultural animosity. Egalitarianism, paradoxically, also helped to undermine liberal immigration policies. During most of the nineteenth century westward ex-

[32] For a review of the recent international trade literature on the relations between trade and factor movements, see Caves, *Trade and Economic Structure*, Chap. V.

[33] Compare Isaac, *Economics of Migration*, pp. 54–58.

[34] Two-thirds of U.S. quota immigration in recent years has been assigned to Ireland, the United Kingdom, and Germany. However, this bias has been partly offset in the past decade by short-term emergency legislation to admit nonquota refugees from Communist countries of Eastern Europe.

pansion in the United States and Canada and the exploitation of rich and relatively accessible agricultural and mineral resources sustained fairly loose-knit societies that could absorb large numbers of immigrants without seriously injuring the income and status of any major occupational groups. Vertical mobility— entry into higher status through farming, trade, or handicrafts —appeared unusually easy to those who had emigrated from more highly stratified societies. Egalitarian pressures were eased by the conviction that, despite great inequality of income, there was a high degree of equality of opportunity. By the end of the century, however, large-scale industry and the end of the "frontier" somewhat dimmed the vision of easy upward mobility. Class lines tightened, and the immigrant appeared a more sustained threat to workers conscious of the greater permanency of their working-class status. Thus, the trade union movement became a major pressure group for immigration restrictions.[35]

Egalitarian pressures affected migration in other ways as well. In most of the major countries of immigration and in western Europe the introduction of social security measures, supplemented after World War II by full employment policies, marked the emergence of the modern welfare state. The distress and inequities generated by technological change were now partly redressed by policies that transferred the gains from economic growth to the mass of the citizenry to a degree that the market mechanism was rarely able to achieve. In western Europe the result was greatly to reduce the impetus to emigrate. Since the establishment of U.S. immigration restrictions in 1921, the annual British, Irish, German, and Scandinavian quotas have rarely been filled.

Welfare-state objectives also require the immigrants to "be

---

[35] For detailed elaboration of this thesis, see Thomas, *Migration and Economic Growth,* Chap. III, VII, IX, XII, XIV.

as far as possible complementary and not competitive with the existing labor force." [36] A major consequence of this vague prescription has been the marked rise in the educational and occupational skills of immigrants.[37] Through labor permits, minimum capital requirements, and other devices, the flow of immigrants to wealthy countries has been regulated to make immigration primarily an instrument for offsetting supply shortages in skilled and professional labor categories.[38] The unskilled may enter only under special dispensation, dictated by the labor requirements of agriculture and service trades or by the desire to make a gesture of solidarity toward former colonies or satellite countries.[39] Instead of functioning as a

[36] From the recommendations of a UNESCO conference of academic and government immigration experts meeting in Havana in April, 1956, as reported in *Cultural Integration of Immigrants*, pp. 291–97. The conferees roundly rejected laissez-faire immigration, the tenor of their views being that immigration must be planned to insure its limitation to educated, skilled migrants capable of being easily integrated economically and culturally into the country of immigration. The numbers of such migrants should further be constrained so as not to exceed the "economic absorptive capacity" of the immigrating country.

The recommendations largely rationalize the aims of existing immigration policies, in which a concern to avoid exploitation of untutored immigrants is supplemented by a much greater concern not to disturb domestic labor markets or to arouse anti-foreigner hostilities.

Borrie, in *ibid.*, Chap. II, III, is a useful summary of existing immigration policies and the attitudes underlying them.

[37] Professional and technical personnel were more numerous than any other occupational category of U.S. immigrants in 1941–61. Only one-third of U.S. immigrants in the same period were classified in various unskilled categories. See U.S. Bureau of the Census, *Statistical Abstract of the United States 1961* (Washington, D.C.: Government Printing Office, 1961), p. 99. A similar composition of immigrants is to be found for Canada, Australia, and South Africa.

[38] Compare Borrie, in *Cultural Integration of Immigrants*, Chap. II, and J. Zubrzcki, "Across the Frontiers of Europe," in *ibid.*, pp. 159–80.

[39] Thus, Great Britain permits the annual entry of a limited number of migrants from its remaining colonies and the poor Commonwealth countries. The United States permits entry outside the quota system to citizens of

safety valve, immigration now tends to draw scarce skilled and professional talent from poorer to richer countries. Less affluent members of the rich nations' club, like Great Britain, are concerned over the loss of academic and scientific talent to the United States, although the loss in Great Britain is offset by an inflow of talent from India and other poor Commonwealth countries. For underdeveloped countries, however, the loss is uncompensated, a recent survey indicating that "no less than 20 to 25 percent of the newly trained cadres of scientists, and the most talented and gifted of them, leave their [under-developed] country." [40] Ironically, Argentina and Brazil, the only two major immigration countries of the nineteenth century that failed to make it into the rich nations' club, still maintain liberal policies toward unskilled immigrants. Brazil, for example, despite its mass of underemployed rural poor, applies no quota or occupational discrimination against Portuguese immigrants and requires that 80 percent of non-Portuguese immigrants be agricultural workers and farmers.[41]

Market changes, trade restrictions, and technological improvements have also reduced the relative importance of international labor migration in the twentieth century. The rising per capita income of the rich nations has not been matched by an equivalent rate of increase in the demand for primary products. Engel's Law has determined this for foodstuffs, and ad-

---

Western Hemisphere nations. France and West Germany allow the entry of unskilled labor from poorer Common Market countries and associate members like Greece. In all these cases, however, entry is closely regulated by labor permits, pre-entry job guarantees by employers, and similar devices.

[40] From a paper by V. Kovda, Director of UNESCO's Department of Natural Sciences to the United Nations' Conference on the Application of Science and Technology, 1962, as reported in the *Manchester Guardian*, February 12, 1962.

[41] Borrie, in *ibid.*, pp. 79–80.

vances in chemical and energy technology, for raw materials. From the end of World War I most branches of agriculture and mining have been under chronic threat of falling terms of trade, alleviated by short-lived boom periods. The result has been the spread of cartels, tariffs, and domestic subsidies to restrict supply and protect domestic agricultural and mining interests, many of the schemes being sanctified by national egalitarian norms. International trade in primary products has thus grown more slowly than in the pre-World War I era, as has the demand for agricultural and mining labor. Technological advances in agriculture and mining, which have helped offset the downward pressure on profits, have further reduced the need for unskilled immigrant labor for these activities in advanced countries.

The same forces have also altered the composition of foreign capital exports. In the nineteenth century British and French railroad entrepreneurs eagerly promoted railroad investment schemes in foreign countries. Governments of these countries, conscious of the great indirect benefits of a railroad network, assisted by providing subsidies and guarantees to railroad investors. The rapid growth of demand for primary exports facilitated the floating of railroad securities in European capital markets by strengthening assurances that dividends and debt servicing could be readily managed by the borrowing countries. Motor transportation in the twentieth century, however, terminated the railroad-building period and ended a major inducement to private capital exporting. The motor road does not attract foreign private entrepreneurship, and the diminished growth of primary exports no longer gives the assurance of ready debt servicing that might open up private capital markets to the large-scale financing of public road construction in primary producing countries.

In the past three decades private capital exporting has shifted from lending to direct investment, primarily in basic petroleum and mining in primary exporting countries and in manufacturing in more advanced countries. Both the flow and distribution of benefits from direct investment have been tied to tariff and tax policies in the capital-exporting and -importing countries to a far greater degree and in a much more complex manner than in earlier epochs. While raising import restrictions discourages investment in primary exports, the reverse is true of manufacturing investment, where "tariff-hopping" into protected domestic markets has been a major motivation behind the establishment of manufacturing branches and subsidiaries. The latter type of foreign investment has been much the greater among the rich nations, but to a limited extent less advanced countries have also managed to induce foreign manufacturing investment by means of import restrictions. Tax policies affect the flow of primary investment and play a crucial role in the distribution of the benefits of such investment. Without fiscal levies, underdeveloped host countries tend to receive only a small percentage of the value of output of foreign-owned primary export industries.[42] The inducement is strong, therefore, to use discriminatory taxes to capture a larger share, to tax, so to speak, some of the economic rent deriving from the relative richness of the natural resources that foreign firms are exploiting. The effective margin for such discriminatory taxation is, however, set in part by the tax policies of the capital-exporting countries. A reduc-

[42] For example, in the 1950s only about 30 percent of petroleum value added of the foreign-owned petroleum sector of Venezuela consisted of local outlays on labor and materials. The percentage averaged even less for the foreign-owned copper mines of Chile. See *United States Business and Labor in Latin America*, a study prepared at the request of the Sub-Committee on American Republic Affairs, U.S. Senate, Committee on Foreign Relations, Eighty-Sixth Congress, Second Session (Washington, D.C.: Government Printing Office, 1960), p. 41, Table 13.

tion of tax rates at home weakens the inducement to invest abroad or forces the host countries to lower their tax take.[43] Tariff-hopping investments in underdeveloped countries, on the other hand, since they do not directly earn foreign exchange from their sales, tend to be influenced by foreign exchange availability and by profit transfer regulations as well as by tax rates in the host countries.[44]

As a result of these and other complicating factors, the course of private capital exporting in recent decades has been marked by frequent controversy and crises of confidence in the capital-exporting and -importing countries. Less developed capital-importing countries seek to increase the domestic yield from foreign-owned enterprises by tax, employment, and profit-transfer regulations. Capital-exporting countries gravitate between the desire to promote private foreign investment for economic gain or as a weapon of foreign policy, and concern with the possible adverse effect of large-scale capital exports on domestic production and employment. More than ever, private foreign investment has become a game for giant firms capable of spreading risks and of maneuvering from a position of strength among the shifting patterns of tariffs, taxes, and ex-

[43] Because U.S. tax laws permit firms to deduct most foreign taxes from their U.S. tax liability, the margin for discriminatory taxation has been high, since foreign taxes reduce U.S. Treasury receipts rather than the profits of firms with foreign investments. U.S. petroleum firms, for example, have paid very little U.S. tax on their very large and lucrative foreign investments in petroleum extraction. Lowering U.S. profit taxes would probably, by shifting more of the burden of host country taxes to the petroleum firms, lessen the attractiveness of investing in foreign oil fields. Removing U.S. import restrictions on foreign oil would, on the other hand, stimulate such investment.

[44] Overcharging foreign branches and subsidiaries for supplies and services is apparently a commonly used device for evading domestic taxes and restrictions on the transfer of profits. Such tactics, for example, are suspected of foreign firms operating in India, according to a recent study. See United Nations, "Postwar Foreign Investment in India," *Economic Bulletin for Asia and the Far East*, XIII (1962), 1–16.

change controls. Despite platitudes about the great mutual benefits from foreign private investment, deep and unresolved conflicts of interest between capital-exporting and -importing countries prevent the establishment of reasonably stable rules of the game comparable to those within which nineteenth-century foreign investment flowed.

Technology, to be sure, may yet make mass settlement of deserts and jungles economic, just as nineteenth-century transportation improvements opened up overseas temperate-zone regions to large-scale capital and labor migration. However, while the areas of heavy population pressure could well use the additional food and raw material produce of the desert and the jungle, they are hardly likely to be able to export the capital necessary to open these regions to exploitation. Neither are they likely to be economically in a position to import the produce at a rate sufficient to make privately profitable the investment by advanced countries on which mass settlement and exploitation of such regions would depend. The institutional arrangements necessary to bring about the requisite flow of capital, trade and techniques for the settlement of the desert and the jungle will have to differ radically from the market system under which the nineteenth-century exploitation of the overseas temperate zone regions took place.

Capital and Labor Migration and
Productivity and Income Differentials

According to the Heckscher-Ohlin theory, both international trade and factor movements reduce international differences in factor prices. Factor movements are presumed to do so in a direct and obvious way; international trade through pressing each country to concentrate more on the production of those commodities that use larger proportions of their most abundant—and thus presumably cheaper—factor inputs. Both trade and factor movements should, therefore, raise world economic welfare, the reduction in international factor price differences representing both a more efficient allocation of productive factors and a reduction in per capita income differences between nations.

The facts have generally been otherwise. In the period when international trade came closest to the free trade ideal and international factor movements were least encumbered by legal obstacles, not only did the rich nations' club pull away from the rest of the world in income and wealth, but income differences between the European and overseas temperate zone members generally widened.[45] Both these diverging trends have continued through the subsequent era of restrictions on trade and factor migration. Similar long-term widening of regional income differences have also been identified within various nations, despite the fact that domestic trade and factor markets are much freer than international markets from the hindrances of language, tax, and legal differences.[46] Trade and factor movements may promote economic growth, but they do so mainly through channels that escape the Heckscher-Ohlin theory. These channels form the subject of much of the recent literature on regional and national economic development.

The basic premises of this literature may be briefly contrasted with that of the Heckscher-Ohlin theory. The latter inhabits a world of full employment, where workers in all countries costlessly acquire the same skills and aptitudes, and entrepreneurs

---

[45] Compare Simon Kuznets, "Quantitative Aspects of the Economic Growth of Nations: Levels and Variability of Rates of Growth," *Economic Development and Cultural Change*, V, No. 1 (October, 1956), pp. 1–93.

[46] The Italian north-south problem is, perhaps, the best publicized case. See Alessandro Molinari, "Southern Italy," *Banca Nazionale del Lavoro Quarterly Review*, II (1949), 25–47.

and managers the same organizational and technological knowledge. Given these and other simplifying assumptions, differences in the proportions of factors with which various nations are endowed explain international differences in factor productivity, and these can be reduced by factor movements or by specialization through trade. Economic development literature, on the other hand, lives in a more readily recognizable world, where differences in social and economic organization generate major qualitative differences in factor skills, and these largely account for international differences in factor productivity. Rich countries are more efficiently organized to import skills and to develop and apply technological improvements than poor countries. Neither rich nor poor countries are likely to stay for long on the frontier of their production possibility space, where Heckscher-Ohlin countries are always to be found. Rich countries suffer from periodic bouts of unemployment and sluggish growth and reach unexpected peaks of productive efficiency primarily in war emergencies, but they are normally able to indulge their preference for individual freedom without sacrificing high rates of economic growth. Poor countries, on the other hand, with their more serious organizational weaknesses, are unable to accommodate both and often enjoy neither.

In the economic development world, shifts in trade affect output in more complex ways than in the Heckscher-Ohlin world. They may alter the rate of investment and hence the level of employment and output in a favorable or unfavorable direction depending on particular circumstances. When unfavorable, efforts to sustain or raise domestic output may require protectionist measures. In the Heckscher-Ohlin world, trade affects only the composition of output and always in a favorable direction, so that protectionism becomes an unjustified interference with the efficient operation of the market mechanism.

In the Heckscher-Ohlin world the high-wage economy will have the lower rate of return on capital, and factor movements will always reduce factor price differences.[47] In the economic development world, where qualitative differences in human skills and in social and economic organization largely determine productivity differences, low wages are often associated with rapidly falling marginal returns from private investment. Capital and labor movements from poor and slow-growing to rich and rapidly-growing regions may progressively widen rather than narrow regional productivity and income differences. The exodus of the more skilled and adventurous and a reduction in the ratio of productive age groups to dependent population in the poorer region may depress the marginal efficiency of investment and sustain the continued outflow of capital and labor. This pattern, reinforced by emigration overseas, approximately describes, for example, the interaction between southern and northern Italy after 1861, when the two regions were united in a single free trade area.[48] Similar dynamic patterns of regional income divergence have been identified for other countries.[49]

Within a nation, however, growing regional differences may

[47] In fairness to Ohlin it should be pointed out that his *Interregional and International Trade* mentions many deviations from the basic model. Ohlin's errors were to attempt to accommodate these deviations within the premises of the Heckscher-Ohlin theory by stretching its premises out of all recognition and to assume that the tendency toward interregional factor price equalization through trade or factor movements was the rule in the real world.

[48] Compare Alessandro Molinari, "Southern Italy," *Banca Nazionale del Lavoro Quarterly Review*, II (1949), 25–47; and Giuseppe di Nardi, "The Policy of Regional Development," *Banca Nazionale del Lavoro Quarterly Review*, XIII (1960), 215–46.

[49] For Latin American examples, see Stephen H. Robock, "Regional Aspect of Economic Development," *Papers and Proceedings of the Regional Science Association*, II (1956), 51–63. France and the United States also have their north-south problems, while in Great Britain the geographic direction is reversed, with the south drawing away from the depressed north.

be checked in time by two countertendencies. The continued growth of the rich region may eventually increase the demand for the labor and the natural resources of the poor region sufficiently to reverse the net flow of private capital between regions. Egalitarian policies may lead to a growing transfer of public capital for developing the natural resources and human skills of the poor region. High-income countries thus tend to have smaller regional per capita income differences than low-income countries.[50] These counterforces are much less effective, however, among nations. Trade and private capital linkages between rich and poor nations are weaker, while the international transfer of public capital has been distorted by military and ideological objectives, and the donor nations are less able to insure that the transfers will be utilized productively.[51]

In the economic development world, therefore, poor nations must rely primarily on their ability to raise the quality of their human skills and economic organization if they are to emerge from economic backwardness. This has at least two major consequences for international economic relations.

The first is that nationalism becomes a major potential force for facilitating economic development in poor regions. In the contemporary world the nation is the largest decision unit with the power potential to bring about the radical institutional changes and the reallocation of domestic resources that may be vital prerequisites for faster or more equitable economic growth, while nationalistic slogans are the most effective rally-

[50] For example, the UN Economic Commission for Europe finds an inverse correlation between national per capita income and regional per capita income differences for European countries. See *Economic Survey of Europe, 1954* (Geneva: United Nations, 1955), Chap. VI.

[51] For a general discussion of the international north-south problem see Gunnar Myrdal, *Economic Theory and Under-Developed Regions* (London: Duckworth, 1957).

ing cries currently available for inducing popular acquiescence to the changes. The pattern has by no means been limited to poor nations. The emergence of the modern welfare state has also taken place under the aegis of nationalist slogans, and with it have come many of the controls that today influence the flow of international trade and factor movements.[52] But nationalism has an even greater appeal to poor nations desperately striving to emerge from economic backwardness. Indeed, there is no case in the twentieth century of successful emergence that has not evolved extensive governmental efforts made under the aegis of a prickly nationalism.[53]

Secondly, capital and capital movements, nebulous enough concepts even in the neat Heckscher-Ohlin world, become even more so in the untidy economic development world. In the Heckscher-Ohlin world, capital is essentially a physical quantity, a stock of produced goods working with labor and natural resources to produce the national output of final goods and services. To insure full utilization of this stock, it is assumed capable of rapid changes from fish to fowl to tractor, large or small as the need may be. A capital inflow from abroad, whether measured from balance-of-payments data or from the increase in net worth of foreign-owned assets, represents a net addition to the nation's malleable capital stock and hence productive

---

[52] On the nationalistic character of the modern welfare state see Gunnar Myrdal, *Beyond the Welfare State: Economic Planning and Its International Implications* (New Haven: Yale University Press, 1960).

[53] The Soviet Union, Japan, Italy, and Israel, the only four countries that in recent decades seem to be approaching rich nation status, clearly substantiate this point. Others like Yugoslavia, Brazil, Mexico, Egypt, and the remaining Soviet-bloc nations, which show some promise of eventually reaching this status, also rely heavily on extensive government-directed development efforts sanctified by strident appeals to national solidarity. Despite ideological qualms, the Soviet-bloc countries in recent years seem to be finding national solidarity a more effective rallying point than the international solidarity of the working class.

capacity. One need not concern oneself with the physical composition of the addition, because market forces insure that the composition will be such as to maximize the yield from the additional capital and effect the optimal reorganization of the existing capital stock.

In the economic development world, however, capital inflows, conventionally measured, may tell us very little about their net contribution to productive capacity. Social yields can deviate substantially from market yields, and the composition of the capital inflow does matter. Tariff-hopping investment may make a much smaller net contribution to productive capacity than an equivalent sum invested in education or roads. A given sum invested in a new export industry may with suitable taxation increase the capacity to import and give more flexibility to the capital stock of a backward nation than the same sum invested in an import-substituting consumer industry yielding a higher rate of profit. Increased import restrictions or a cyclical downturn in advanced countries may force other nations to seek foreign loans merely to sustain domestic activity, so that the increased borrowing is associated with no discernible increase in the rate of growth of the capital stock, although foreign claims against its output rise.[54]

But the most dramatic and, for backward countries, the most important cases involve clashes between the desire to attract foreign capital and the need to raise the quality of national skills and organization through radical reforms. Periods of intense

---

[54] John Knapp, "Capital Exports and Growth," *Economic Journal*, LXVII (1957), 432–44, analyzes a number of types of what he calls "excess borrowing." According to Knapp much of the nineteenth-century capital lending involved "excess borrowing," which could be said to have contributed to the economic growth of the borrowing countries only in the sense that the prevailing "rules of the game" prevented nations from dealing with cyclical fluctuations and other economic imperfections more efficiently.

and widespread social and economic reform are intended as transitional steps to a new and more stable institutional framework, the pace and extent of the reforms varying with the ideology of the reforming governments and their appraisal of national needs and political possibilities. But these critical periods of rapid institutional reform are characteristically marked by a falling away of new foreign investment and by capital flight. Foreign investors do not consider a society in the hands of radical reformers to have "a favorable climate for foreign investment," and frustrated reformers and revolutionaries in backward societies are well aware that an essential for establishing a "favorable climate" is to slow the pace and extent of the reforms. What is the net addition to productive capacity of an inflow of foreign capital whose prerequisite is a weakening of efforts to alter the institutional status quo?

Foreign Aid and the Cold War

In principle, intergovernmental loans and grants should be free of fears that cause private capital inflows to dry up when the effort to reform backward societies is most intense and foreign capital assistance could be most productive. In practice this has been true only to a limited extent of the post-World War II flow of foreign aid, and usually for reasons having less to do with genuine ideological tolerance than with Cold War strategy. The recent recommendation of the Clay Committee that the United States avoid financing public investment in underdeveloped countries that might compete with private enterprise is illustrative of a view widely shared by Congress and the U.S. business community.[55] Internal disagreements over

[55] *Scope and Distribution of United States Military and Economic Assistance Programs*, Report to the President of the United States from the Committee to Strengthen the Security of the Free World (Washington, D.C.: Government Printing Office, 1963).

foreign aid policy have not yet impelled the Soviet Union to air its linen in public so freely, but there is little reason to doubt that Soviet leaders regard aid to mixed economies like Egypt or India with at least something like the distaste with which U.S. politicians have regarded U.S. aid to Yugoslavia—or India. Usually, the range of ideological tolerance of each of the Cold War giants has been narrower when their economic and military dominance of a region has been more pronounced, as U.S. behavior toward Latin America and Soviet behavior toward eastern Europe illustrate. But even in regions toward which the Cold War rivals find it politic to broaden their range of ideological tolerance, underdeveloped countries genuinely committed to economic development must still work to maintain the "credibility" of their ideological neutrality in order to keep aid flowing in from both sides. Whether this imposes a desirable degree of caution and eclecticism on the development effort or merely increases its inconsistencies it is difficult to say. It would be exceedingly strange, however, if the mixtures of ideology and Cold War *Realpolitik* motivating the Cold War rivals should, like an invisible hand, always bring about a set of institutional reforms and development programs in the neutral underdeveloped countries superior to what they would be able to devise if they were freer from competing Cold War pressures.

It is no doubt true that the Cold War has been a major force for increasing the flow of aid from rich to poor nations; but it is doubtful if the additional volume of aid stimulated by the Cold War has contributed much to the economic development of underdeveloped countries. Most of the additional aid has been directed to countries considered strategically important to one or another side in the Cold War, and these are not necessarily countries seriously committed to economic development. Indeed, there is probably an inverse correlation between lack of commitment and strategic importance. Countries whose governments are primarily concerned with protecting the institutional status quo against mounting internal pressures for reform and modernization tend sooner or later to become strategic battlegrounds in the Cold War by their very conservatism. By far the largest share of U.S. aid to underdeveloped countries has had as its primary purpose the protection of recognizably status-quo-oriented but friendly governments against overthrow by internal upheaval or external force.[56] As such it has usually earned its dividend. To have expected it also to accelerate economic development was to ask for a double dividend in the most unlikely circumstances. Yet mounting frustration at not getting this double return and chagrin at discovering that capital inflows may merely permit the recipient, if so minded, to divert more resources to unproductive and even frivolous uses underly much of the current pessimism in the United States concerning the economic effectiveness of foreign aid. Having at first stimulated a larger flow of foreign aid, the Cold War may, by insuring its misdirection, victimize in the longer run the flow of genuine U.S. development aid. This would indeed be the unkindest cut of all.

Ironically, it is the former colonial powers, France and the United Kingdom, who are currently extending aid to poor countries—mainly, to be sure, to their former colonies—with a magnanimity and ideological tolerance which contrasts favorably with the attitudes currently manifested by the United States and the Soviet Union.[57] American readers staggering

[56] The Clay Committee estimates that over 70 percent of U.S. aid in 1962 was either for direct military purposes or to ease the financial burden of governments accepting military aid.

[57] One may compare, for example, the generous sentiments and political maturity of the report of the Jeanneney Commission on foreign aid to the President of the French Republic, published early in 1964, with the narrowness and Pecksniffian overtones of the Clay Committee report.

under the burden of foreign aid might be relieved to note that in 1961 France devoted 2.41 percent and the United Kingdom 1.32 percent of their gross national products to loans, grants, and investments in underdeveloped countries, as compared with only 0.97 percent for the United States.[58] Unfortunately, the combined French and British gross national products is only one-fifth that of the United States.

Conclusion

Thus, neither the market system for directing international trade and factor migration nor the international donor system as presently constituted seem capable of effectively implementing world economic welfare norms. The former, even when relatively free from government interference, has tended, in a world of gross qualitative differences in human skills and organization among nations, to widen the gap between poor and rich nations. The controls of immigration, trade, and capital exporting imposed by wealthy nations to further their domestic welfare have only augmented the tendency for the gap to widen. The system of intergovernmental loans and grants to poor nations has been too distorted by the national interests of the donor nations, exacerbated by Cold War rivalry, to be an effective counter to the unequalizing tendencies.

It is not difficult to visualize international arrangements that, without giving up the nation-state, could effectively implement international welfare norms. Wealthy nations, now spending more annually on armaments than the combined national income of China, India, and Southeast Asia, could in a more pacific world considerably increase their capital assistance. They could open their borders more freely to the exports and

[58] Calculated by the Development Action Group of the Organization for Economic Cooperation and Development.

absorb more of the unskilled from poor nations without reducing their own economic growth rates below current levels. A modest fraction of the talent and outlays now going to warfare science would surely suffice to develop the technology needed for economic exploitation and mass settlement of the desert and the jungle, thereby allowing mass migration to ease the development problems of densely populated Asiatic countries as it did for nineteenth-century European countries. Nor do nations ready to spend astronomical sums on anti-anti-missile missiles have the moral right to bridle at the cost of developing and distributing effective birth-control devices in poor countries.

For rich nations the international north-south problem is as much a moral and political as a technical problem, for the resources and the engineering techniques at least for eliminating poverty are at hand or in the offing. Rich nations that assume the moral duty to save the poor nations from their ideological rival's "ism" at the cost, if need be, of destroying them for their own salvation can hardly absolve themselves of their share of responsibility for the fact that the north-south problem continues to worsen. To be sure, the problem of effectively transmitting these resources and technology cannot be solved by the rich nations alone. Unless the poor countries are willing to modify and even sacrifice many of the values of their current way of life in the interest of their economic development, efforts to transmit resources and technology to them will continue to yield disappointing results. But until they are given greater freedom to make their own institutional adjustments and rich nations are more generous in mobilizing their resources and technology to assist the development effort, it would be quite premature to conclude that the north-south problem's seeming intractability is due primarily to the unwillingness of the poor nations to change. Lacking such measures, the conclusion bears rather a depressing resemblance to the fatalistic incantations by which wealthy classes prior to the welfare state era expiated themselves of guilt for the poverty around them.

V

THEODORE MORGAN

Economic Relationships among Nations: The Pattern of Commodity Trade*

THE MOST AMBITIOUS estimates of world trade go back nearly a hundred years. Further back, they are replaced by scattered statistics and descriptions and by general reasoning. The remote origin of trade, in any region or society, is a simple concept. Transfer of goods from one person or group to another can originate in coercion, exchange, and gifts. Gifts have an obvious limitation, for, as Alice observed, the more there is of yours, the less there is of mine. Mankind has never been rich enough to make unrequited gifts more than a small part of exchange. Coercion has plain limitations in that the coercee is not likely to come that way again—unless there is a net advantage to him none the less. The robber who wants to stay in business therefore has incentive to moderate his toll and to

* I am indebted to M. C. Madhaven and Nyle Spoelstra for valiant work in collecting and organizing the statistics in this essay.

protect his victims against other robbers—and so exchange has pushed its nose under the tent: law and order are exchanged for a tax.

Voluntary exchange of good for good, with advantage to both sides of the swap, plainly has much to say for it. When groups not previously in contact with each other trade, the advantage can be very great indeed. Before their discovery by European navigators, the native Hawaiians had to use bones, including those of their ancestors, for making fishhooks. Bone fishhooks are greatly inferior to iron fishhooks. In the early days after discovery, a bent nail from a whaling ship or from a sandalwood trader could buy a wagonload of vegetables and fruit. In exchange, the fresh provisions rescued the seamen from scurvy, and hence were infinitely valuable to those who otherwise would have died.

As times goes on and trade continues and grows under free conditions, the incremental advantage diminishes toward zero, since if there is gain at the margin, there is incentive to carry on a still greater volume of trade. But average and total advantage can expand greatly. The very existence of any modern economy in anything like its present form depends on a on-going pattern and volume of trade.

Statistics on trade movements have been rapidly improving in recent years. The shrinking quantity and quality of trade data as one goes back through the decades are less burdensome in that historical "international" trade has a strong arbitrary element from the economic point of view: if the boundaries of nations change or nations consolidate or split up, international trade as defined is swelled or contracted. When Texas and Vermont join the Union, "international trade" shrinks, but there need be no change in actual trade flows at all.

Long-Run Volume Trends of Commodity Trade

International trade should increase in volume with lowered cost and increased quantity of communications and with greater rationalization of production, including the growth of social order that makes rationalization possible. Trade should increase most rapidly among the regions of the world where political stability, economic preoccupations, and economic rationality are growing most rapidly. Since there are economies of scale in transportation—the steamship versus the rowboat, the railroad freight car versus wagons—trade should grow more rapidly still in regions where its volume is rising through critical points where more efficient means of transportation become economic. Transportation innovations, by cutting the cost of movement, expand the volume of trade.

On the other hand, protectionism and autarchy, including probably government trading not sensitively responding to price comparisons, should contract the volume of trade. They should contract the volume of recorded trade more than the volume of actual trade in view of the unrecorded efforts of smugglers.

Suppose we evaluate these expectations against statistics. Table 1 gives League of Nations data. This is a picture of substantial success in the world economy, even when we allow that the benefits were concentrated in the more economically progressive regions. Over the whole period to 1958–59, trade in primary commodities rose 2.0 percent a year, in manufactures, 2.5 percent a year, and total commodity trade 2.2 percent a year. At the same time world population was growing at the rate of only 0.7 percent a year.

Information on manufactures production in major countries over approximately this same period indicates that world man-

Table 1. The Secular Trend in the Volume of World Trade
(1876–80 = 100)

	1876–80	1913	1926–29	1936–38	1958–59
Quantum of world trade in:					
Primary commodities	100	320	361	374	511
Manufactured commodities	100	311	324	287	715
Total commodity trade	100	317	347	343	581

Source: Up to and including 1936–38, adapted from *Industrialization and Foreign Trade* (New York: League of Nations, 1945), p. 14 and Annex, Tables I, VII, VIII. The world index for primary and manufactured commodities is a weighted arithmetic average of the national indexes. The total commodity trade index is a weighted average of the primary and manufactures index.

The 1958–59 calculations, made by us separately, are only roughly comparable with the earlier data: 1953-base figures were adjusted to an 1876–80 base; fuels were excluded from being counted in primary commodities; and 1938 instead of 1936–38 was, through lack of the full data, used as the base for the 1958–59 relatives. Source of data: United Nations, *Statistical Year Book*, 1961, p. 426.

ufactures output was rising much more rapidly than world trade in manufactures (Table 2). The contrast is sharp. Over the whole period world *production* of manufactures was rising

Table 2. The Volumes of World Manufactures Production and
World Trade (1876–80 = 100)

	1876–80	1913	1926–29	1936–38	1958–59
Quantum of:					
World trade in manufactures	100	311	324	287	715
World production of manufactures	100	385	567	755	1,978

Source: Data on trade from Table 1. Data on production from *Industrialization and Foreign Trade* (New York: League of Nations, 1945), Table I, p. 130; and from Karl W. Deutsch and Alexander Eckstein; "National Industrialization and the Declining Share of the International Economic Sector, 1890–1957," *World Politics*, XIII (1961), 260. The basic sources for the Deutsch-Eckstein series are GATT, *Trends in International Trade* (Geneva, 1952) for data up to 1938; and United Nations, *Monthly Bulletin of Statistics*, various issues, for data from 1948 on. For production of manufacturers, 1936 data are used as an approximation for 1936–38; and 1959 data are used for 1958–59.

2.8 times as fast as world *trade* in manufactures. The explanation appears to be high domestic income elasticities of demand for manufactures—which have been effective toward keeping a rising share of them at home despite their nonperishability and hence their transportability as compared with many kinds of foodstuffs.

Parallel data for primary products are lacking, but indirect reasoning leads to a reverse conclusion. During the period 1876–1959 over two-thirds of the world's population lived in traditional economies, where farm and fiber outputs were not rising much more rapidly than their populations and where their populations were growing on the average at close to the rate of that of the developed areas, that is, at close to the rate of the world as a whole. In some areas where population pressure on the land was severe, output rise must have been less than population growth. A generous allowance for rising primary product production in high-income regions still leaves world primary product production growing much less than the 2.1 percent a year rise in primary product trade. In brief, relatively stagnant *world* primary production contrasts here with relatively rapid growth of primary product exports into high-income areas—of food and fiber from newly-settled regions to European consumers, and of specialized tropical products to high-income regions generally.

The contrasting trends of the ratios of international trade to production of manufactures and primary products in this period is a basic phenomenon of commodity trade worth remembering against very recent data.

A GATT (General Agreement on Tariffs and Trade) study breaks down primary products into main divisions and finds in recent decades (1928 to 1955) sharp differences in the separate trade trends. Petroleum exports have been booming commodities, with their volume rising sixfold. Agricultural raw materials, tropical foodstuffs, and minerals increased about 40 percent. Nontropical foods fell 15 percent in volume.[1]

Long-Run Price Trends of Commodity Trade

A conventional view holds that in world trade generally the prices of primary products have been secularly falling compared with manufactures prices. To the extent that, as is roughly true, exports of high-income countries are manufactures and exports of low-income countries primary products,[2] the implication is that price changes have been secularly benefiting the rich countries and injuring the poor ones. This alleged experience can be interpreted, *à la* Marx, as exploitation by monopolists in the rich countries or (most conspicuously by Prebisch) as the result of effective labor-union packing up of wages and costs in rich countries or of high-income elasticity of demand for manufactures imports in the poorer, primary-producing countries. The policy conclusion plausibly follows that low-income countries should shift their specialization toward manufactures and so gain the advantage of being on a rising-price escalator.

We shall not comment here on these interpretations, because the price data themselves do not support, with anything like

---

[1] Prices were higher for all these commodities over the period. Petroleum, tropical foodstuffs, and minerals were more than double their 1928 price; the rest increased by less. GATT, *Trends in International Trade* (Geneva, 1958), p. 4 and Chap. II. The report concludes that the growth in the world's volume of commodity exports "fell considerably short" of the growth in the world's commodity production.

[2] For example, in 1935, 61 percent of the exports of 12 high-income countries were manufactures, and 88 per cent of the exports of other countries were primary products. (Of course, primary product prices were specially depressed at this time.) Compare a different emphasis, based on European experience, in C. P. Kindleberger, *The Terms of Trade, a European Case Study* (New York: Wiley, 1956), pp. 263–64.

adequate regularity and simplicity, the thesis of falling terms of trade for primary products versus manufactures. In some countries, notably the United States, it is easier to see in the data rising terms of trade for primary products; in the classical trading country, Britain, a long-wave pattern is the plausible generalization. In five other countries for which we have considerable data, there are significant declines in the terms of trade since the beginning of this century into the 1930s for three but improvements for two. Since the 1930s there has been notable improvement in the terms of trade for primary products.

There have been clearly greater improvements in the general terms of trade for "underdeveloped" countries since the 1930s than for "developed" ones (Table 3).

Table 3. Median Values of Terms of Trade (1937 = 100)

	1937	1948	1951	1954	1957	1959
Developed countries	100	102	98	102	97	101
Underdeveloped countries	100	108	160	128	127	123

Source: Theodore Morgan, "Trends in Terms of Trade and Their Repercussions on Primary Producers," in International Economic Association, Roy Harrod and D. C. Hague, eds., *International Trade Theory in a Developing World: Proceedings of a Conference Held at Brissago, 1961* (London: Macmillan, 1963). Basic secular terms-of-trade data are given in an earlier paper, "The Long-Run Terms of Trade between Agriculture and Manufacturing," *Economic Development and Cultural Change,* VII (October, 1959), pp. 1–23.

However, Table 3 also shows sharp deterioration in the typical terms of trade of underdeveloped countries since 1951, the peak year of the Korean War primary-product price boom. Since then their median terms of trade have fallen 23 percent, while those of developed countries have risen 3 percent.

The 1950s general experience for underdeveloped countries of deteriorating terms of trade and the contrast with stable terms of trade for developed countries explains much of the current publicity and worry over terms of trade as related to development. But the publicity is in the main misleading. The terms-of-trade problem is primarily a short-term one and an issue for special commodities.

This conclusion does not deny the special problem of instability of export earnings, which imposes a heavier burden on underdeveloped countries than on developed ones. In his careful study of trade instability since World War II, Coppock calculates "instability indexes," which are, approximately, the average year-to-year percentage variations, adjusted for trend, in export, import, or total trade values.[3] The larger the index, therefore, the greater is instability. Table 4 portrays export-earnings instability by continents. By commodities, the highest export instability indexes are for minerals (27) and for crude materials (21), the least for manufactures (19) and for food, drink, and tobacco (16).[4] Instability in export earnings obviously interferes with the continuity of development programs and makes planning for the future more difficult.

Table 4. Export Earnings Instability by Continents, 1946–58

	Instability indexes	
	Median	Range
Asia (22 countries)	25	12–74
Africa (12 countries)	23	10–40
South America (13 countries)	13	10–41
Europe (26 countries)	19	6–46
North America (10 countries)	14	8–27

Source: Adapted from the table in Joseph D. Coppock, *International Economic Instability: The Experience after World War II* (New York: McGraw-Hill, 1962), p. 51. All indexes rounded to the nearest whole figure.

[3] Joseph D. Coppock, *International Economic Instability: The Experience after World War II* (New York: McGraw-Hill, 1962), pp. 23–25. The formula is given on p. 24. An earlier study, by the United Nations, is *Instability in Export Markets of Under-Developed Countries* (New York, 1952).

[4] Coppock, *International Economic Instability*, p. 103. Indexes rounded to the nearest whole figure.

*Shares of World Trade Captured by
Individual Countries, Long-Run Data*

To talk in terms of shares breaks up the vision of the world as a unit—whose experience tradewise has been one of obvious remarkable growth in the past hundred years or more—into an emphasis on more for one, less for another, of the segments of the whole. And yet the success of individual units is a force toward expansion for the whole; and expansion of the whole is correlated with better specialization among the nations and regions of the world, with increasingly pervasive monetary systems and flows-of-capital patterns, and expanding flows of entrepreneurship and technical knowledge. It also means changing consumer tastes and increasing consumer knowledge as more goods and types of goods become available in the world generally; and an increasing quantity of economic alternatives is the central meaning of economic progress.

We explore below the shares of major trading countries during the past eighty years in the manufacturing trade of the world. The hope is that out of their various experiences of success and failure there can emerge some suggestions for countries today whose domestic policies for growth are sharply limited by balance-of-payments straitjackets and who therefore seek to expand exports. The data are those of Arthur Lewis, mainly based on an earlier study by Tyszinski.

The main trends implied or illustrated in Table 5 are (1) the capture by England of three-eighths of the manufacturing trade of the world between the Napoleonic wars and the late nineteenth century and decline since to less than half that share, (2) the rise of Germany between the 1880s and World War I, (3) the considerable increase of Japan's share between 1913 and 1937, and (4) the rise of the U.S. share at the end of the nineteenth century and since World War II.

The most curious aspect of Table 5 is the constant share of "Others" up to World War II. As Holmes said, the curious incident was that the dog did nothing. Why should "other" countries have retained precisely the same proportion of world manufactures for a half-century after 1883? This we should not have predicted. A plausible interpretation is that there was a constant rate of imitation and adaptation of skills, capital, and organization from the leading industrial countries.

As for success and failure among the leading seven countries, Lewis suggests that to the economist's usual emphasis on "keen prices" (because they are easy to measure) we should add a

Table 5. Percentage Shares of World Exports of Manufactures

	1883	1899	1913	1937	1954	1958–59
United States	3	10	11	17	26	20
United Kingdom	37	28	25	19	16	14
Germany	17	20	23	20	12[a]	14[a]
France	15	13	11	5	7	7
Belgium	5	5	4	5	5	4[b]
Canada	0	0	1	4	5	4
Japan	0	1	2	6	4	5
Others	23	23	23	23	26	32
Total	100	100	100	100	100	100

Source: The 1899 to 1954 data were compiled and classified by the late H. Tyszinski, *Manchester School of Economics and Social Studies*, XIX (September, 1951), 277–80; reproduced by W. Arthur Lewis in "International Competition in Manufactures," *American Economic Review*, XLVII (1957), 579. The 1883 and 1954 data are Lewis' estimates. 1958–59 (average) data are our own calculations, with classifications slightly different from those of the earlier years, being the sum of SITC groups 5, 6, 7, 8, 112, and 122. In 1958–59, Communist countries provided 12 percent of world exports of manufactures (*Yearbook of International Trade*, 1959; United Nations, *Monthly Bulletin of Statistics*, March, 1962). All data in this and the following tables are rounded to the nearest whole percent. (Detail may not add to total because of rounding errors.)

[a] West Germany.

[b] Belgium-Luxembourg data are adjusted downward (by 10.5 percent on evidence from parallel data) to arrive at an estimate for Belgium.

flood of salesmen, large-scale organization of selling, attention to customers' wishes, and liberal credit. He thinks central interest lies in *why* at one time or another a country launches and persists in effective selling techniques or loses its past momentum.

Hilgerdt's study for the League of Nations also gives us data on shares of various nations in primary commodity trade. Table 6 shows both import and export data.

We could reasonably assume for manufactures that a rising proportion of the world's export originating in one country represents economic success for that country. It implies relative efficiency in production of these commodities—that is, in skills, organization, and capital—plus effective selling methods. And effective skills, organization, capital, and selling methods mean economic advance.

But interpretation of primary-product trends is more complicated. A sustained or rising share of world primary-product exports may indicate effective utilization of natural resources, failure to achieve reasonable progress in goods requiring skill, organization, capital, and sales effort, or a combination of the two. A rising share for a country of world primary-product imports may indicate rising consumption with higher real income. It may also indicate, more specifically, a growing demand for industrial raw materials as industrialization proceeds.

The nine listed countries put together have been providing a sharply falling share of world exports of primary commodities; this presumably means a falling off of relative advantage in primary production as industrialization proceeded. They have also been importing a smaller share of world primary products as other parts of the world have been drawn into the international economy (but the United States has expanded its share by a third since before World War II).

Table 6. Percentage Shares of World Trade in Primary Commodities [a]

	Exports				Imports			
	1881–85	1911–13	1936–38	1958–59	1881–85	1911–13	1936–38	1958–59
United States	16	14	11	12	9	10	12	16
Germany	7	6	3	1	13	17	11	10
U.K. and Ireland	3	4	4	3	29	20	23	18
France	7	4	3	3	16	10	8	7
Russia and USSR	7	7	2	...	4	3	1	...
Austria-Hungary	3	2	...	...	3	3	...	...
Canada	...	...	6	7	...	2	2	3
Italy	4	2	2	2	3	4	3	4
Belgium	...	4	3	1[a]	...	6	4	2[a]
Rest of world	54	57	68	71	23	26	35	40
Total world	100	100	100	100	100	100	100	100

Source: Data of 1881 to 1936–38 calculated from *Industrialization and Foreign Trade* (New York: League of Nations, 1945), Table VIII, p. 157, and Table XIII, p. 166. Primary products are groups I, II, and III of the international (1913) classification. Where figures are lacking for a given country, its percentage is omitted from separate presentation and estimated for inclusion in "Rest of world." Data for 1958–59 are for SITC's 0, 1, 2, and 4 groups in United Nations, *Monthly Bulletin of Statistics*, March, 1962.

[a] Belgium-Luxembourg data are adjusted downward (by 10.5 percent for exports and 9 percent for imports on evidence from parallel data) to obtain an estimate for Belgium. (Detail may not add to total because of rounding errors.)

Trade of Developed versus Trade of
Underdeveloped Areas in the 1950s

Since World War II the country coverage and accuracy of international trade statistics have improved sharply over the prewar statistics, in large part because of the encouragement of the United Nations. Data of the 1950s throw light on two questions:

1. Is the world becoming increasingly split up or more unified with respect to income and production trends? Trade data are superior in quality to national income estimates, which for many a developing country are only crude measures of economic performance. Hence, we have in trade data of the world an alternative and at least equally reliable measure of the rates of economic advance of major regions.

We suspect from income data and other evidence that underdeveloped areas are falling increasingly behind the economic progress of developed areas despite official and unofficial world concern with accelerating the growth of the former. What is the evidence from trade data as to comparative rates of growth of the two groups?

Table 7 shows exports and imports of developed and underdeveloped areas for 1950, 1955, and 1960. The evidence is consistent. Trade from and into developed areas is growing much more rapidly than trade from and into underdeveloped areas. The implication is convincing that income trends show the same divergence; this prosperous decade shows substantial growth in both but much more rapid growth in the developed areas.

The divergence is no more than a continuation of a pattern several centuries old. Five hundred years ago the standard of living throughout the world was close to a minimum for survival—save for the statistically insignificant islands of gold of the nobility and landowners and rich traders scattered in the

Table 7. Exports and Imports of Developed and Underdeveloped Areas

	Developed areas		Underdeveloped areas	
Year	Exports from these areas	Imports into these areas	Exports from these areas	Imports into these areas
	Values (in billions of current dollars, F.O.B.)			
1950	35.4	37.9	18.3	15.7
1955	56.1	57.1	22.9	21.8
1960	79.8	78.4	25.8	27.2
	Indexes of values			
1950	100	100	100	100
1955	159	151	125	139
1960	226	207	141	173
	Indexes of quantums			
1950	100		100	
1955	139		116	
1960	192		141	

Source: United Nations, *Monthly Bulletin of Statistics*, August, 1962, pp. 18, 19. For classification of developed and underdeveloped countries, see Appendix A of this essay.

general ocean of poverty. Since then, some regions and peoples have gotten ahead; others have lagged behind. This kind of division of the world is still widening.

2. We might plausibly reason (as Robertson did in the 1930s) that as techniques of production are copied and become more nearly alike among the most progressive countries, comparative advantage differences among them will shrink. The next step is to conclude that trade among these countries will shrink relative to trade with widely different kinds of economies. Table 8 shows the growth of trade in the 1950s from and to the two areas.

Any effect on trade from shrinking comparative advantage among the developed countries is more than offset by the stimulating effects from their relatively rapid rise in incomes and by

Table 8. Value of Exports of Developed and Underdeveloped Areas by Destination (*1950 = 100*)

| | Exports of developed areas | | Exports of underdeveloped areas | |
	To developed areas	To under-developed areas	To developed areas	To under-developed areas
1950	100	100	100	100
1960	238	199	149	119

Source: United Nations, *Monthly Bulletin of Statistics*, August, 1962, pp. 18, 19. For classification of developed and underdeveloped countries, see Appendix A.

the associated increasing differentiation of products. The plausible a priori prediction turns out to be wrong. The doubling of trade from developed to underdeveloped countries indicates the substantial benefit of economic development programs supported by high-income countries, since it is much larger than the growth of total exports from low-income countries.

The lowest rate of increase is shown by the trade of underdeveloped countries among themselves. Such relative stagnation indicates a worrisome problem. The underdeveloped countries have generally been experiencing a low rate of growth of production and of consumption. They need investment goods, but these are obtainable only from developed countries; their products are typically competitive rather than supplementary. Adjacent tropical poor countries—to take a typical picture—are apt to trade halfway round the world rather than with each other. The extent to which mutually advantageous trade can take place among underdeveloped countries has considerable relevance to the success of their economic hopes. Aside from the comparative advantage gains, economizing on foreign exchange needed for imports from industrial countries will ease the balance-of-payments constraint on their growth possibilities.

World Commodity Trade versus World Trade in Invisibles

So far we have spoken of our central topic, commodity trade, as if that were the only trade item in the balances of payments of the world. In this we have been conventional. Invisibles are often neglected because the data, compared with those on commodities, are more recent, being generally very rough before World War II, less detailed, less frequent, and evidently subject to more error.[5]

But the invisibles—transportation, tourism, investment income, banking and insurance services, and perhaps some other items—are a large part of total trade. Devons, using a limited definition of invisibles,[6] finds them to make up 28 percent of world receipts from exports in 1958. There is wide variation in the dependence of particular countries on invisibles, from Korea's 96 percent of export earnings to Venezuela's 4 percent.[7] As with commodity trade, invisible trade is heavily concentrated in a small number of high-income countries. It seems to be increasing.[8] In the 1950s all the main items—foreign travel, transport, and investment income—were growing, with travel growing most rapidly.

THE "LAW" OF DIMINISHING FOREIGN TRADE

If there is some evidence that invisibles are increasing as a proportion of world trade, there is much clearer evidence that

---

[5] Ely Devons, "World Trade in Invisibles," *Lloyd's Bank Review*, XIII (April, 1961), 37–50.

[6] Because of lack of comparability of different national statistics if the definition is broadened. Devons, *ibid.*, includes only transportation, tourism, and investment income.

[7] Among the 15 major trading countries of the world, plus 16 other countries heavily dependent on invisible trade. Devons, *ibid.*, p. 40.

[8] Devons compares two boom years for the 1950s, 1951 and 1957, and (excluding government grants, which have a falling trend) finds invisible trade rising from 22 to 26 percent of world exports; *ibid.*, p. 41.

for many high-income countries services are making up a rising proportion of domestic national income. Since services are not a part of commodity trade among nations, the conclusion might plausibly follow that commodity trade should be a falling proportion of world incomes as the decades go by.

A number of writers have discussed a possible "law of falling importance of international trade," among them Sombart as far back as 1913.[9] Recently, Deutsch and Eckstein have offered statistical and logical evidence for such a law. Using data from a number of countries, they conclude that there is a tendency for the proportion of trade to national income to rise in the early stages of industrialization and eventually, when industrialization reaches a fairly high level and grows further, for the proportion to fall.[10]

The causes are said to be as follows:

1. In the early stages of industrialization, commercial activity rises fastest in sectors in contact with foreign markets. Capital goods are imported, then fuel and spare parts; often textiles, consumer manufactures, and even food are imported for newly employed wage labor, as well as hand tools and other equipment. At the same time domestic expenditure tends to lag; roads and railroads are improved mainly to the seaports, and housing and education outlays in the traditional economy remain small.

2. Later, as industrialization increases, there is increasing domestic activity. Secondary communications are developed—

---

[9] In *Die Deutsche Volkwirtschaft im 19 Jahrhundert* (3d ed., Berlin, 1913), p. 371. Cited by G. Haberler, "Terms of Trade and Economic Development," in H. S. Ellis and H. C. Wallich, eds., *Economic Development for Latin America* (London: Macmillan, 1961), p. 285.

[10] Karl W. Deutsch and Alexander Eckstein, "National Industrialization and the Declining Share of the International Economic Sector, 1890–1957," *World Politics*, XIII (1961), 167–99. Kindleberger, *Terms of Trade*, pp. 293–94, has doubts about the generalization, finding diverse results for France and England from different data.

roads, railroads, canals, airports—and spending rises for government buildings, including barracks and schools, for housing, and for dams needed for power and irrigation.

3. In the third and last stage, industry is well along in development and still keeps growing. Services increase rapidly as a share of domestic national income (housing, mass education, government), and these are mainly produced and consumed domestically. Internal transportation and communication improve more rapidly than foreign transportation and communication. Local substitutes for imports are developed, and refining and finishing stages in secondary production grow more important. And, to the extent that governments desire to insulate their economies from the world economy—owing to instability abroad, war, or hostile ideologies—they shift to autarchic policies.[11]

Robertson's argument, mentioned above, leads to the same prediction for stage 3: if skills and knowledge of production techniques are spreading ever more widely in the world, comparative advantage differences are lessening, and so the incentives for trade are also diminishing. Hence, international trade should be shrinking in importance in the world economy.

It is easy to think of conditions in which these plausible events would not dominate the trade pattern. With respect to the first stage: in the eighteenth and early nineteenth centuries in the United States, Argentina, and Australia, fuel and food did not need to be imported at all, domestic production of textiles quickly became a major home industry, and after the first decades it is doubtful that roads, canals, and railroads were oriented mainly toward the seaports. In the third stage, the effect of a rising share of services in income could easily be more than

---

[11] This last argument modifies and generalizes the Deutsch-Eckstein reasoning.

offset by the rapid growth of comparative advantages in specific exports or by the rapid growth of imports due to exhaustion of some local material or by a shift of taste toward some foreign commodity (financed by more exports or in some other way).

COMMODITY EXPORTS AS A PERCENTAGE OF NATIONAL INCOME—
DEVELOPED AND UNDERDEVELOPED COUNTRIES, FOUR PERIODS

The following data present a statistical test for the "law of falling importance of international trade" over a thirty-year period, 1929 to 1958–59. That is, the data measure whether national economies are becoming more or less interwoven into the world economy, whether interdependence is increasing or decreasing.

If interdependence is decreasing with national economies becoming more isolated from each other, we might reasonably worry about the political and social implications and feel that national and international action is required to strengthen international economic ties.

Data for a maximum of 42 countries are summarized below, 21 developed and 21 underdeveloped,[12] excluding Communist-bloc countries, for which data are not adequate. The figures were put into the form of exports as a percentage of national income, both measured at current prices.

The range is wide. To take the extremes: in 1958–59 the U.S. figure is 4.5 percent and the India figure 4.7 percent, but Venezuela attains 42.5 percent and the Belgian Congo 58.0 percent. Countries with large populations and large areas normally have low indexes; small countries and those with high advantage in certain (export) commodities have high indexes. Table 9 gives measures of typical values and trends.

[12] But only 17 developed and only 4 underdeveloped countries had usable data for 1929.

Table 9. *Exports as a Percentage of National Income* [a]

	Developed countries				Underdeveloped countries			
	1929	1937–38	1948–49	1958–59	1929	1937–38	1948–49	1958–59
Highest quartile	31	23	24	26	(44)[b]	35	33	26
Median	22	18	17	22	(25)[b]	28	20	20
Lowest quartile	20	13	7	13	(19)[b]	19	11	12

[a] For basic data, see Appendix A at the end of this essay. All data rounded to nearest whole percent.
[b] Based on only four countries.

What generalizations can we make out of these figures?

1. The most striking is that both developed and under-developed countries had by 1958–59 a nearly identical degree of integration in the world economy—in dispersion as well as on the average.[13] Although this result is surprising, it seems trustworthy in view of the large number of countries in both groups by that time and the improving quality of the data. Of course, if we looked more closely at the 21 underdeveloped countries, we should often find a dual-economy pattern, with an export sector isolated from the traditional economy, in contrast to the greater domestic integration of the developed countries.

2. The road by which different countries arrived at this identical degree of integration with the world economy differs.

---

[13] The degree of integration looks still more alike if one takes into account the nearest tenth of a percent: for developed countries the more exact value is 21.5 percent, for underdeveloped, 20.1 percent.

As to dispersion, the interquartile range shrinks for the underdeveloped countries (though not for the developed ones) between 1929 and 1958, despite the increasing numbers of countries sampled, which in itself tends toward wider dispersion. Taking into account the increasing representation of countries and the improved data of post-World War II, the trend throughout the world appears to be toward greater similarity in the likeness of exports to income.

Developed countries have typically, in the past ten and twenty years, *increased* their dependence on foreign markets. This trend probably reflects the dislocations associated with the 1930s depression and with prewar and immediate postwar conditions, in contrast with the increasingly free trade of the 1950s. But underdeveloped countries have typically reduced their dependence on foreign markets since 1937–38 and not changed it since 1948–49. The pattern exists despite typically rising prices for their exports since 1937–38 and even since 1948.[14] Why? An adequate answer rests on detailed study of the individual countries, but probably growth of domestic economies and actions hostile to foreign enclaves and exporting companies are relevant trends.[15]

The Deutsch-Eckstein theorem, however, predicts the reverse pattern: falling dependence on exports for developed countries and (at least frequently) rising dependence for underdeveloped countries. We conclude that the theorem is not supported in the typical trade-income patterns of the past several decades. Other influences with inverse effects must have been more important than those Deutsch and Eckstein thought dominant.

Changed Exports as Cause of Changed National Income

It is generally taken for granted—or proved with a simple

[14] Theodore Morgan, "Trends in Terms of Trade and Their Repercussions on Primary Producers," in International Economics Association, Roy Harrod and D. C. Hague, eds., *International Trade Theory in a Developing World: Proceedings of a Conference Held at Brissago, 1961* (London: Macmillan, 1963), p. 60, Charts la, lb. The above does not deny falling primary prices in the late 1950s.

[15] Over the past two decades, countries that have moved into a clearly lower ratio of exports to income are Honduras, Thailand, Argentina, and Japan—three of the four "underdeveloped." Those that have increased their ratio substantially are Denmark, the Netherlands, Ireland, South Africa, the United Kingdom (since 1938), and Germany.

multiplier model—that higher exports, other things being equal, will cause a higher national income (and vice versa). Consideration of the balance-of-payments effect reinforces the simplest analysis. Lamfalussy gives a compact statement of the standard case, applied to Europe in recent years:

> Exports can safely be regarded in the case of all European countries as the decisive factor in encouraging expansion. For one thing, a satisfactory rise in export receipts improves the external balance of the country, and enables the government to let home demand expand freely. On the other hand, exports usually represent a sizeable share of total demand and therefore exert a direct influence on home investment and on the level of activity of home industry.[16]

We consider below, first, some complications and diverse views to add to the simplest reasoning and, second, summary statistical relationships for various countries in recent years.

Consider the favorable effects of an export rise in some detail, assuming demand rises abroad:

1. There is full employment in the home country. The rise in the value of exports must be associated with some improvement in the terms of trade. Real domestic income rises. There is stimulus toward greater investment in the export sector and probably development of greater skills there—further causes for higher real income. There may be internal economies or diseconomies in the export sector or economies or diseconomies external to the sector. Economies seem likely to dominate; if so, another cause of higher income.

2. Perhaps there is underemployment in the home country, which is shrunken by the higher export demand. Then higher employment adds to the causes for increased income listed above.

---

[16] Alexander Lamfalussy, "Europe's Progress: Due to Common Market?" *Lloyd's Bank Review*, XIII (October, 1961), p. 3.

3. The shock of conspicuously higher exports may decrease immobility. Resources flow more readily to the export sector (assumed more efficient in their use than competing sectors). Income rises even if the terms of trade deteriorate. The shock of an export boom can encourage the search for innovations, for lower costs of production, and for marketable variations on existing products.[17]

On the other hand, there may be unfavorable effects from a rise in exports:

1. Suppose the rate of rise is less than in a previous period. Then a (negative) acceleration effect can lead to an absolute fall in activity in supplying sectors; or, a modest variant, the slower rate of growth of foreign earnings from exports can force a slower rate of growth of imports of investment and consumption goods and so limit the rate of growth of domestic income that can be sustained. Once again there can be further (negative) acceleration effects.

2. Dislocating effects of export expansion can dominate. Brief expansion can be followed by contraction, so that dislocation costs exceed rising export gains. The cause of the temporary export rise could be war or successive changes of tastes abroad or of techniques.

3. Perhaps export demand deludes countries into dead-end specialization—for example, in food and raw materials in a stagnant plantation system—without desired linkage and external economy effects or with sharply falling prices in prospect. Thus, it prevents them from developing the possibilities of eventually more productive domestically orientated industries. There may seem to be little scope for technical progress in the

---

[17] Compare the analysis in C. P. Kindleberger, "Foreign Trade and Economic Growth: Lessons from Britain and France, 1850 to 1913," *Economic History Review,* XIV (1961), 189–290.

export industry, and secondary benefits of investment there may be realized mainly back in the foreign investing country.[18]

4. A rise in exports can cause or add fuel to an unwanted and injurious inflation.

5. Myrdal finds an adverse *sector* effect—not necessarily an adverse effect on the whole economy—as a possible consequent of growing exports. One part of a country (say, northern Italy during the late nineteenth century) can be enriched by growing exports; but as its efficiency grows, the markets of another sector (say, southern Italy) can be lost, and immobility of factors there can be so great that it sags into deeper poverty.[19]

The above are possible relationships between export and income changes. We might test empirically how applicable these theories or sub-theories appear to be by studying in detail special cases.[20] Another approach is to use the rapidly improving

[18] These are close to the arguments of Hans Singer, "The Distribution of Gains between Investing and Borrowing Countries," *American Economic Review*, XL (1950), 476–77.

[19] Gunnar Myrdal, *Rich Lands and Poor: The Road to World Prosperity* (New York: Harper and Row, 1957), p. 28. One may well ask critically whether immobility is not the active cause rather than increased exports from the whole economy. Is immobility only a conditioning influence?

Hal Myint more moderately blames the "internal pattern of economic development rather than . . . the external pattern of international trade" for the smaller share of gains from international trade than might reasonably be expected that have gone to the people of certain backward countries: "The Gains from International Trade and the Backward Countries," *Review of Economic Studies*, XXII (1954–55), 141. These domestic causes are "monopolistic and monopsonistic factors" and "dynamic pressures of the need to expand export production rapidly, acting on the institutional rigidities of the internal economic structure."

Paul Baran, from a Marxist viewpoint, finds foreign investment (associated with export expansion) to have its principal impact in "hardening and strengthening the sway of merchant capitalism, in slowing down and indeed preventing its transformation into industrial capitalism"; *The Political Economy of Growth* (New York: Monthly Review Press, 1957), p. 194.

The above quotations were brought to my attention by Mr. Youngil Lim, of the Department of Economics, University of California at Los Angeles.

[20] As does Kindleberger in "Foreign Trade and Economic Growth," *Eco-*

international trade data of post-World War II to see the typical relationships between export changes and national income changes. If the dominant relationship (in our time period and for our sample countries) is that of a stimulus from exports and if other influences—domestic investment, government, consumption expenditures, and import policies—are random or constant, then there will be an observed positive correlation between export changes and income changes. Since other influences are never so random as to cancel out, we should expect a higher correlation between changes in exports and changes in income in those countries in which exports bear a higher proportion to income.

Table 10 carries out this modest experiment. Data for 34 countries for the period 1948–49 to 1958–59 are divided into three groups, on the criterion of the average proportion of exports to income.[21]

The results are contrary to what we have anticipated. The correlation is positive for all three groups of countries; but standard errors for *b* are very large, and lowest correlation is found for those two groups of countries whose export-to-income ratios are high. Evidently, domestic causes of income changes have been important and not correlated with export changes, or sometimes the influence of exports on income has been negative, in accord with the theories above.

The Patterns of Commodity Trade in High-Skill-and-Capital and Low-Skill-and-Capital Manufactures

The rest of this essay consists of several inquiries into the composition of world trade, in recent years and since 1900,

---

nomic History Review, XIV (1961), 189–200, and in "Foreign Trade and Growth," *Lloyd's Bank Review*, XIV (July, 1962), 16–28.

[21] The groups are: $\Sigma X/Y < 15$ percent (for 10 countries), 15 percent $< \Sigma X/Y < 25$ percent (for 19 countries), and 25 percent $< \Sigma X/Y$ (for 5 countries).

Table 10. The Correlation between Changes in Exports and
Changes in National Income (Real Data) [a]
(Formula: $\Delta Y = a + b \Delta X$)

Ratio of total exports to national income	a	b	r	r^2
Low ratio (10 countries)	12.8 (2.9)	0.34 (0.30)	0.75	0.56
Moderate ratio (19 countries)	52.9 (3.0)	0.03 (0.25)	0.07	0.005
High ratio (5 countries)	66.8 (11.2)	0.09 (0.50)	0.22	0.05
All countries (34)	44.1 (17.1)	0.16 (0.16)	0.32	0.10

[a] Standard errors of *a* and *b* are given in parentheses. For data of the separate countries and for sources see Appendix B of this essay.

with emphasis on patterns related to the skill and capital categories of manufactures trade.

THE BOXES

The central problems we face in a study over time in this area are those of classification and of accuracy of data:

1. Many products are heterogeneous with respect to factor proportions used in their production: the manufacture of household salt is one thing in the United States, in Indonesia another.[22] We must reply on average skill-capital requirement estimates: problems of heterogeneity are less because many of the data from less well-developed countries, which would be dubious on qualitative grounds because of fringe-end produc-

[22] I have watched on the beach south of Jogjakarta in Java an ingenious salt factory, which used little capital and after the first innovator, modest skill. It was a one-man project. A villager piled beach sand, in which the salt content was high because of the evaporation of sea water, in a wicker basket and then poured and repoured several gallons of sea water through the sand, collecting it each time in a jug below the basket. When he judged the salt content in the water high enough, the manager-and-work-force set the water aside in a shallow tray to evaporate.

tion functions, are simply not available and so do not enter our results.

2. The broad classes we use will, as time goes on, gain new products, sometimes with uncertainty as to their classification, and lose old products.

Other things being equal, a critical condition is that trade restrictions (including exchange rates) should not change systematically with reference to our skill-capital classification. We can and, so far as we can, shall take this consideration into account.

The advantage of a trend-over-time approach is that it should lead to more sophisticated predicting of probable future developments than a point-of-time analysis can.

In the background of this study and giving, we hope, a practical cast to it is the export policy of Japan during her uniquely successful period of growth in the 1950s. According to the *Economist*,[23] the Japanese Planning Agency has aimed through a number of government measures to shift Japan's exports away from "light industrial" exports (textiles, etc.) to "heavy industrial" products (machinery, metals, metal products, and chemical goods). The *Economist* demonstrates that six developed countries have experienced this shift to a pronounced degree between 1928 and 1959; it is portrayed as moving to a "more modern" structure of exports. Our statistics below attempt to test the fact of such a vision of trade trends and to evaluate the sense of this export policy as a means of accelerating economic growth.

Choice of the manufactures commodities to be used in this study cannot be made without reference to the form in which statistics on exports appear. Definitions of the Standard Inter-

[23] September 1, 1962, pp. 808ff.

Table 11. Certain Manufactures Classed by Skills and Capital Requirements

Commodity group	Corresponding SITC code and name	Skill level: percentage of skilled and supervisory workers to total gainfully employed	Capital intensity: capital per worker, ranked from min = 1 to max = 11
Leather	61: leather, leather manufactures, and dressed furs	0–10	2
Textiles	65: textile yarn fabrics, made-up articles, and related products	0–10	3–7
Paper	64: paper, paperboard, and manufacturers thereof	10–20	6–8
Chemicals	Section 5: chemicals	10–20	11
Base metals and metal manufactures	68: base metals 69: metal manufacturers	20–30	5–11
Machinery and transportation equipment	Section 7: machinery and transport equipment	30–40	6–7

Sources of data:

SITC classifications: United Nations, *Statistical Papers*, Series M, No. 10, 2d ed., June, 1951.

Skill level evaluations: National Resources Planning Board, *Industrial Location and National Resources* (Washington, D.C., 1942). Data compiled from A. M. Edwards, "A Socio-Economic Grouping of the Gainful Workers of the United States, 1930," U.S. Bureau of the Census, 1938, and presented in K. A. Bohr, "Investment Criteria for Manufacturing Industries in Underdeveloped Countries," *Review of Economics and Statistics*, XXXVI (1954), No. 2. Considerable approximations by like industries were needed for these classifications.

Capital-intensity measures: Bohr, *ibid.*, adapted from a frequency distribu-

national Trade Classification (SITC) were used as the basis for picking out the commodity groups to be studied. We evaluated the UN groupings of manufactures with respect to (1) skill level, measured by the ratio of skilled and supervisory people to total gainfully employed, and (2) capital intensity, measured by the amount of capital per worker.

The classifications in Table 11 are based primarily on skill requirements, on the now-conventional ground—after the contributions of Abramovitz, Schultz, and Solow—that these are a more important determinant of comparative advantage than capital. Where the skill comparison is not clear, the capital requirement dominates.

A threefold division of the commodities—(1) leather and textiles, (2) paper and chemicals, and (3) machinery and metals—seems a useful pattern. It emphasizes the skill criterion and enables one to compare data for two clearly low-skill-and-capital groups (leather and textiles) with data for two clearly high-skill-and-capital groups (machinery and metals).

SKILLS AND CAPITAL EMBODIED IN MANUFACTURES EXPORTS SINCE 1900

Table 12 shows the proportions of the above three groups of manufactures and of other commodities in the exports of 10 industrial countries, 1900–59.

tion of rankings of industries in five countries (Australia, Canada, Hungary, Palestine, and Rumania), 1936–37, with original data in K. Mandelbaum, *The Industrialization of Backward Areas* (London: Oxford University Press, 1945). "Base metals and metals manufactures" is an especially heterogeneous class, with rank ranges in the Bohr material from 5 to 11 (including semi-manufactures of metal products). But the SITC class adheres more closely to the Bohr "metal extraction" category, with rank concentrated on 9. Canada is an awkward country among the five, since its huge aluminum industry and huge newsprint industry both require heavy capital investment and have no counterpart in the other countries. Its skill-capital position is not weighted heavily on the above estimates.

Table 12. Exports from 10 Industrial Countries, 1900–59: Percentage Distribution of Total Values of Commodities Classified by Skill and Capital Requirements [a]

Commodity group	1900	1928	1958–59	1900 to 1928	1928 to 1958–59	1900 to 1958–59
				Percentage increase or decrease		
Manufactures:						
Low skill and capital requirements:						
1. Leather			(0.2)			
2. Textiles	19.9	18.0	7.0	−9.5	−61.1	−64.8
Moderate skill and capital requirements:						
3. Paper and paper manufactures (including newsprint)			(2.5)			
4. Chemicals	3.9	4.2	7.9	+7.7	+88.1	+102.6
High skill and capital requirements:						
5. Metals and metal manufactures	9.7	10.6	14.1	+9.3	+33.0	+45.4
6. Machinery and vehicles	6.7	13.5	31.6	+101.5	+134.1	+371.6
Subtotals (5+6)	16.4	24.1	45.7	+47.0	+89.6	+178.7
Subtotals (2+4+5+6)	40.2	46.3	60.6	+15.2	+30.9	+50.7
Miscellaneous and unspecified	14.6	15.0	12.4	+2.7	−17.3	−15.1
Food, drink, and tobacco	21.0	15.5	11.0	−26.2	−29.0	−47.6
Raw materials	24.2	23.2	16.0	−4.1	−31.0	−33.9
Totals	100.0	100.0	100.0			

Sources:

For 1900–28 data: Robert E. Baldwin, "The Commodity Composition of Trade: Selected Industrial Countries, 1900–1954," *Review of Economics and Statistics*, XL (1958), 52–68. The countries are Belgium-Luxembourg, Canada, France, Germany, Italy, Japan, Sweden, Switzerland, the United Kingdom, and the United States. The classifications are not the SITC, but Svennilson's modification of a system used by the United Kingdom before 1954; I. Svennilson, *Growth and Stagnation in the European Economy* (Geneva: United Nations, 1954), which in turn is close to that used by Charles Kindleberger, *The Terms of Trade, a European Case Study* (New York: Wiley, 1956).

The 10 industrial countries covered have been increasing the share of their exports represented by manufactures in general and most rapidly in the high-skill-and-capital area. Textiles (low skill and capital) and all other classes of exports have falling shares. The trend is the same, with minor qualification,[24] in both near-thirty-year segments of the twentieth century. Why should this trend exist? Elements in the explanation include (1) the rising share of manufactures in total world trade during the recent thirty-year period and the falling share of primary products (Table 1), (2) the falling prices of many, not all, primary commodities in the first thirty years but not in the recent thirty-year period,[25] and (3) increasing comparative advantage for high-skill-and-capital commodities in the most advanced countries.

SKILLS AND CAPITAL EMBODIED IN WORLD TRADE DURING THE 1950S

Data are available for world trade in the 1950s with a similar but not identical division of kinds of commodities.

The 1950s decade is likely to appear in retrospect a time of

The 1928-to-1958–59 comparison is built up from statistics and information in *Year Book of International Trade*, 1950, 1951, 1959; United Nations, *Monthly Bulletin of Statistics*, 1956; United Nations, *Statistical Year Book*, 1958; *International Financial Statistics*, Supplement to 1962–63 issues.

The 1958–59 (average for the two years) data for chemicals and metals are not exactly comparable to 1900 and 1928 data, since detail of SITC categories 55, 66, and 67 are not available for all 10 countries. Care was taken to adjust the 1958–59 data to a basis comparable to Baldwin's 1900 and 1928 figures, which follow Svennilson's classification. Notice that the above percentages, being for 10 industrial countries only, and based on Svennilson rather than SITC classes, are not strictly comparable to percentages for similar commodity groupings found elsewhere in this essay.

[24] "Miscellaneous and unspecified" shows a small rise in 1900–28, in contrast to a fall since.

[25] Theodore Morgan, "The Long-Run Terms of Trade between Agriculture and Manufacturing," *Economic Development and Cultural Change*, VII (October, 1959), 1–23; and in *International Trade Theory*, pp. 52–95.

Table 13. *Percentage Composition of World Trade, by Values of Selected Groups of Commodities, 1948–49 and 1958–59*

Commodity group	1948–49		1958–59		Change	
Manufactures:						
Low skill and capital requirements:						
1. Leather and leather products	0.3		0.2		−33.3	
2. Textiles and clothing	8.4		5.8		−31.0	
Subtotal (1+2)		8.7		6.0		−31.0
Moderate skill and capital requirements:						
3. Paper and paper manufactures	2.1		1.9		−9.5	
4. Chemicals	4.2		5.9		+40.5	
Subtotal (3+4)		6.3		7.8		+23.8
High skill and capital requirements:						
5. Metals and metal manufactures	8.9		12.2		+37.1	
6. Machinery and transportation equipment	14.7		21.1		+43.5	
Subtotal (5+6)		23.6		33.3		+41.1
Subtotal (1+2+3+4+5+6)		38.6		47.1		+22.0
Other manufactures (wood products, books, etc.)		5.7		6.7		+17.5
Food, drink, and tobacco		} 46.3	19.3		−23.8	
Raw materials			16.0			
Fuel		9.5		10.9		+14.7
Subtotal (food, etc., raw materials, and fuel)		55.8		46.2		−17.2
Total		100.0		100.0		

Sources: See note to Table 12.

The data do not include the export trade of the USSR, East European countries, mainland China, and (for 1958–59) North Korea and North Vietnam. All figures are rounded to the nearest tenth of a percent. The 1948–49 figures are the averages for 1948 and 1949 taken separately; similarly for 1958–59. The purpose of taking two years is to diminish the variability of one-year data.

reasonably normal experience. Its early years saw reduction of trade controls and other trade restrictions and major progress in getting exchange rates, set to a large extent arbitrarily after World War II, into line with prices and income levels. There was only one respectable-size war, the Korean incident; and there were rapid rates of economic expansion in many countries. It is not unreasonable to hope, in the world of the New Economics, that substantial growth rates will come to seem normal.

Table 13 offers a percentage breakdown of world trade over a ten-year period ending in 1958-59. These data show the same striking pattern as those of Table 12. Suppose we put to one side the miscellaneous "Other manufactures" and "Fuel" (mostly oil), both of whose values have been rising moderately.

We are left with two major groups of sharply different trends. Manufactures requiring high skills and large amounts of capital have been rising rapidly (+41 percent) in their share of world commodity trade. Manufactures with low requirements for skill and capital and foods, drink, tobacco, and raw materials have been falling rapidly (−31 and −24 percent, respectively) in their share of world trade. Falling primary-

---

The data have been adjusted to take account of the known differences between SITC and earlier classifications. In some cases the details of export trade value of particular commodities are not known for a given year; then previous-year percentages were applied. For the French Zone of West Germany, German bizone data are used to estimate percentages. Where the exact value of one group is not clear because it is thrown together with others, reasonable values were estimated. For Iran, it was necessary to rely on the trend of petroleum exports to obtain an estimate for 1958–59.

For a number of countries, especially underdeveloped ones, details of manufactures exported are not given. The omission introduces a slight bias in the subclassification data, but the above results are close to the similar but not identical classifications in 1958–59 data of the United Nations *Monthly Bulletin of Statistics,* March, 1961, pp. 16, 17.

product prices are *not* an explanation over these years of falling *values* for primary products.[26]

Why should there be such a contrast in the trend of major groups in this decade of prosperity? An analysis of the trends of the subitems of these groups would contribute to an answer; so would a detailed study of the changes in major trading countries of relative exchange rates, exchange controls, and protective policies in general.

A tentative pattern of explanation, looking at the summary data here, would consider the following possibilities:

1. Whether higher exports of metals, machinery, and chemicals are associated with the drive for higher growth rates and industrialization in less developed areas of the world.

2. Whether for low-skill-and-capital manufactures, whose volume was already small in 1948-49, the decline in trade was due to rising production of these easily produced goods in moderate-income countries and perhaps to associated increased protectionism.

3. Whether falling shares of food and raw materials reflect more agricultural production in Europe and perhaps substitutions made possible by technical progress of cheaper and less raw materials for those that are dearer and needed in greater quantity. The fall in leather textiles and clothing, for example, probably indicates increasingly effective competition of plastics and synthetic fibers.

The consistency of the trends in the 1950s with those for the longer period back to 1900 suggests that much of the same influences have been operating both in the 1950s and in the entire six decades of this century.

---

[26] In *International Trade Theory*, p. 79, Table A-5.

A TEST OF THE HECKSHER-OHLIN TRADE THEORY: SHARES IN EXPORTS
OF LOW-SKILL-AND-CAPITAL EXPORTS AND HIGH-SKILL-AND-CAPITAL
EXPORTS, SELECTED COUNTRIES, 1928–59

The Hecksher-Ohlin trade theorem states that the patterns
of trade among countries depend basically on the relative factor
endowments of the countries as compared with the relative
factor requirements of different kinds of traded items. The
theorem becomes complicated as soon as we grant that production functions may differ in different countries and that taste
patterns may also differ.

A test of the theorem at any point of time faces statistical
and interpretation hurdles, as most conspicuously, the Leontief
evidence from U.S. 1947 data indicates. Leontief concluded,
to the surprise of his readers, that "America's participation in
the international division of labor is based on its specialization
on labor-intensive, rather than capital-intensive, lines of production."[27]

There are advantages in carrying out a test over time and for
a number of countries. Some countries are increasing their proportions of skills in the work force, of capital used in productive
processes, and of organization improvements and other aids to

[27] Wassily Leontief, "Domestic Production and Foreign Trade; the American Capital Position Re-Examined," *Proceedings of the American Philosophical Society*, XCVII (1953), No. 4. This study was organized in terms of two
factors only, capital and labor. There was no subdivision of labor by level of
skills. Leontief's interpretation was that, owing to better organization, training,
entrepreneurship, and the like, one man-year of American labor was the
equivalent of several man-years of foreign labor—that is, in fact, the United
States is comparatively well endowed with labor! A simple alternative explanation, which perhaps should replace a great deal of complex discussion, is
offered by Irving Kravis: 1947, immediately after World War II, was an
anomalous year, in which comparative *availability* of different goods was a
major determinant of what goods moved in trade and what did not. Comparative availability need have had no systematic relation to comparative
advantage.

the production of complex commodities and services. Others are not or are doing so only at a modest rate.

Current trade data enable us to improve on the simple labor-capital dichotomy of factors used by Leontief for the U.S. economy. We consider below the amounts and trends in trade of commodities embodying a relatively large and a relatively small quantity of work skills *and* of capital from selected countries.

The countries that are most rapidly increasing their proportions of productive skills, of capital, and of organization used in production should be increasing their incomes most rapidly. They should also be growing in their ability to compete internationally in the high-skill-and-capital commodities. Conversely, the countries that are increasing their proportions of these factors least rapidly or not at all should have low or zero rates of increase of income and should be falling behind in international competition in the high-skill-and-capital commodities.

We have tested this prediction. The chief consideration for the selection of countries was the availability of consistent series of relevant data. In consequence, the number of countries was limited sharply. We found data we thought reasonably reliable for 26 countries; the highest income and most rapidly growing countries (nearly identical classifications) are best represented.

We ranked these countries in groups from those growing most rapidly, 1928 to 1959, to those growing most slowly or not at all.[28] The groups were: "very rapid recent growth as-

---

[28] The period is, of course, heterogeneous: a great depression, a great war, and a decade of political tension, minor wars, and remarkable growth among high-income areas make up the three decades. From the point of view of the study, the heterogeneity is not necessarily a disadvantage. The shaking-up that depression and war gave the world economy might have led comparative

sociated with war recovery" (3 countries), "other countries growing rapidly" (2), "growing but less rapidly" (9), "probably growing" (8), "may be growing" (2), and "not growing" (1).[29] The statistics are lengthy and are not presented here; certain summary material for 1948–59 is in Appendix C of this essay.

For low-income countries the data are fragmentary and thus generally inconclusive. The significance of 1938 data, and still more, of 1948 data as an indication of trend is modest. In 1938 exchange-rate and exchange-control vagaries, the Spanish War, and World War II preparations influenced and distorted the flows of trade from their longer-run normal. Pronounced deviations from trend are shown in 1938 for one or more of the textile, paper, metal, and machinery categories in the accounts of Italy, Germany, Norway, Sweden, and Spain. Most of these deviations are plausibly interpreted from demand and supply factors of the time. It comes as no surprise that Spain's textile exports were low (civil war), Italy's metals exports low (retention for military uses), and Norway's and Sweden's metals exports high.

In 1948 war dislocations and destruction, various degrees of availability of goods, often arbitrarily set exchange rates, ex-

---

advantage factors to work out no less effectively than if there has been stable peace.

Sources of estimates of growth: E. E. Hagen, "Some Facts about Income Levels and Economic Growth," *Review of Economics and Statistics,* XLII (1960), 62–67; John H. Adler, "World Economic Growth—Retrospect and Prospects," *Review of Economics and Statistics,* XXXVIII (1956), 173–285; Simon Kuznets, "Quantitative Aspects of the Economic Growth of Nations: I. Level and Variability of Rates of Growth," *Economic Development and Cultural Change,* IV (October, 1956), especially Table 1, p. 10, and Table 9, pp. 38–40; our own estimates of 1948–59 rates of growth from UN data of money GNP or GDP, recalculated to a real basis.

[29] The full data are obtainable from the author on request.

change controls, and the various paces of inflation all conspired to distort normal trade flows. Eight countries—Germany, Italy, Japan, France, Norway, Sweden, Spain, and India—show pronounced deviations from trend. Two low-skill-and-capital commodities (textiles and paper) show upward deviations from trend; three high-skill-and-capital commodities show downward deviations—each of these deviations in two to six countries. One suspects that high international demand explains the former commodity deviation and that low domestic production plus high domestic demand explains the latter.

The full-period comparison, 1928 to 1959, is therefore a more reliable measure of normal change than intermediate-year comparisons. The full-period comparison avoids the biases listed above. Also, both 1928 and 1959 were prosperous years in the world economy as a whole.

I draw three conclusions from the full period:

1. The orthodox doctrine of international trade—here interpreted with a strong emphasis on the skill factor—receives surprisingly strong support from this historical study. (Surprisingly strong, because one usually would expect to find major discrepancies and gaps when a general theory meets the complexity of fact, which, as Francis Bacon once advised us, "exceedeth many times over the subtility of argument.") The support lies in a consistent pattern: "certainly growing" countries show a fall in their export reliance on low-skill-and-capital commodities and a rise in their reliance on metals and machinery, the high-skill-and-capital categories. Among these 14 countries, there is only one commodity in one country that shows exception to the expected trend of a rising share of high skill-and-capital items.[30] Lack of data for the small "Leather"

---

[30] Switzerland shows a falling share of exports in the "metals" classification.

item, and often for the "Textiles" item also, makes generalization here uncertain; but Germany, Italy, France, Switzerland, and the United Kingdom show the normal decline we should expect.

2. The increasing realization of comparative advantage possibilities, latent at the beginning of the period, explains some trends. The rise of "Paper" in Canada and Finland data are cases in point. The same explanation is plausible for the rise of "Textiles" in the data for Portugal and India.

3. It is easy to read too much into figures. For that reason we have resisted the temptation to develop averages and correlations. Improving international statistics should make interpretations five and ten years hence more rewarding. For example, the remarkable success of Japan in the 1950s in raising exports of metals and machinery doubtless indicates less any increasing comparative advantage in these lines than firm government measures to encourage such exports.[31] Similarly, the high proportion of exports of "Metals" and "Machinery" from Yugoslavia in 1959 may reflect not relative efficiency but government controls. The trend of chemicals from Chile (mainly iodine) and from Argentina (recently, entirely quebracho) doubtless says something about world demand but little about the trend of the chemical industry as a whole in those countries.[32]

[31] The *Economist* lists "winks and nods passed along Japan's extensive 'old boy' network," special exemptions from corporate income tax, special depreciation allowances, ready permission to import technical know-how, tight protection against imports, and, finally, differential interest rates and firm channeling of loans to the most promising industries (September 1, 1962, pp. 803–11).

[32] We have made a supplementary test, with summary data, of the same theorem—that rising income should be positively correlated with a rising share in their exports of high-skill-and-capital commodities—for the period 1948–49 to 1958–59. The data for this period are sharply improved over

Summary

What are the main patterns in world commodity trade that stand out in the course of our inquiry?

1. Its volume has expanded remarkably in the past eighty-odd years, by about six-fold. Trade has been growing much more rapidly than world population; but trade in manufactures has been rising more slowly than manufactures production, while trade in primary products has been rising more rapidly than their production.

2. The terms-of-trade experience of primary products versus manufactures shows great variety. From the beginning of this century down to the 1930s, primary product prices typically fell, relatively, though with significant exceptions. Since the 1930s they have typically risen.

3. Major trends in the shares of world manufactures trade held by main trading nations include a prolonged decline for the United Kingdom from its uniquely dominant position (37 percent) in 1883, the rise of the United States (until recently) and Japan, and the remarkably constant share of other countries than the seven leading ones up to World War II.

4. Since the 1880s high-income countries have been export-

---

earlier years; but, as we have reasoned above, the starting point is a time of acute disequilibrium in domestic production and in trade. The changes for each of 19 countries in the weighted average share in exports of the three highest skill-and-capital commodities is correlated with the change in income. (The data are given in Appendix C.)

The results are disappointing. Correlation, though positive, is low: $r^2 = 0.19$. Very likely the most important cause of the low correlation is, as we have argued above, that in 1948–49 the dislocations of war were only partly overcome. The unequal paces after 1948–49 of inflation, exchange control, and exchange rate changes, and the unequal chances of penetrating new markets for industrial commodities, as compared with regaining old prewar markets where buyer and seller knew each other and their commercial and product habits—all these would lead to deviations from "normal" (comparative advantage) performance during the 1950s.

ing and importing a falling share of world trade in primary commodities.

5. Data of the 1950s for developed and underdeveloped countries indicate that developed countries are increasing their incomes *and* their share of world trade (in this prosperous decade) much more rapidly than the underdeveloped countries. The ratios, by different kinds of data, run from roughly one and a third to over double. The centuries-old divergence between the countries that are getting ahead rapidly and the rest of the world that is not is still increasing. General modernization of techniques is *not* causing a relative decline of trade among the high-income countries.

6. Since before World War II, trade as a share of income has been rising among developed countries. Recent data do not support the "law of falling importance of international trade." But trade in relation to income does seem to have been declining among underdeveloped countries since before World War II.

7. The empirical relationship between changed exports and changed income was modest in the 1950s, even among countries whose trade is very large compared with their incomes. Other causes of changed income have probably dominated.

8. The main industrial countries have, since 1900, been increasing sharply the share in their exports of high-skill-and-capital goods and reducing the share of all other goods. Nearly the same pattern holds for total world trade in the 1950s: high-skill-and-capital goods have taken a greater relative share of world exports; nearly everything else has taken a smaller share.

9. The Hecksher-Ohlin trade theorem is supported by data, 1928 to 1959, emphasizing the skill-and-capital component of exports. The comparatively rapidly growing countries for which data are available show a fall in their export reliance on low-skill-and-capital commodities and (most clearly) a rise in their reliance on high-skill-and-capital goods.

TRADE AND ECONOMIC GROWTH

Marshall's uncharacteristically firm dictum, "The causes that determine the economic progress of nations belong to the study of international trade," [33] was based on the experience of the nineteenth century. Marshall seems to have been thinking in terms of the stimulus to nonindustrial countries from the rising demand for primary products of industrial countries. The falling share of underdeveloped countries in world trade (Tables 7 and 8) makes reliance on this kind of stimulus to growth more dubious than it appeared fifty or more years ago.

Hence, as a generalization for the twentieth century, Marshall's judgment looked curious to Nurkse;[34] but trade remains relevant to growth experience and policy. Not only have primary products made up a falling proportion of world trade, but other low-skill-and-capital commodities have also been shrinking relatively in the twentieth century to date. In both value and volume, high-skill-and-capital commodities are continuously and rapidly rising in their share of world trade. The trend gives justification to Japan's effort, as a means of economic advance, to move in the direction of "heavy" commodity exports as rapidly as these goods, with encouragement and support from government, can become competitive internationally.

Comparative advantage is not a fixed thing. A logical policy for individual countries is a continuous effort to shift comparative advantage in the direction of products with the most rapidly growing world demand. It is equally in the interest of mankind as a whole that resources should be constantly reallocated in pursuit of the changing pattern of human wants.

---

[33] Alfred Marshall, *Principles of Economics* (8th ed., New York: Macmillan, 1920), p. 270.
[34] In his Wicksell lectures; Ragnar Nurkse, *Patterns of Trade and Development* (New York: Oxford University Press, 1961), p. 16.

A central difficulty in achieving world interest with fair success is inherent in the increasing rapidity of scientific and technical change. The accelerating rate of change hardly needs documentation: one crude estimate is that chemical knowledge has doubled since 1950, another that at least half of all scientific knowledge has been developed since 1910. People now in their middle years have lived through half the world's scientific and technical history. In the United States, by date from a combination of Defense Department and National Science Foundation estimates and a McGraw-Hill forecast, research and development outlays were 900 million dollars in 1941, were 13.4 billion dollars in 1960–61, and will be 22.2 billion dollars in 1969. The corresponding ratios are 1, 15, and 25.[35] Slichter generalized that the technology of the American economy in the past 150 years breaks up into three overlapping phases: in the first main reliance for progress was placed on increasing capital, in the second on increased use of energy, and in the third on revolutionary changes in "the art of management and a sensational growth of technological research."[36]

An advance of knowledge differs from the other two sources of growth listed by Slichter in that it spreads quickly among advanced countries[37] but less readily to underdeveloped countries. The blocks from educational lags, communications hurdles, limited markets, and inability and unwillingness to commit resources to new ventures are greater in those countries.

We have seen that the underdeveloped countries closely

[35] All three groups of statistics are presented together in Edward F. Denison, *The Sources of Economic Growth in the United States,* Supplementary Paper No. 13 of the Committee for Economic Development (New York, 1962), p. 240.

[36] Sumner H. Slichter, *Economic Growth in the United States* (Baton Rouge: Louisiana State University Press, 1961), p. 74.

[37] Compare Denison, *Sources of Economic Growth,* Chap. 21, pp. 229ff.

resemble the developed ones in the proportion their exports bear to income. But the recent (1950s) tendency is for this proportion to be stable or fall in underdeveloped countries and to rise in developed countries (Table 9). Since the incomes of the underdeveloped countries are relatively stagnant and those of the developed countries have been rapidly growing, it should come as no surprise that the underdeveloped areas have a shrinking part of total world trade (Table 8).

In brief, the increasing rapidity of technical change presents a special disadvantage in trade to those countries whose incomes are lowest. From the point of view of mankind as a whole, however, it is just these countries that should be lifting their incomes most rapidly.

The guild of students of economic history are inclined to emphasize the strategic influence of export expansion in setting off and stimulating economic growth. A conclusion from Lamfalussy, applied to Europe, was given above. A broader generalization is given by North:

There are few exceptions to the essentially initiating role of a successful export sector in the early stages of accelerated growth of market economies. . . . An expanding external market has provided the means for an increase in the size of the domestic market [previously small, scattered, based on a mainly rural economy, with a high degree of family and village self-sufficiency], for growth in money income, and spread of specialization and division of labor.[38]

The above reasoning leads us to a portrait of the expected normal world economy of the next several decades. The underdeveloped nations will on the average continue to fall further behind the developed ones with respect to income levels. There will be occasional windfall gains and losses from trade when commodities they produce happen to have increased or de-

[38] Douglass C. North, *The Economic Growth of the United States* (Englewood Cliffs, N.J.: Prentice-Hall, 1961), p. 2.

creased demand abroad because of technological or other change.

To diminish the expected increased divergence between the developed and the underdeveloped economies is a high-priority goal for the world community. Private, government, and international efforts can advantageously support the activities that will enable underdeveloped countries to adapt more flexibly to new opportunities in trade, including new products, new techniques, and new marketing patterns. Among these activities are research and development on commodities for which world demand is growing most rapidly, pilot projects to test costs and markets, and training and encouragement of the needed skills and of innovatory and energetic habits of mind.

APPENDIX A

Table A1. Value of Exports as a Percentage of National Income; Developed and Underdeveloped Countries: 1929 to 1958–59

	Developed countries				Underdeveloped countries			
	1929	1937–38	1948–49	1958–59	1929	1937–38	1948–49	1958–59
Highest quartile	31.1	23.2	23.9	25.8	(43.5)	35.0	33.1	25.8
Median	22.1	17.8	16.9	21.5	(25.1)	28.3	20.0	20.1
Lowest quartile	20.1	12.5	7.4	12.8	(18.6)	18.5	11.3	11.7

Developed countries include, at maximum, 22: Australia, Austria, Belgium-Luxembourg, Canada, Denmark, Finland, France, West Germany, Greece, Italy, Japan, the Netherlands, New Zealand, Norway, Union of South Africa, Sweden, Switzerland, the United Kingdom, the United States, Yugoslavia, and Ireland. Only 17 countries had usable data in 1929.

Underdeveloped countries include, at maximum, 22: Argentina, Brazil, Burma, Ceylon, Guatemala, Honduras, India, Pakistan, Indonesia, Jamaica, Mexico, Peru, the Philippines, Thailand, Turkey, Venezuela, Cuba, the Republic of the Congo, Colombia, Costa Rica, the Dominican Republic, and Ecuador. 1950 instead of 1948–49, and 1959 instead of 1958–59 data have been used for the last-mentioned five countries. The number of countries included in 1929 and 1937–38 are 4 and 12, respectively (Table A1).

The figures from which Table A1 was calculated are given in Table A2.

*Table A2. Value of Exports as a Percentage of National Income
(Current Prices)*

Country	1929	1937–38	1948–49	1958–59
Argentina	. . .	21.6	11.3	14.0
Australia	20.2	19.3	28.7	17.1
Austria	30.7	21.4[a]	16.4[b]	23.4
Belgium-Luxembourg	45.2[e]	37.5[a]	30.3	36.2
Brazil	. . .	. . .	12.4	7.1
Burma	. . .	40.9[a]	24.7	25.9
Canada	24.6	22.9	24.5	19.8
Ceylon	. . .	47.9[a]	37.7	32.8
Denmark	32.8[e]	24.8	19.8	31.8
Finland	31.4	30.6	23.3	26.1
France	20.5	8.7[e]	10.2	13.0
Germany	17.8[e]	12.9[e]	13.9[b]	21.2
Greece	15.7	14.3	5.3[f]	8.8
Guatemala	16.3	15.4	15.5	19.3
Honduras	57.5	32.0	34.9	21.9
India and Pakistan	. . .	. . .	5.2	4.7
Indonesia	29.4	30.7	. . .	19.6
Italy	. . .	8.0	10.0	12.3
Jamaica	. . .	26.2	23.0	25.7
Japan	. . .	20.9	9.9[b]	12.7
Mexico	20.8	14.7	9.9	8.8
Netherlands	32.6[g]	23.5	25.5	42.3
New Zealand	. . .	33.4	32.5	27.4
Norway	21.5	17.8	18.1	24.6

Source: Computed from data drawn mainly from *International Financial Statistics,* August, 1962; Supplement to 1962–63 issues of I.F.S.; and United Nations, *Statistical Year Book,* 1955, pp. 453–54; 1957 (pp. 396–425, 483–84); 1960, pp. 457–58.

[a] 1937 *or* 1938 data.

[b] Refers to 1950–51.

[e] 1930 data.

[d] An unofficial estimate for 1937 is averaged with the official data for 1938.

[e] Official data for 1938. The 1929 figure is drawn from W. S. and E. S. Woytinsky, *World Population and Production: Trends and Outlook* (New York: Twentieth Century Fund, 1953), p. 386. The 1929 estimate for undivided Germany is apportioned between West and East Germany in the ratio of their population in 1950.

[f] Refers to 1951–52.

[g] Trade figure is taken from League of Nations, *Memorandum on International Trade and Balance of Payments, 1927–29,* Vol. III, *Trade Statistics* (Geneva, 1931), p. 216.

Table A2 (continued)

Country	1929	1937–38	1948–49	1958–59
Peru	. . .	. . .	21.7	25.1
Philippines	. . .	. . .	10.2	10.5
South Africa	20.0	10.6	16.1	23.1
Sweden	22.1	18.0	16.9	21.5
Switzerland	22.3	15.4	19.7	23.8
Thailand	. . .	23.5[a]	18.2	14.8
Turkey	. . .	8.9[a]	7.4	6.2
United Kingdom	20.1	12.1	17.6	18.0
United States	6.0	4.5	5.5	4.5
Venezuela	. . .	39.9[a]	45.7	42.5
Cuba	. . .	30.4	40.5	33.7
Yugoslavia	. . .	13.6	6.0	6.8
Ireland	29.4	15.1	16.6	25.4
			1950	1959
Belgian Congo	. . .	. . .	44.5	58.0
Colombia	. . .	. . .	11.3	12.8
Costa Rica	. . .	. . .	27.7	20.8
Dominican Republic	. . .	. . .	31.2[h]	21.0
Ecuador	. . .	. . .	16.3[h]	20.1

[h] 1951 data.

APPENDIX B

Table B. Percentage Changes in Exports and National Income, Real Values

Country	1958–59 compared with 1948–49		1958–59 compared with 1928–29	
Group 1: $\Sigma X/Y < 15$ percent:	Change in exports	Change in income	Change in exports	Change in income
Argentina	26.7	1.8		
Brazil	−15.4	55.5		
Colombia	35.2	31.2		
France	156.8	39.0	49.7	149.5
Greece	107.7[a]	58.2[a]	. . . .	157.8
India	31.5	24.3		
Italy	202.9	131.7		
Japan	218.2[b]	96.4[b]		
Philippines	118.0	77.9		

Sources: United Nations; *Statistical Yearbook*, 1955, 1957, and 1960. *International Financial Statistics*, Supplement to 1961–62 issues.

[a] Ratio of 1958–59 to 1951–52 data.
[b] Ratio of 1958–59 to 1950–51 data.

Table B (continued)

Country	1958–59 compared with 1948–49		1958–59 compared with 1928–29	
Group 1 (cont.):	Change in exports	Change in income	Change in exports	Change in income
Turkey	....	110.9		
United States	20.0	42.5	87.5	116.8
Group 2: 15 percent $< \Sigma X/Y < 25$ percent:				
Australia	3.7	39.4	....	138.4
Austria	154.9[b]	34.6[b]	93.2	
Burma	19.4	62.9		
Canada	36.8	78.1	116.7	191.2
Denmark	166.7	30.0	....	79.2
Ecuador	114.3	65.1		
Finland	118.3	65.1	....	138.4
Germany	200.0[b]	96.4[b]	140.8	89.1
Guatemala	19.5	16.0		
Honduras	5.0	53.0	....	174.2
Jamaica	137.2	97.9		
Norway	102.1	16.9	102.1	103.2
Peru	78.6	34.8		
South Africa	116.2	30.5	162.3	167.8
Sweden	96.6	42.8	....	134.4
Switzerland	108.8	64.3	....	89.0
Thailand	38.1	100.6		
United Kingdom	41.1	28.3	29.7	
Costa Rica	36.3	93.3		
Dominican Republic	30.7	62.3		
Group 3: 25 percent $< X/Y$:				
Belgium-Luxembourg	93.1	45.5	....	95.8
Ceylon	22.1	67.9		
Cuba	17.2	45.1[c]		
Netherlands	242.9	67.5	....	80.8
New Zealand	26.7	44.7	118.9	
Venezuela	94.8	134.3		

[c] Ratio of 1958 to 1948 data.

In Table B, export data exclude military aid. Where independently calculated (sector) price deflators had not been used, national income data were deflated to real values by the use of the domestic wholesale price index, save in a few countries where the retail price index alone was available and was used.

If a country fell in Group 2 in one period and in Group 1 or 3 in the other, it was classed in Group 2.

APPENDIX C

Table C uses data from 19 countries. The rate of increase in real national income, 1948–49 to 1958–59, is correlated with the weighted average rate of change in exports of three high-skill-and-capital classes of commodities. The three classes were machinery and transport equipment, chemicals, and metals and metal manufactures. The weights used were the average share of each of these classes of commodities in total commodity exports of the country, in 1948–49 and 1958–59. The countries below are grouped in order, from those whose total exports are smallest compared with national income (under 15 percent), to a middle group (between 15 and 25 percent), to a highest group (over 25 percent).

Table C. Relation of Rising Income to Share in Commodity Exports of High-Skill-and-Capital Commodities

Country	Percent change in real total national income	Weighted average percent change in share of high-skill-and-capital exports
Chile	+61.6	+2.4
France	39.0	27.5
Italy	131.7	88.9
Japan	81.3	116.1
Mexico	69.9	−33.3
Turkey	110.9	+135.3
United States	42.5	17.8
Australia	39.4	97.4
Austria	49.9	98.4
Canada	78.1	12.7
Denmark	30.0	46.3
Germany	239.6	150.0
Norway	16.9	139.5
Sweden	42.8	36.5
Switzerland	64.3	0.4
South Africa	30.5	47.5
United Kingdom	28.3	20.4
Belgium-Luxembourg	45.5	34.0
Netherlands	67.5	86.5
Arithmetic means	66.8	41.5
Medians	49.9	46.3

Source: See Appendixes B and C.

VI

BERNARD SEMMEL

On the Economics of "Imperialism"

MANY WRITERS have questioned whether "imperialism" is a term that scholars ought to use. In recent years, it has become even more a term of abuse and less one which may be profitably employed to describe complex relationships. The Marxists have seized upon it and have constructed a theory of "imperialism" so narrow and partisan as to have increased rather than diminished the difficulties of analysis. In pursuing polemical purposes, they have directed arclights of dazzling brilliance upon special areas of the problem, and the glare has not only intensified the surrounding darkness but has distorted even the illumined area. Many opponents of the Marxist view have been no less guilty of this kind of scholarship, offering polemical anti-Marxist interpretations to counter polemical Marxist ones. Certain economists and sociologists have tended to think in terms of special and peculiar causes or motivations and have been able to substantiate limited hypotheses by references to equally limited times and places. Historians have either been too much in the debt of partisan theorists or, on the other hand, have rather nihilistically determined to prove that no theory corresponded to the facts. The result has been a confusion which a short essay cannot, unfortunately, dispel.

It is easiest, if not wisest, to plunge *in medias res*, into the tangled question of the relationship between capitalism and imperialism. This is the most familiar part of the problem and the one that has evoked the most heated controversy. In 1901, after the conclusion of the Boer War, which he had witnessed as a correspondent for the *Manchester Guardian*, J. A. Hobson, an English liberal economist and journalist, had written of modern imperialism, epitomized by British aggression in South Africa, as promoted by manufacturers of war materials, industrialists who required export markets, and capitalists with idle funds. These business interests and these interests alone profited enormously by imperialism, he asserted, while the remainder of the nation lost. "The economic root of imperialism," Hobson wrote, "is the desire of strong, organized industrial and financial interests to secure and develop at the public expense and by the public force private markets for their surplus goods and their surplus capital." Hobson placed the chief onus upon the holders of "surplus capital," who wished more profitable investments than were available at home. These capital surpluses and consequently imperialism were, he declared, the result of the maldistribution of the national product, which left huge amounts in the hands of the possessing classes. A more just distrbution would remove this surplus income and at the same time broaden the home market sufficiently to permit it to absorb the goods and capital which had heretofore been shipped abroad. "Trade Unionism and Socialism are thus the natural enemies of Imperialism," he wrote, "for they take away from the 'imperialist' classes the surplus incomes which form the economic stimulus of Imperialism." [1]

The Neo-Marxists—Luxemburg, Hilferding, and others—writing in the decade following Hobson's treatise, saw imperialism as the latest and probably the last stage of capitalist development. In this stage, free competition no longer existed; trusts, cartels, and monopolies were the rule. New technological advances, Hilferding argued, following Marx, had resulted in a fall in the rate of profits as a result of the increasing proportion of capital invested in machinery rather than in labor. Capital had therefore been compelled to turn to undeveloped areas, to the exploitation of native labor under more primitive conditions, in order to realize satisfactory returns. Most neo-Marxist theorists of imperialism, indeed, simply extended to the international stage the analysis prepared to explain "exploitation" at home. Luxemburg, on the other hand, came to a conclusion similar to Hobson's. She asserted that capitalism's fatal tendency toward irrational accumulation, a tendency she associated with a vast working class living on the bare minimum of subsistence, had resulted in a tremendous capacity to produce goods without the simultaneous development of domestic markets to absorb this production. Hence the necessity for markets abroad. All this gave rise to imperialism and war, from which the capitalists derived relief, however temporary, from the pressures created by the system. The arguments of Lenin's famous essay on imperialism, written in 1917, were essentially those of Hobson and Hilferding. The writings of Hilferding and of such other Marxists as Kautsky and Bauer, however, possessed an insight and a sophistication well beyond the crude and somewhat

[1] J. A. Hobson, *Imperialism: A Study* (London: Allen and Unwin, 1938, originally published in 1902), pp. xv, 81–84, 89–90, 106, 140–45.

hysterical assessment of imperialism of Lenin's treatise, which was to become virtually unalterable Communist dogma.[2]

Hobson and the Neo-Marxists, then, although differing among themselves as to the causes of the phenomenon, agreed in seeing imperialism as a phase of capitalism in which the capitalists found it desirable to export capital to countries where they were likely to gain a significantly higher return from their investment than was available to them from home investments. This export of capital was frequently accompanied by the use of national force at the instance of the capitalists to safeguard investments. This was "imperialism." Indeed, Marxists were ready to believe that capital export per se was imperialism, whether or not aggressive force accompanied the process. The Marxists insisted, furthermore, that imperialism was a necessary and inevitable concomitant of capitalist development. Many noncommunist writers today, particularly in former colonial territories, in India, for example, have become convinced of the accuracy of this view of imperialism. This conviction has resulted in their failure to object to crude Soviet expansion in Eastern Europe, while at the same time they have been ready to denounce international efforts to guide the use of foreign aid as malevolent neocolonialism.

The rejoinder of Western social science has increasingly come to be a questioning of the reality of economic motives in modern imperialism. In this, they have taken their cue from Schumpeter, an Austrian economist, who was an early opponent of the Hobson and neo-Marxist view of imperialism. In an essay

---

[2] Rudolf Hilferding, *Das Finanzkapital, eine Studie über die jüngste Entwicklung des Kapitalismus* (Vienna, 1910); Rosa Luxemburg, *The Accumulation of Capital* (New Haven: Yale University Press, 1951, originally published in 1913); O. Bauer, *Die Nationalitatenfrage und die Sozialdemokratic* (Vienna, 1907); Nikolai Lenin, *Imperialism, the Highest Stage of Capitalism* (New York: International Publishers, 1939, first published in 1917).

upon the sociology of imperialism, written in 1919, Schumpeter suggested that far from imperialism's being an inevitable stage in the development of capitalism, capitalism was by its inner nature anti-imperialist. Had not such nineteenth-century liberals as Cobden and Bright, the spokesmen of the rising British capitalism, been the most vociferous opponents of militarism and colonialism? Modern imperialism, Schumpeter urged, was not a product of rational, economic factors but of irrational sentiments that had managed to survive from feudal, precapitalist times. Placing his opposition to the position of the Marxists in their own language, Schumpeter wrote: "Imperialism thus is atavistic in character. . . . In other words, it is an element that stems from the living conditions, not of the present, but of the past—or, put in terms of the economic interpretation of history, from past rather than present relations of production." Schumpeter explained modern imperialism as an alliance between "expansive interests" within capitalism, selfish interests constituting a minority of the capitalists, and the survivals of feudal, precapitalist classes. Imperialism, he held, was rooted in the irrational sentiments still lodged in the breasts of these feudal and military classes.[3]

Thucydides, in speaking of the Athenian empire, described its origin in motives of "fear, honor, and interest." [4] Certainly, irrational and political factors have played a large role in modern imperialism as well. It is difficult, however, to balance motives upon an apothecary scale to determine whether aggressive feelings of racial superiority are, in troy ounces, more or less weighty than the desire to sport as much colonial plumage

   [3] J. A. Schumpeter, *Imperialism and Social Classes* (Oxford: Blackwell, 1951), p. 84 and *passim*.
   [4] Thucydides, *The Peloponnesian War* (New York: Modern Library, 1951), p. 44.

as a neighbor or the hope of obtaining an exploitative profit. Sometimes, to add to the confusion, one motive poses as another. (An example is a recent well-received historical proof that England went into Africa in the 1880s for strategic reasons—Thucydides' "fear"?—rather than economic ones; that is, that English policy in Africa was grounded upon her determination to maintain the sea route to India. Why bother to maintain the sea route to India, however, if not on grounds of "interest"?) [5]

It is unfortunate that the dogmatic declarations of social scientists during the 1920s and 1930s in favor of the Hobson-Lenin hypotheses as all-embracing explanations of imperialism have produced, as by an ideological version of Newton's Third Law, an equally emphatic rejection of these hypotheses. What must, indeed, be avoided is seeing imperialism as an entirely economic phenomenon. It would be foolish to assert that Cromwell's imperial activities in Ireland were dominated by the needs of a nascent British capitalism rather than on grounds of religion or strategy and equally foolish to deny the primacy of economic motives in Leopold's Congo. It is certainly more hopeful, given our focus of "mankind" in this essay, to investigate the economic—the rational—motives, which are at our state of knowledge more capable of adjustment and control, than to plunge into the darknesses of the irrational.

"Empires" have been among the oldest forms of political and economic organization, and the ancient world provided numerous examples of empire-building of rather different types. In both the Assyrian and the Persian empires, the gains of dominion consisted of expropriated lands, slaves, and tribute. The

[5] J. Gallagher and R. Robinson, with Alice Denny, *Africa and the Victorians* (London: Macmillan, 1962).

great trading city of Tyre, later rivaled by its own colony of Carthage, reaped the profits of the middleman; Tyrian ships sailed to Spain to obtain silver and even beyond Gibraltar to obtain Cornish tin, establishing trading stations along the way, and maintained a naval and commercial predominance in the Mediterranean for centuries. Nearly all the Greek cities, suffering from a surfeit of population, established colonies from the ninth century B.C. onward in Ionia or in Sicily and Southern Italy to relieve the pressure of numbers. The links of these colonies with their mother cities were largely sentimental; of a rather different order was the Delian League, of the fifth century B.C., an association of tribute-paying "allies" under the naval dominance of Athens. (The "allies" were, furthermore, subject to trading restrictions designed to benefit Athenian producers and merchants.) Rome's empire was erected on the same foundations as Persia's, with the differentiating element, especially during the republican period, that privileged individuals or combines were permitted to exploit colonial territories as tax-farmers and operators of mines and latifundia with slave work forces.

The imperial form which had appeared in the maritime predominance of Tyre and Carthage in the ancient world and in the Athenian naval and trading confederacy was to blossom in the great trading empires of Venice and Genoa during the late Middle Ages. From the eleventh through the fifteenth centuries, these cities monopolized the distribution of the luxury products of the Orient and of Byzantium into Europe and returned to Constantinople and other eastern ports with Sicilian wheat and Flemish woolens. The discovery of the New World and of ocean routes to the East undermined the trading monopolies of the Italian cities. Portugal sought its fortune through control of the Spice Islands of the Indies and its mastery of an ocean route to them. During the sixteenth century, the Spanish Empire in the Americas concentrated, in the Roman pattern, upon the exploitation of great landed estates and rich mines worked by Indian and Negro slaves. Spain, however, missed the opportunity of establishing a domestic industry and of developing her agriculture and continued to be supplied with manufactures and even with part of her food from abroad, principally from Genoa, in exchange for her American gold. In the seventeenth century, the Dutch erected a commercial empire—the epitome of the empires of Mercantilism—not only upon the spice monopoly, seized from the Portuguese, but also upon a magnificent merchant marine which served as a common carrier for all nations, upon previously unexampled facilities for financial transactions, and upon great accumulations of capital.

The empires of Mercantilism, those of seventeenth- and eighteenth-century Holland, France, and England, were largely naval and commercial in character, yet they also followed the example of the ancient Roman latifundia. Slaves from Africa's Guinea Coast worked West Indian sugar plantations, and the natives of Java and Borneo were compelled to work the East Indian spice plantations. These plantations, however, were far removed across wide oceans from the imperial metropolises and therefore made extensive merchant marines and battle-ready navies necessary for effective management. In most cases, the imperial metropolises, following the example of the Greek city-states, transferred part of their population as colonists to their overseas empires. Thus, the older techniques for the utilization of empire and for imperial gain were not forgotten but adapted and supplemented. Mindful, perhaps, of the mistakes of Spain and of the means they themselves had employed to profit by Spain's weaknesses and conscious of the advantages, in an age when the rivalry between powers was so keen, of an extensive population profitably employed, the commercial empires of the seventeenth and eighteenth centuries set down the lines of economic behavior which Adam Smith was the first to call the "Mercantile system." The colonists were to provide those goods—primarily raw materials—which the mother country was incapable of producing herself and which she needed to maintain her power, such as ship timber and naval stores, or which in surplus could be sold abroad, such as sugar, tobacco, and indigo. In this way the metropolis would not lose bullion by purchasing goods from the foreigner as Spain had and could perhaps even gain precious metals from other countries. In addition, the colonists were committed to purchasing manufactured commodities from the metropolis, thus keeping employed what the Mercantilist planners hoped would be a large and growing population. As a conserver of bullion and a preserver of naval readiness for war, it was provided that domestic shipping always be favored over foreign in all these trading transactions.[6]

A leading principle behind these practices of Mercantilism was presented in the early seventeenth century by Francis Bacon: "The increase of any estate must be upon the Foreigner," Bacon wrote, ". . . (for whatsoever is somewhere gotten is somewhere else lost)." [7] Economic conditions were regarded as static by the Mercantilist, and economic theorists devoted themselves to describing exchanges of wealth rather than, as was later to be the case, its production. It was everywhere taken for granted that one man's, or country's, gain in-

---

[6] The best discussion is in E. F. Heckscher, *Mercantilism* (London: Allen and Unwin, 1935). It should be noted that Dutch policy at times departed from some of these principles.

[7] Quoted in C. J. Friedrich, *The Age of the Baroque* (New York: Harper and Row, 1962), p. 1.

evitably meant another man's, or country's, loss, as Bacon had asserted. For most Mercantilists, trade itself was imperialistic and the profits of trade a species of plunder: international trade was an unrelenting war to obtain possession of a limited supply of the precious metals; and the manufacturer and the merchant exacted not a "natural" price for his goods, a price for the raw material and labor applied, but whatever the traffic would bear.

In the mid-eighteenth century, it might have still been unexceptionable to say, as the Physiocrats did, that manufacturing simply transformed raw material, adding no more value to it than the number of man-hours required for that transformation. Indeed many "advanced" economic thinkers (among them Edmund Burke, as late as the 1780s) continued to maintain that what a nation must seek were not profits of production, which were meager, but rather the more sizable profits of exchange. Holland was the model of the riches that might be acquired by the transporter and merchant. With the coming of the Industrial Revolution, however, such a view became outdated. By the end of the eighteenth century, and certainly during the first two decades of the nineteenth century, the focus of economic activity and of economic theorizing had shifted from exchange to production. It had become clear that the new power-driven machinery would make possible a tremendous increase in the scale of the profits of production and that Great Britain would be the first nation to reap these profits.

From the middle of the seventeenth century, England had striven to rival Dutch commercial and financial predominance. By the middle of the eighteenth century, the Bank of Amsterdam had been eclipsed by the London money market, and the British merchant marine had edged ahead of the Dutch. Even as her merchant mariners inherited the Dutch monopoly of world commerce and London bankers usurped Amsterdam's financial predominance, English manufacturers, pioneers in the new industrial revolution, set out to make England the "workshop of the world" and to multiply many times the profits of trade by procuring for themselves the profits of production as well. (The economic triumph of Holland over the southern provinces of the lowlands in the seventeenth century had been the triumph of the merchant over the manufacturer; now the immense productivity of the new steam-driven machinery of the Industrial Revolution placed the manufacturer in the controlling position.)

Furthermore, by the last half of the eighteenth century, England, like Holland in the previous century, had accumulated, whether through commercial enterprise or the plunder of Indian riches, as has been variously maintained,[8] great hoards of capital which it sought to invest abroad because of low domestic interest rates. In 1803, in his highly perceptive *Inquiry into the Colonial Policy of the European Powers*, Brougham wrote that in ancient times colonies were formed because of overflowing numbers of people but that "none of the ancient nations appear to have reached such a pitch of wealth, as to give rise to the emigration of an overflowing capital." Indeed, he continued, "if we except Tyre and Carthage, none of them seem to have had sufficient stock to engage in the more distant trades."[9] Brougham then, a century before Hobson, identified the new empire-building with the new capitalism. The Industrial Revolution and "an overflowing capital," the fruits of large-scale commercial and industrial growth, were to be, as we have seen, regarded as the hallmarks of the new imperialism.

[8] See J. M. Keynes' discussion in his *Treatise on Money* (New York: Harcourt, Brace, 1930).

[9] Henry Brougham, *An Inquiry into the Colonial Policy of the European Powers* (Edinburgh, 1803), I, 217–18, 222.

There are no wholly new contemporary theories of imperialism. Those of the past sixty years which have seemed novel have had in reality a surprisingly long history. Furthermore, despite the differing outlooks of the various theorists and the constantly altering circumstances, the theoretical descriptions of the new empire-building of an industrial society by the economists of the first half of the nineteenth century are much less contradictory of each other and of more recent theories than might be imagined. The differences are largely of emphasis. This conclusion may surprise those who see the beginning of modern imperial activity in the division of Africa in the 1880s and the beginning of the modern theory of imperialism in Hobson. The new industrialism created conditions which substantially increased the economic intercourse between regions at widely differing levels of social and economic development. The founders of the new economic science, constructed to describe the new industrial society, quite naturally directed themselves to an analysis of this new intercourse, which loomed large in the consciousness of the time and was closely associated in the minds of the first generations of political economists with the success of the new system.

Despite obvious family resemblances to "imperialisms" of the past, the new empire-building of early industrialism had important differentiating elements. There was ample, though hardly unqualified, justification for the view of the classical economists that the new imperial economic relationship between metropolis and colony—formal or informal—was not the parasitism of the older empires but was, rather, symbiotic in character. No longer are we dealing with the comparatively simple mechanisms of a merchant capitalism but with powerful forces, growing out of a complex, only partially understood economic system, which were compelling an industrial society to turn outward. At any rate, so an important school of political economists, led by Wakefield and Torrens, saw the issue in the early nineteenth century. The new industrialism, they argued, was giving rise to conditions which made it essential that new lands be found upon which to settle ever-growing surfeits of population, new markets to vend surpluses of goods, and new fields of activity to invest mounting accumulations of capital. Without the safety valve of colonial areas, these surpluses of men, goods, and capital threatened to glut the home economy and to produce the direst consequences—economic crises and possibly social revolution. All these matters were the common currency of economic writings nearly a century before *spätkapitalismus*.

For many Mercantilists, foreign trade was the virtually exclusive means of increasing the national wealth because only when precious metals could be elicited from another country could a nation really be understood to have profited. There was thus no national advantage in trade between persons within the same nation-state, however essential it might be and however profitable to individuals. The classical theory of international trade, Ricardo's theory of comparative costs, was different in character. Foreign trade was the mechanism that made possible an international division of labor, enabling every country to produce what it was most capable of producing. Each country, the classical economist held, profited by an exchange, although the benefits of trade might not be divided equally. Many English economists, as we shall see, were convinced that England's industrial monopoly would give her a preponderant advantage in most international exchanges.

The new school of classical economists, led by James Mill, Ricardo, and Torrens, was, with one or two exceptions, in favor of transforming England into a commercial and industrial state in conformance with the principle of comparative advantage. In thus tying England's destiny to manufactures and to foreign trade, the classical economists subscribed to the view—implicit, if not always explicit—that foreign trade was in some fashion more profitable than the home trade.[10] Economists associated in one way or another with agricultural interests, men like Spence, Chalmers, and Malthus, protested against this effort, climaxed by the repeal of the Corn Laws in 1846, to transform Great Britain into the workshop of the world to the great detriment and the possible extinction of British agriculture. Loyal to the full-blooded anti-Mercantilism of the earlier Physiocracy, they urged a balanced development of agriculture and industry and chanted the virtues of the home trade over an uncertain and insecure foreign trade.[11] They were unsuccessful, and policy during the nineteenth century was directed toward Great Britain's becoming the world's workshop. The maintenance of the wages of factory-hands at a bare minimum was defended as necessary if England were to undersell industrial competitors. Free trade was adopted and agriculture permitted to die so that England might establish regular trade channels with food-exporting countries. The failure to develop Ireland properly—a magnificent field for British capital investment and a considerable potential market for British industry—is, of course, explicable in terms of the special vested interests of British landlords, but there is reason to believe that there also lurked the atavistic view that energies ought to be given pri-

[10] See especially Robert Torrens, *An Essay on the External Corn Trade* (London, 1815).

[11] See W. Spence, *Britain Independent of Commerce* (London, 1808); W. Chalmers, *An Enquiry into the Extent and Stability of National Resources* (Edinburgh, 1808); T. R. Malthus, *Observations on the Effects of the Corn Laws* (London, 1815). See also R. L. Meek, "Physiocracy and the Early Theories of Under-Consumption," *Economica*, XVIII (1951), 229–69.

marily to *foreign* trade. In the heyday of England's industrial and commercial predominance, only diehard "reactionaries" suggested that English factories might find a market for their products among English factory-hands, among English agricultural laborers, or in Ireland.

One of the bulwarks of the defenders of the new industrialism, and of the new political economy, was to be Say's Law, a proclamation of faith that the new industrialism was a harmonious, virtually automatic economic order. Say's Law became the heart of orthodoxy and received the support of James Mill, Ricardo, McCulloch, and their followers.[12] For many decades a refusal to accept its validity was to convict oneself of the grossest ignorance of political economy. Indeed, almost a century later, when Hobson dared to question Say's Law, he discovered that he had committed an unpardonable offense in the eyes of academic economists.[13] There were, of course, a number of economists during the first half of the nineteenth century who espoused the heretical doctrine that Say's Law was not valid. Malthus, for one, suggested that glut and crises were an inescapable part of the commercial system and argued for a balanced economy as the method by which gluts might be mitigated. Such arguments were regarded as reactionary, as we have noted, and the orthodox Ricardians were proponents of the Law, which reassuringly foretold the smooth passage of an industrial England, an England that would not be dependent on foreign or colonial markets, although, of course, it might choose to develop such profitable outlets.[14]

[12] See correspondence among James Mill, Ricardo, and McCulloch in P. Sraffa, ed., *The Works and Correspondence of David Ricardo* (London: Cambridge University Press, 1952), VIII, 139, 167, 366, 376, and *passim*.

[13] J. A. Hobson, *Confessions of an Economic Heretic* (London: Allen and Unwin, 1938).

[14] See, for example, [T. R. Malthus], "Political Economy," *Quarterly Review*, XXX (1824), 297–334; and J. S. Mill's reply in "The Quarterly Review—Political Economy," *Westminster Review*, III (1825), 213–32.

Glut—of goods, of capital—appeared to be a frequent occurrence in the England of the 1820s, 1830s, and 1840s. A new school of economists arose who, unlike Malthus, were enthusiastic supporters of the new industrialism and yet—and this has been generally forgotten—questioned the validity of Say's Law. Wakefield and Scrope were most prominent among these, and Wakefield was the more influential of the two. Production, Wakefield declared, was "limited not merely by capital," as the Ricardians had insisted, "but also by the field of employment for capital itself," that is, the land, which was "the chief element of production." An advanced commercial system, beset by glut, had outgrown its "field of employment" and required new lands for its population, new markets for its excess production, and new fields in which to invest rapidly accumulating capital; consequently, it must build an empire. Despite an increase of national wealth "the state of capitalists and labourers may grow worse, provided that the field of production be not extended at the same rate with the increase of people and capital." Wakefield's insistence upon the importance of the "field of production," or the "extent of the market," a notion borrowed from Adam Smith, convinced many economists that empire-building, if only in an informal sense, was a necessary concomitant to industrial growth.[15] (Of course, it was also understood that the production of a surplus for foreign markets would make possible a more intensive division of labor and consequent economies of scale.)

Malthus, Wilmot-Horton, and others of their party had long been concerned about England's overpopulation. They, along with James Mill, regarded colonies as a safety valve for this population surplus although, especially in Malthus' view, not a

[15] See notes to E. G. Wakefield's edition of Adam Smith, *Wealth of Nations* (London, 1835), I, 223–41, 251–53, 390, 395.

permanent solution.[16] Wakefield and his disciple, Torrens, made an imperial asset of what the Malthusians had considered a grave social problem. "Multiply and replenish the earth" was their injunction, and they envisioned a far-flung empire composed of men of British stock who would stand ready in Canada, in Australia, and in New Zealand to provide cheap food for the expanding population of the metropolis in exchange for the surplus manufactured goods of the homeland. Wakefield insisted upon the necessity of nonindustrial areas to the new capitalism. Trade between such new agricultural countries and Great Britain would be most profitable, and Wakefield suggested a permanent division of employment between, for example, England and America, which he declared would be "equally useful to both": "Americans would raise cheaper corn than has ever been raised: and, no longer wanting a tariff, might drive with the manufacturers of England the greatest trade ever known in the world." Furthermore, Wakefield asserted, American agriculture would be a most useful field for investment of superabundant English capital, for he was convinced, as Adam Smith, Malthus, and Chalmers had also been, that the domestic rate of profit declined as a result of the ever-increasing competition among capitalists, thus making necessary an export of capital to relieve the glut at home. This, too, was a denial of Say's Law, which held a surfeit of capital to be as impossible as a surfeit of goods.[17]

These ideas of Wakefield and his disciples were largely accepted—and this, too, appears to have been forgotten—by the

---

[16] See James Mill, "The Article 'Colony,' Reprinted from the Supplement to the *Encyclopedia Britannica*" (London: 1821?). Also R. N. Ghosh, "Malthusian Emigration and Colonization: Letters to Wilmot-Horton," *Economica*, XXX (1963), 45–62.

[17] E. G. Wakefield, *England and America* (New York, 1834), pp. 23–30, 42, 47, 61–63, 68, 82–84, 93–130, 190–98, 221–31 (London edition published in 1833).

main stream of classical economists, including J. S. Mill. In his
Principles of Political Economy, in which he paid a generous
tribute to Wakefield, Mill declared that "Colonization, in the
present state of the world, is the best affair of business, in which
the capital of an old and wealthy country can engage." In advanced countries, he observed, arguing from the standpoint of
the principle of diminishing returns, not capital but fertile land
was deficient, and the legislator ought not to promote "greater
aggregate savings but a greater return to savings . . . by access
to the product of more fertile land in other parts of the globe."
In specific terms, he observed that if one-tenth of England's
workers and capital were transferred to the colonies, wages and
profits would benefit from the "diminished pressure of capital
and population upon the fertility of the land." Acknowledging,
in non-orthodox manner, that a surfeit of capital in England was
pushing profits to the minimum, he asserted that one of the
"counter-forces which check the downward tendency of
profits" was the "perpetual overflow of capital into colonies or
foreign countries." "I believe this to have been for many years
one of the principal causes by which the decline of profits in
England has been arrested." Indeed, capital export, for Mill,
was a precondition to the healthy functioning of advanced
economies: "As long as there are old countries where capital increases very rapidly, and new countries where profit is still high,
profits in the old countries will not sink to the rate which would
put a stop to accumulation." The "exportation of capital" was
an "agent of great efficacy in extending the field of employment" for the capital that remained at home and would help put
off the advent of what the classical economists called "the stationary state." [18]

[18] J. S. Mill, *Principles of Political Economy* (London: Longmans, Green,
1909, first edition in 1848), pp. 727–28, 738–39, 741–42, 746, 748, 749.

Mill's disciple, Cairnes, was to write, in the manner of Wakefield, that "the great trades of the world are carried on between countries pretty widely removed from each other either in the scale of civilization or in respect to their natural resources and productions, while in proportion as countries approximate to each other in natural resources or in industrial qualities of their inhabitants, the scope for international trade is narrowed: it is even possible that it should fail altogether." For Cairnes, as for Wakefield, the most valuable of trades was one between England and a predominantly agricultural United States.[19]

The repeal of the Corn Laws in 1846, enabling corn from abroad to enter England free of duty, was to serve as a foundation for an informal English trade Empire. The undeveloped, agricultural areas of the world, whether owing allegiance to the British Crown or not, were to acquire in this fashion a stake in the British industrial monopoly. Not only was the appeal of free trade directed at newly opened regions in Australasia or South America, but England could also henceforth assure the more economically advanced wheat-exporting countries of Europe and North America—Germany, the United States, Russia, and others—a large and regular market. In exchange, these agricultural countries would be enabled by the income obtained from British food purchases to buy from England manufactured goods at prices substantially below those at which they would be capable of producing such goods themselves. Having adopted free trade, Britain now urged upon all nations the advantages of a free international economy and an international division of labor. Britain's keen interest in free trade was well understood in Europe, and powers who wished for

---

[19] J. E. Cairnes, *Some Leading Principles of Political Economy* (London: Macmillan, 1884), p. 300.

various reasons to maintain English favor—Cavour's Piedmont, for example, or the France of Napoleon III—opted for trade freedom.

Liberal England stood for freedom in all spheres of life. The very cornerstone of the new capitalism, for example, was the free labor contact. At considerable expense, the Royal Navy employed its dominance of the seas to halt the comings and goings of slave ships and to destroy slave-trading stations along the coast of Africa. Similarly, England worked to end everywhere, in so far as she was able, the tightly regulated, formal colonialism of the Mercantilist era and to replace it by free commercial intercourse between less well-developed regions— formerly colonies, perhaps, but more and more acquiring political independence—and the European metropolises. Just as the freeman working upon a free contractual basis had proved a more profitable employee than a serf or slave, the liberal economists declared, so would colonial peoples who bought and sold according to the law of the free marketplace prove the more desirable trading partners. The opponents of the new capitalism —men like Carlyle, for example—saw in the free labor contract sham and hypocrisy. In reality, they insisted, the workingman under "free contract" in the factory or mill was in a more wretched position than the slave, in whose welfare a master at least had some interest. Similarly, economists such as List and Carey saw the international free market in the first half of the nineteenth century as a mere blind to disguise the subordination of all the agricultural nations of the world to the British industrial colossus.

The relationship between "advanced" industrial nations and less well-developed agricultural nations had for some time been a subject of analysis. In the middle of the eighteenth century, there had been a noteworthy controversy concerning "rich" and "poor" countries between two distinguished economists, David Hume and Josiah Tucker. The origins of the controversy were in conclusions elicited by Hume from the theory of the automatic mechanism. If the amount of precious metals in England were to be halved overnight, that theory suggested, the low wages and low prices that would result, following the quantity theory, would so promote English exports that the influx of gold and silver would soon restore the former hoard of treasure as well as the former wage and price levels. Arguing similarly though less carefully, Hume insisted that, under conditions of free trade, wealth would be transferred from a richer to a poorer state until the riches of both states were equal. In this reasoning, Hume, a Scotsman, saw the economic salvation of his native undeveloped country growing out of its commercial association with a rich England.

Josiah Tucker, the Dean of Gloucester, took issue with Hume's argument. He saw all the advantages lying with the richer country. The richer country would be aided by "long Habits of Industry," by its possession of "an established Trade and Credit," "experienced Agents and Factors," "commodious Shops," "the best Tools," "Engines for abridging Labour," "good Roads, Canals," "Quays, Docks," and "Ships, good Pilots, and trained Sailors." The richer country had "Superior Skill and Knowledge (acquired by long Habit and Experience)," it had the capital "to make further Improvements" and to embark upon "expensive and long-winded Undertakings," it had access to a profitable home market. "In the richer Country," furthermore, "the Superiority of the Capital, and the low Interest of Money, will ensure the Vending of all Goods on the cheapest Terms."

Tucker had no wish to keep backward nations from progressing. He urged that the English lend some of their capital to

Scotland, "at moderate Interest" and supply the Scots "with Models and Instructors." The increasing prosperity of England's neighbors would make them better customers. Hume, while willing to admit the advantages favoring the richer nations, was unwilling to strike his colors. There would come a limit, a *ne plus ultra*, at which point the rich nation would check itself

by begetting disadvantages, which at first retard, and at last finally stop their progress, [for example,] the dear price of provisions and labour, which enables the poorer country to rival them, first in the coarser manufactures, and then in those which are most elaborate. . . . Were it otherwise, commerce, if not dissipated by violent conquests, would go on perpetually increasing, and one spot of the globe would engross the art and industry of the whole.

In such circumstances, Scotland would have little to hope for, Hume protested. To this, Tucker replied, in an anticipation of the classical view, that "every Nation, poor as well as rich, may improve their Condition"; there were local advantages, or "the natural Turn and peculiar Genius" of a country that it was "at Liberty to cultivate," and it would have the capital of the richer country to help them to do so. Privately, in a letter to Lord Kames, on July 6, 1758, Tucker anticipated the program that was to be put forward by such economic spokesmen for undeveloped countries as Alexander Hamilton, List, and Carey. Tucker observed:

It is true likewise, that all of them [the poor countries] have it in their power to load the manufactures of the rich country upon entering their territories, with such high duties as shall turn the scale in favor of their own manufactures, or of the manufactures of some other nation, whose progress in trade they have less cause to fear or envy.

He concluded that "thus it is, in my poor apprehension, that the rich may be prevented from swallowing up the poor; at the same time, and by the same methods, that the poor are stimulated and excited to emulate the rich." [20]

It is interesting to observe the assumption on both sides of the controversy that the richer country had a highly developed commerce and system of manufactures and that the poorer country was almost exclusively agricultural. This point of view was to persist into the nineteenth century. (Even Malthus, who was to vaunt agriculture and the terms-of-trade advantages of agricultural exports, had agreed by 1817 that with the exception of the United States a purely agricultural nation was an impoverished nation.) [21] Classical trade theory proclaimed relative indifference as to the type of export by which a country secured its imports, yet even the classical economists, as we shall see, were to suggest, largely in obiter dicta, that both the immediate division of the benefits of trade and the long-run gains from trade tended to favor richer, that is, manufacturing, countries. They were preceded in this not only by Tucker but also by Alexander Hamilton.

Hamilton's *Report on Manufactures* (1790) strove to prove the advantages of manufacturing to a country hazily convinced of the superiority of agriculture. Manufactures permitted a more extensive use of division of labor and of machinery and consequently, were

susceptible, in a proportionately greater degree, of improvement in its productive powers. . . . The substitution of foreign for

---

[20] See Josiah Tucker, *Four Tracts Together with Two Sermons on Political and Commercial Subjects* (Gloucester, 1774), pp. 11–47; J. Y. T. Greig, ed., *The Letters of David Hume* (Oxford, 1932), I, 27–72; A. F. Tytler, *Memoirs of the Life and Writings of the Honourable Henry Home of Kames* (Edinburgh, 1807), Vol. II, Appendix, p. 5.

[21] T. R. Malthus, *Essay on the Principle of Population* (London, 1803), pp. 447ff., and the change in view in *Additions to the Fourth and Former Editions of an Essay on the Principle of Population* (London, 1817), pp. 97ff.

domestic manufactures is a transfer to foreign nations of the advantages accruing from the employment of machinery. . . . Nations, merely agricultural, would not enjoy the same degree of opulence, in proportion to their numbers, as those which united manufactures with agriculture.

The very nature of the trade between an agricultural and a manufacturing country placed the former at a disadvantage: foreign demand for agricultural products was rather "casual and occasional than certain or constant," while the growth of manufactures would provide a home market for the farmer; a manufacturing nation had the advantages of "the more numerous attractions which a more diversified market offers to foreign customers, and the greater scope which it affords to mercantile enterprise," and "the greatest resort will ever be to those marts where commodities, while equally abundant, are most various." The terms of trade of American agricultural exports were also put at a disadvantage by the distance from European markets and by the high transport costs caused by the "bulkiness" of raw produce. Hamilton observed a chronic factor of imbalance in what J. S. Mill was later to call the equation of reciprocal demand between an agricultural America and a manufacturing England—

a constant and increasing necessity on their part, for the commodities of Europe, and only a partial and occasional demand for their own, in return could not but expose them to a state of impoverishment, compared with the opulence to which their political and natural advantages authorize them to aspire.

Hamilton called upon Congress to establish a system of protective duties (the remedy Tucker had spelled out in his letter to Lord Kames), prohibitions, bounties, and drawbacks; to encourage inventions; to promote the building of canals and roads; and to establish a tax policy to encourage investment. He wanted, most particularly, to encourage European investment: "It is a well-known fact," he observed, "that there are parts of Europe which have more capital than profitable domestic objects of employment; . . . it is equally certain that the capital of other parts may find more profitable employment in the United States than at home." Americans ought not to regard foreign investment as a rival but as a "most valuable auxiliary." [22]

In his *National System of Political Economy*, first published in 1841, Friedrich List, a Swabian bureaucrat turned professor of political economy at the University of Tübingen, presented as his grand conclusion, derived from life in both Germany and the United States, that England, the premier commercial and industrial country, held less industrially advanced countries in perpetual bondage in a commercial empire of free trade:

In all ages there have been cities or countries surpassing others in manufactures, trade and navigation; but the world has never witnessed a supremacy to be compared with that existing in our time. In all ages states have aspired to domination, but no edifice of power has ever been constructed upon so broad a base. How miserable appears the ambition of those who attempted to establish universal domination upon the power of arms, in comparison with the great attempt of England to transform her whole territory into an immense manufacturing and commercial city, into an immense port, and to become to other nations what a vast city is to the country, the center of arts and knowledge, of an immense commerce, of opulence, of navigation, of naval and military power; a cosmopolitic country supplying all nations with manufactured products, and asking in return from each country, its raw materials and commodities; the arsenal of extensive capital, the universal banker, regulating, if not controlling the circulating money of the whole

[22] Alexander Hamilton, "Report on Manufactures," in *Papers on Public Credit, Commerce, and Finance* (New York: Columbia University Press, 1934), pp. 177–276.

world, and making all nations tributary to her by loans and the payment of interest.

List rejected the theory of the classical economists, which he characterized as one of mere exchange values, and substituted that of productive powers. Convinced that "the power of creating wealth" was "vastly more important than wealth itself," he, too, urged the building of a manufacturing industry behind tariff walls. Immediate sacrifices, he declared, would be justified by future benefits. Furthermore, the growth of manufacturing would mean freedom from "tributary" status to an industrial England.[23]

Henry C. Carey, a Philadelphia protectionist and a disciple of Hamilton's, had a view of British "imperialism" similar to List's. England, he maintained, was at war "against the agricultural communities of the world, for the reduction of the prices of their rude products"; the objective of this war was to enable "the people of England to obtain three pounds" of cotton or tobacco "for the price they before had paid for one." He therefore favored every policy which aimed at securing the growth of manufacturing.[24]

J. S. Mill, in his analysis of the determination of the terms of trade by "reciprocal demand," confirmed, in part, the earlier analysis by Hamilton, which Carey had largely accepted. We must note, for example, Mill's emphasis upon the advantages enjoyed by a country that possessed a variety of exports and whose exports, furthermore, "contain greatest value in smallest bulk" and were "the most susceptible of increase from additional cheapness." [25]

[23] Friedrich List, *National System of Political Economy* (Philadelphia, 1856).

[24] See Henry C. Carey, *Letters to the President on the Foreign and Domestic Policy of the Union* (Philadelphia, 1858), pp. 126, 131, 79–86; *Commerce, Christianity and Civilization versus British Free Trade* (Philadelphia, 1876).

[25] J. S. Mill, *Principles*, pp. 583–606.

Nassau Senior saw England's superior trading position as residing in the increasing use of steadily improving machinery, which made English labor "more than ten times as efficient in the production of exportable commodities." It was this, he wrote, which enabled Englishmen to obtain foreign products "not merely at the expense of less labour than it would cost to produce them" in England, which was what was maintained by Ricardian trade theory, "but often at the expense of less labour than they cost in the producing countries."[26] Nor did Senior accept the classical view that if a foreign nation manufactured, say, cotton textiles more cheaply than England, England could, with profit, buy from them and devote its own industry to producing other goods. For Senior, the nations were "competitors in the general market of the world," and he appears to have opposed the exportation of machinery.[27]

This was also the position of Torrens, one of the formulators of the classical trade theory, when, speaking in the House of Commons in 1826, he declared himself against the export of machinery, approving, rather, "the policy of each country reserving to itself the sole benefit of these exclusive advantages, which either from nature or by acquisition, it might enjoy."[28]

Addressing himself to the question of a tariff, J. S. Mill agreed with the protectionist economists as to the necessity of tariff support for infant industries, suggesting, as they did, that

---

[26] Senior confirmed List's and Carey's view of the international division of labor when he wrote: "When a nation in which the powers of production, and consequently the wages of labour, are high, employs its own members in performing duties which could be as effectually performed by the less valuable labour of less civilized nations, it is guilty of the same folly as a farmer who should plough with a race-horse."

[27] Nassau Senior, *Industrial Efficiency and Social Economy* (London, 1929), II, 149–50; *Three Lectures on the Cost of Obtaining Money* (London, 1830), pp. 11–16, 18–20, 23–24, 26.

[28] *Parliamentary Debates*, N.S. XVI, December 7, 1826, pp. 294–95.

"the superiority of one country over another in a branch of production often arises only from having begun it sooner." [29]

Mill's disciple, Cairnes, examined the special circumstances that affected the trade between advanced and undeveloped nations from another standpoint. In surveying the English balance of payments, with its great excess of imports over exports, he spoke of the "interest on borrowed capital, dividends on stock, and so forth," which appeared in the shape of an excess of imports as an "annual tribute" to England from borrowing countries. He pictured an America compelled to yield such a tribute and therefore compelled to lower the prices of her exports in order to persuade her creditors to accept the tribute—compelled, indeed, to lower her prices to the point of inviting the hardships of commercial crisis.[30]

This picture of an "informal imperialism" was confirmed by Giffen, a Board of Trade economist, who, writing during the depression of the 1870s, set forward some of the same reasons which Hamilton had presented nearly a century earlier to explain why raw-material-producing countries were much harder hit by the trade depression than manufacturing countries—most particularly, "the greater liability of raw material to be produced occasionally in excess of demand." In addition, the dependence of less advanced countries upon the capital exports of more developed nations was a liability, since at times of crisis "capitalists call in instead of extending their advances." [31]

During the nineteenth century, then, even during the so-called "anti-imperialist" mid-century, we can see the operation of this British "imperialism of free trade," the chief objective of which was to make trade secure. In many instances, in Latin

[29] J. S. Mill, *Principles*, p. 922.
[30] Cairnes, *Principles*, pp. 355-72.
[31] Robert Giffen, *Essays in Finance* (London: Bell, 1880), pp. 137-41.

America, for example, annexation was unnecessary to the expansion and security of British trade and investment. In other cases, along the Indian frontier, for example, wars and annexations were the rule even in mid-century. Different techniques were employed to suit different conditions, but there was continuous expansion, both "formal" and "informal." In the last part of the century, during the time of the partition of Africa, the use of more informal techniques was seriously undermined by international competition for colonies and markets. As a result there had to be greater reliance upon a policy of war and annexation, whence came the view that imperialism replaced anti-imperialism during the 1880s and 1890s. What was actually happening was that the neo-Mercantilist imperialism of certain continental nations, marked by a revival of protection, development of techniques of dumping, etc., was challenging a "cosmopolitan" British imperialism. A policy that sought commercial monopoly was battling a policy whose objective was the securing of free and safe access to markets. In a word, an imperialism of annexation and war was opposing the old imperialism of economic penetration and establishment of informal political controls.

The cosmopolitan imperialism of the mid-nineteenth century was more appropriate to the time of British industrial hegemony, the neo-Mercantilist to the time of keen international competition, competition not only for political control of strategically placed lands in Africa or Asia but for potential markets and sites for investment. Trade once more became war. The homeland and its colonies were "protected" by tariffs; invasions in the form of the dumping of goods were made whenever possible, and a tariff assault was met with instant retaliation. For the neo-Mercantilist, as for the Mercantilist before him, a nation's welfare could be purchased only at the expense of her rivals; and the neo-Mercantilist could reinforce his arguments by the dicta of a "scientific" social Darwinism. During the decade after 1903, Joseph Chamberlain made a determined effort to turn even England from free trade to a neo-Mercantile program of tariff protection and imperial preference, but he failed. Economists of the classical school—such men as Marshall, Bastable, Cannan, Edgeworth, and Pigou—continued to advocate free trade and to look toward foreign investments and the profits of the carrying trade and international financial transactions as the means by which England's well-being might best be advanced. The historical economists—such men as Ashley, Cunningham, and Hewins—taking their inspiration from the German historical school of Schmoller, were, in neo-Mercantilist fashion, suspicious of capital export except within the empire and sought by means of an Imperial Zollverein to reserve colonial markets for British manufactures, with Britain receiving, in exchange, Canadian, Australian, or South African agricultural commodities. (Schmoller had suggested, it might be noted here, that only the United States, Russia, and the British Empire had sufficient population, territories, and economic diversity to attempt successfully such a quasi-autarchic arrangement.) Neo-Mercantilism, as we have noted, had carried the day on the European continent before 1914; and by the early 1930s, protection and an imperial preferential system were adopted by Great Britain.[32]

The most noticeable aspect of this neo-Mercantilism was, of course, the struggle for colonies and later for mandates, con-

---

[32] J. Gallagher and R. Robinson, "The Imperialism of Free Trade," *Economic History Review*, VI (1953), 1-15; B. Semmel, *Imperialism and Social Reform* (Cambridge, Mass.: Harvard University Press, 1960), pp. 18, 141-53.

cessions, and spheres of influence among the European powers in Africa, Asia, and Latin America. This was the "classical" period of imperialism that Hobson and Lenin described, and the political situation from, say, 1880 until 1945 was one in which there was little to inhibit struggles among the great industrial European powers and Japan at the expense of economically backward continents.

This "classic imperialism," both free trade and neo-Mercantile, during approximately the first half of our century can be regarded as having brought peoples outside the international economy—outside history in some cases—into the great world market and the main stream of world history. With the benefit of hindsight and the passage of the years, which somehow obscures almost all but the most blatant outrages associated with pre-1914 imperialism, at least to Western eyes, the "imperialism" of the 1880s and onward takes on somewhat the appearance of a necessary stage not only for the development of Western industrialism to its fullest potentialities but also for the dissemination of Western ideas and techniques and for laying the foundations for what, we hope, will become a universally beneficial international division of labor. Since 1945, however, political and economic conditions have changed enormously. The world is now composed of several score self-conscious sovereign entities whose independence and integrity are guaranteed, not only formally by the United Nations to which they belong but also, although not with unfailing success, by the two great power blocs, each determined not to let any state slip into the enemy camp. In addition, the inner drives of the industrial economies for expansion no longer operate in the old ways: the widening of the domestic market through more equitable distribution of national income, the employment of Keynesian remedies, and the discovery of alternative uses for surplus capital and labor power have invalidated the doctrine that capitalism in its "later stages" must inevitably turn to a neo-Mercantile capital-export imperialism to avoid industrial crises. Hobson's imperialism is dead, which is not the same, of course, as to say, as some scholars do, that it never existed, although, as the analyses of Wakefield and J. S. Mill might suggest, such an imperialism —one impelled primarily by the inner needs of capitalism— may, in fact, have preceded the imperialism of Hobson's time, when other motives tended to predominate.

Attitudes toward the export of capital—the "classic" mechanism of imperialism—have fluctuated considerably during the past century and a half. The classical economists rarely wrote of investing in colonies or foreign countries, although such investments were already considerable by the 1820s and 1830s; indeed, Ricardo had set down the principle that capital would long hesitate before leaving its own country—of course, he granted, it would do so if the increased rate of profit proved sufficiently attractive.[33] During the nineteenth century investments abroad were regarded as a service to the country in which they were made and did not bear the taint of "empire-building" until such investments became the justification for political intervention as in Egypt in the 1880s or in South Africa during the Boer War. It was Hobson, with the experience of the Boer War before him, who altered the formerly favorable view of foreign investment; and even he, some ten years after writing his *Imperialism*, was to revert to the earlier opinion, which regarded such investments as beneficent instruments of a cosmopolitan capitalism.[34] In the years before 1914 only the Marx-

---

[33] David Ricardo, *The Principles of Political Economy and Taxation* (London: Dent, 1937), p. 83.
[34] J. A. Hobson, *The Economic Interpretations of Investment* (London: Financial Review of Reviews, 1911), pp. 116ff.

ists were convinced that efforts to secure political control were
an inevitable accompaniment to investment in backward economies. With the new international political order, investment
in less well-developed regions is once again regarded as highly
desirable both by the governments of the advanced nations—
interested, doubtlessly, in currying favor with uncommitted
parts of the world—and by the new governments of the undeveloped parts of the world, who fully recognize, as both Tucker
and Hamilton had in the eighteenth century, that economic
growth in its early stages is difficult without capital advances
from more advanced nations. What was regarded as exploitative
imperialism about a half-century ago is now regarded on almost
all sides virtually as benevolences extended to economically
backward nations starved for development capital.

Today there is difficulty about supplying this capital. Industrialism in the nineteenth and early twentieth centuries produced huge capital surpluses that glutted the home market and
searched eagerly for foreign investment, sometimes of a highly
speculative sort. Have such surfeits ceased to be produced since
1945? For one thing, as we have indicated, there has been a re-
distribution of the national income throughout the West, and
Western Europe is today attempting to keep pace with the
United States in supplying its peoples with the widest variety
of consumer goods, previously inaccessible to the lower classes.
Secondly, we are now experiencing a great technological—
electronic and cybernetic—revolution, which will undoubtedly
dwarf the industrial revolution of the nineteenth century. This
revolution, too, is absorbing a great deal of the capital that is
being generated. Individual investors are consequently not particularly interested in assuming risks in undeveloped countries
beset by violence and stirred by new nationalist passions. There
are, however, other hoards of capital less advantageously occu-

pied, immense quantities that are at this time committed in all the advanced industrial nations, on both sides of the Iron Curtain, to the systematic waste of production of war materials. Indeed, the greater the capital resources of an economy and the more advanced its state of development, the more necessary has such waste production seemed for maintaining continued economic health. If *these* resources could be diverted to investment in backward regions, the twin goals of maximization of income and more equitable distribution could both be served.

The old imperialism certainly helped to maximize world production and income, but there has not been anything like a proper or equitable distribution of this increasing income. Today, without the benefit of complex Mercantile regulations or the presence of imperial proconsuls or troops to insure favorable trading arrangements, UN economists assure us that the gap between the backward and the advanced nations of the globe continues to widen rather than to narrow, that the most essential characteristic of the usual trade between the two— between commodity and manufacture-exporting countries—is chronically disadvantageous to the former, despite the fact that occasionally trade conditions do favor them. Indeed, the plight of the commodity exporters has in recent years provided grounds for suspicion that an important basis for the prosperity of some of the more advanced nations of the West is their enjoyment of highly favorable terms-of-trade vis-à-vis the more backward exporters of commodities. The new political and economic conditions of the middle of the twentieth century, which have made the analyses of Hobson and Lenin virtually obsolete, appear to have restored to primacy of position the arguments, first debated by Hume and Tucker, which stirred both classical and national economists.

Jacob Viner, who may be considered one of the foremost contemporary champions of the tradition of the classical economists, has acknowledged that the traditional economics had an "almost exclusive orientation to the interests, the needs, and the complacencies of countries advanced industrially and with relatively high income levels" and has observed that "Listian" economics, which had a rather different point of vantage, now possessed numerous disciples in underdeveloped countries. Viner is ready to grant that protection would be quite acceptable if it were "a poor country which benefits from its adoption" under circumstances where "the countries which are injured thereby are rich countries." Here, "the improvement in the international distribution of income which results may be an adequate offset to the reduction in the aggregate world income." It would seem that by granting this, Viner has yielded a great deal. Certainly, the issue to be taken with a free international trading system is not that it detracts from aggregate world income, at least in short range, but precisely that it results in a lopsided distribution. Yet Viner proclaims himself none the less unconvinced of the essential practicality of even the "Listian" protection of infant industry, and he similarly rushes behind the orthodox barricade in denouncing the view of certain members of "the technical staff of the United Nations" that "the relation of productivity to prices is such in 'underdeveloped' countries that the exchange by such countries of primary products for the manufactures of developed countries, while especially profitable for the latter, is positively injurious to the former."

Viner assails the "dogmatic identification of agriculture with poverty" and denies that agricultural poverty can be explained by "inherent natural historical laws by virtue of which agricultural products tend to exchange on ever deteriorating terms for manufactures" and that technological progress tended "to confine its blessings to manufacturing industry." If this were so, why are Denmark and New Zealand and Australia—all commodity-exporting nations—so prosperous? Viner emphasizes quite rightly the advantages, more often than not, for an undeveloped country to apply its limited capital to developing its ability to feed itself and even to securing a more efficient production of a staple export, where market conditions justify such investment. Yet the examples of agricultural prosperity that he has cited constitute rather special cases in terms of the character of their exports, for which the demand is relatively stable, and their location. Indeed, in the case of Denmark, New Zealand, and Australia, despite the agricultural character of their principal exports, only a relatively small proportion of their total labor forces is properly agricultural. What, however, of the many truly "agricultural" countries, often producing but *one* commodity for export and competing to sell their coffee or sugar or petroleum, which frequently glut the world market with disastrous effects upon prices, to the richer nations of the world? Even Viner is ready to admit—as Giffen had some three-quarters of a century earlier—that primary commodities had "a wider amplitude of fluctuation in their prices during the business cycle than do manufactured commodities." [35]

Gunnar Myrdal, the noted Swedish economist and the former director of the UN Economic Commission for Europe, Viner's leading adversary, has taken strenuous issue with the orthodox view. While protesting that the classical theory of international trade has provided no explanation for the present-day realities of ever-widening inequalities in wealth between the advanced and backward regions of the world, Myrdal is not ready to dis-

[35] Jacob Viner, *International Trade and Economic Development* (New York: Free Press of Glencoe, 1952), pp. 24, 55–62, 142.

card this theory entirely. Classical economics might still provide
the lumber for a new edifice; specifically, Myrdal has suggested
that "the development of the 'infant industry' argument contained *in nuce* hints of a much more realistic approach to the
problems of the underdeveloped countries." He has stressed the
importance of formulating a "general theory of economic
under-development and development" which was consistent
with the classical theory of international trade. When such a
general theory emerged, it would be found, he continued, to
have "salvaged many familiar arguments and theorems." "In
economics, as in social theory generally, old thoughts are rarely
discarded altogether, and no ideas are entirely new and
original." [36]

When such a general theory is finally constructed, it does not
seem unlikely that it will be found to have retained not only the
"infant industry" argument, but a number of the others presented between, roughly, 1750 and 1850 by both classical and
national schools of political economy. Among the leading pioneers of such a general theory will be, in all likelihood, Tucker,
Hamilton, List, Senior, and J. S. Mill. (All accepted, in whole
or in part, the "infant industry" idea.) Tucker will then be
lauded for his understanding of the advantages of the lead and
his insights into the take-off period and after, List and Senior
for their appreciation of the qualitative differences that the
immense productive powers of the new machinery made in the
economies and in the international trading positions of the advanced countries of Europe, Hamilton and Mill for their analysis of the many factors that entered into the determination of
"reciprocal demand" in international trade, the mechanism that
sets the terms of trade and, as Hamilton pointed out, oper-

---

[36] Gunnar Myrdal, *Economic Theory and Under-Developed Regions* (London: Duckworth, 1957), pp. 149–58.

ated more often than not against the exporters of primary staples. When such a general theory of economic development is formulated, furthermore, it will probably be found to include not only a theory of international trade, but also, in large part at any rate, a theory of "imperialism," comprehending the theories of Brougham, Malthus, Wakefield, and Hobson.

There have been several species of trade "imperialism"—the empires of ancient Tyre, of the Delian League, of Venice, and of seventeenth- and eighteenth-century Mercantilism. In many of these cases, elements of compulsion were employed, somehow, in rigging the terms of trade to the advantage of the metropolis, but today, as we have noted, this "rigging" is a result of the ordinary functioning of the free international market economy. (Tariffs and other restrictions upon the exports of undeveloped countries—as they exist, for example, in the European Common Market—must also be noted.) It certainly may be regarded as a kind of trade "imperialism" when the well-being of the advanced industrial nations of Europe and America is promoted by the chronically bad terms of trade under which the producers of most primary staples exchange their produce for manufactured goods. Hume, Hamilton, List, or Carey would have so described it and so would have, on a less theoretical plane, the Populist leaders of the American Midwest during the 1890s, who spoke of the western and southern farm regions as "colonies" of an industrial East, not only because of rigged railroad rates and the like but also because of the numerous disadvantages suffered by the American farmer under free market conditions.

The free market within the United States during the nineteenth and early twentieth centuries had the effect of maximizing national income, while on occasions before and especially after World War I tending to hit hard at the farmer and to a somewhat lesser extent at a considerable part of the working class. The workingman responded to his unpleasant exposure to the swings of the business cycle by the formation of trade unions. In almost every one of the industrialized nations, the farmers, finding themselves similarly exposed by the operation of the market system, at last combined politically to effect crucial amendments in the system which would assure them of a higher proportion of the national revenue. In the United States, the Populist movement finally achieved its objectives in the early years of the New Deal; farmers, in significant numbers, are now protected by a system of price supports, which assures their keeping pace with the other producers in the economy. This system is bulwarked by one of regulation of crop production and marketing and supplemented by government storage of surpluses. Similar systems are in effect in other countries.

The undeveloped countries, exporters of vulnerable agricultural commodities, can be similarly protected from the swings of the international market economy to which they are so precariously exposed. Efforts to regulate production and marketing have already been undertaken by those countries which are exporters of petroleum. Recently, in the latter part of 1962, the coffee-exporting countries have, under UN auspices, made similar arrangements. These isolated efforts on the part of producers to regulate production and marketing must, of course, be encouraged by international bodies and by the advanced nations. There have been bilateral attempts to support the prices of particular commodities—as, for example, the arrangements by which the United States imported Caribbean sugar at a price higher than the prevailing market price.[37] Great

---

[37] The Cuban government, it will be recalled, regarded the existence of such a privileged price as vicious imperialism; it was to repeat the charge in even

Britain, to cite another example, has acted to grant tariff preferences to the staple exports of her present and former West African colonies without exacting similar preferences for goods she exports to them, an effort to compensate, within the Commonwealth, for extreme disparities in the terms of trade. Certainly, an effective system of price props—on a multilateral basis rather than the largely politically inspired bilateral arrangements outlined above—must be constructed to make possible a more equitable division of the benefits of world trade. Suggestions have recently also been made that as a temporary expedient the richer, more developed countries make grants to the poorer countries to compensate them for their deteriorating terms of trade.

It is precisely this—a more equitable division of the benefits of trade by such arrangements as have been outlined and a planned international program of the capital development of backward areas to help, among other objectives, to diversify undeveloped economies so as to enable them better to meet the fluctuations of the international market—which would end this sophisticated trade "imperialism" which has replaced the older, classic imperialism of capital export with its underpinning of force. The problem of vast inequalities of development and consequently of well-being is fortunately capable of solution on the basis of immediate and immediately foreseeable technological resources. The problem, as we have seen, is not a new one; it has been a subject for economic analysis for almost 200 years, and on an intranational basis practical solutions have already been successfully explored. The general direction of in-

---

more energetic terms when the arrangement was abrogated. Of course, the motives of the United States in this matter have been called into question; the privileged price was not only a prize for Cuban sugar growers, mostly large American companies, but was also meant to protect higher cost domestic sugar producers.

ternational action is comparatively clear. Fairly immediate steps on a global basis must be taken if catastrophe is to be averted and if the great goal of the classical economists, a universally beneficial international division of labor, is to be at last achieved.

VII

EMILE BENOIT

The Economics of
Disarmament and Coexistence*

THE CONCEPT of humanity stands at the extreme pole from the ethnocentric world view that regards one's own society, tribe, clan, village, city, or nation as the center of the world, the focus of value, and the standard of right conduct. Some primitive societies use the name of their own tribe to designate humanity and refer to outsiders in a wholly different way. Even the civilized Greeks of the Age of Pericles viewed *hoi barberoi* as not fully human, and it was this half-articulate premise that alone made Aristotle's defense of the naturalness of slavery seem plausible.

A wider knowledge of men and societies led the Hellenistic philosophers to a broader social viewpoint and to at least an abstract grasp of the concept of humanity, an idea also achieved in more concrete and moral terms in the working out of the Judeo-Christian prophetic tradition. While this idea has been accessible to a small minority of intellectually or spiritually gifted men for two milleniums, it has had only a limited influence on popular thought and social institutions. Progress has been chiefly in broadening out ethnocentric attitudes beyond their original focus on the tribe, the village, or the city-state and extending them—without basic change in emotional content— to the wider group of the province and the nation-state.

The Concept of Humanity and the Goal of Disarmament

Today the technological revolution is rapidly creating the conditions for a general acceptance of the humanity concept as a simple reflection of observable facts. Three aspects of this technological revolution are most relevant in this connection:

1. The release of new destructive forces of cosmic magnitude has suddenly rendered all men of all nations essentially insecure and is forcing on them a recognition of the powerlessness of any man or group of men to achieve security other than in cooperation with their fellows.

2. The well-known "shrinkage of the earth," derived from enormously expanded power of communication and locomotion, renders all men in a real sense neighbors.

3. There has been a virtual revolution in wealth production, based not only on the accumulation of capital, but also on scientific-engineering achievements such as automation, on organized research, on improved business and administrative techniques, and on new economic insights and tools by means of which depressions may be avoided and growth accelerated. An enormous rise in living standards, which this progress has made possible, is rapidly reducing the gross disparities in health, education, nutrition, and even attire that buttressed the regimes of hereditary social classes in the past. Even the differences in wealth among nations, which still remain tremendous (and in absolute terms are probably still increasing), are for the first

---

* I am greatly indebted to Bert F. Hoselitz, David Felix, and Theodore Morgan for helpful comments.

time in history subject to a vast cooperative effort to reduce them. Indeed, the sudden emergence in the 1950s and 1960s of the idea of "economic development" as a moral imperative, implying an obligation of rich countries to help poor countries to get rich, is as startling and important an innovation in human history as was the sudden appearance of the idea of progress in the nineteenth century.

Even though the *concept* of humanity has won increasing acceptance, there has been a notable lag in its practical application. Only gradually and reluctantly has it been recognized that if it is membership in humanity that is primary and group differences that are secondary in the attributes of man, then many traditional social arrangements will have to be profoundly modified or even abandoned. For example, if other peoples and races are recognized to be truly human, unlike cattle or horses, which we compel to serve us, then slavery can have no morally sound justification despite its long history as a respected human institution. Similarly, an organization of society along caste lines, in which opportunities are unequally shared between groups distinguished by superficial biological characteristics, is seen to involve profound injustices. Yet, even in the United States it was not until the nineteenth century that the practical implications of the humanity idea were fully drawn in the matter of slavery, and it is only in the second half of the twentieth century that residual caste elements in our society are being finally abandoned.

It will be the work of perhaps the rest of this century to draw the practical implications of the humanity idea for the abolition of the social institution of war. War in the sense of organized large-scale killing of "strangers" or "outsiders" has always been distinguished from the occasional deliberate killing of fellow members of a group under limited circumstances and with limited casualties, for example, infanticide, euthanasia, and execution of criminals and duels, feuds, or formalized contests of individuals, families, or other groups.[1]

Warfare in the earliest stage of mankind appears to have been a more or less automatic response to contacts with outsiders.[2] Later it was glorified as a sort of sport and valued for the opportunities it provided for heroic achievement. Gradually it became a highly organized technique for achieving economic gain by the enslavement of captives or their quasi-enslavement under serfdom, by looting any accumulation of wealth, by the monopolization and sale of tax rights or the imposition of other monopolies by the victor, by imposing indemnities, or by the mere takeover of fertile land for exploitation by the conquerors.

Two of these elements—the heroic and the materialistic—have colored our interpretations of war long after they have ceased to be truly relevant. Modern warfare offers little of the adventure of personal combat and makes no sense economically. The Franco-Prussian war of 1870 was probably the last of the wars between advanced societies to have any significant net economic payoff for the victor. The cost of preparing for war and waging it has become very high, and the gains of receiving indemnification have become very low relative to what ad-

---

[1] There are, it must be admitted, some borderline cases, such as banditry and civil war. The first refers to outlaws who have deserted their society and are waging guerrilla warfare against it. The second may be best understood as the splitting of a society into two parts, which form for a time two antagonistic societies mutually at war. The extraordinary ferocity of such wars may well express the sense of moral outrage at the opponents for being traitors to their own kind.

[2] There are a few cases, such as that of the Eskimos, where the physical environment is so severe as to absorb all vital energies in the task of survival, where the tribes are so isolated as not to experience much contact with outsiders, or where the "outsiders" are ethnologically so closely related as not to to be real outsiders. In such cases the practice of warfare may be virtually unknown.

vanced nations can contribute to one another by voluntary trade based on specialization and comparative advantage.

The organization of production by peaceful means and by the free activities of individuals in response to market demand has become enormously more efficient than any sort of directed or enslaved labor. This modern type of production depends heavily on continuity and the absence of disruption, as well as on voluntary saving and investment, productivity improvement, the acquisition of advanced education, and the acquisition and practice of complex and subtle skills. It can therefore function successfully on the basis of positive motivation rather than of fear and physical coercion. In short, exploitation of people is not an effective basis for running a modern economy, and winning a war in order to achieve a position from which one can better exploit people no longer makes sense economically in view of the vastly greater rewards available from the cooperative exploitation of nature. Moreover, actually waging modern war, especially if any effective counterblows have to be sustained, has become—even from a narrowly economic viewpoint—prohibitively expensive.[3]

Thus, we have come in the second half of the twentieth century to a stage where war no longer makes the least sense economically but does not for this reason automatically disappear, for, in fact, our societies are organized on the basis of institutions that are inherently war-inclined. Thus, so long as our national institutions remain as they are, war can be avoided only by a continuous series of difficult adjustments achieved by the art of diplomacy.

[3] People who worry about whether we can afford to disarm need to be reminded that if modern armaments are ever actually used, the losses in purely economic terms are likely to be of an order of magnitude quite incommensurable with the cost of the arms themselves and transcending anything in recorded experience.

A built-in institutional proneness to war in our society arises from a fundamental characteristic of the nation-state: its "sovereignty." This is essentially an ethnocentric right to judge its own case and to take what measures it wishes, including resort to war, to safeguard what it itself judges its vital interests to be. Under national sovereignty a state cannot be bound by its prior treaties and commitments, including nonaggression treaties, and retains the right to denounce such treaties and commitments and to resort to "self-defense," that is, war, when it (and it alone) judges such self-defense to be necessary. These rights are, despite some contrary appearances, retained in the UN Charter, which is based on the principle of the "sovereign equality of nations" (presumably meaning that UN members are to be equal *and* sovereign) and explicitly upholds the rights of national and collective self-defense, while providing no objective standard for distinguishing self-defense from aggression. Indeed, the Charter takes care to assure that no such method of determining aggression will be possible by providing for the right of an alleged aggressor to veto a decision establishing him as such in the Security Council.[4] The unconstitutional evasion of this provision of the Charter by the "Uniting for Peace" resolution, which throws security affairs into the General Assembly after a Security Council veto [5] is one that I am persuaded the United States will sooner or later regret.

To this observer at least, the actions and the failures to act of the General Assembly in security matters have been hardly indicative of its judicial temper and objectivity when confronted with charges of threats to international peace, nor would it seem possible for a body constituted as it is not to be

---

[4] This protection would be unavailable only in the unlikely instance that the aggressor had neither a seat nor an ally on the Security Council.

[5] Unconstitutional because not obtained by the regular amendment procedure provided for in the Charter.

influenced by self-interest, wire-pulling, log-rolling, and simple prejudice, which would seriously detract from any claim that might be made for it to represent, in any sense, the "conscience of humanity."

The danger of national sovereignty is that it is put at the service of the power drive of the world's political leaders. Political leaders are generally those who have the strongest urge for power and the greatest ability to succeed in the power struggle. After having achieved the top posts in their own power hierarchy, it is natural for them to seek to expand the power of the nation they lead, thereby increasing their own. The power conflicts thus generated assume an international form and may lead to war in the absence of outstanding diplomacy. This drive for power is a professional compulsion that it requires exceptional wisdom and character to resist.

The danger is especially great in totalitarian societies, where leaders are not accustomed to relinquishing power voluntarily nor emotionally inured to the experience of hostile criticism. They may be strongly tempted to try to suppress criticism by taking over the outside societies from which it still emanates. As William Alanson White, the eminent American psychiatrist, once remarked, "Deference is a specific for anxiety!" In so far as totalitarian leaders suffer from neurotic anxiety—and the evidence suggests that they frequently do—their pursuit of deference by seeking to eliminate or silence their critics (including their foreign critics) lends an inevitable militancy to their foreign policy. This is particularly dangerous in conjunction with an essentially paranoid ideology (such as Nazism or Leninism-Stalinism), which endows its proponents with a strong sense of grievance (thereby emotionally justifying hostile feelings and actions), a sense of mission, and a conviction of inevitable final triumph.

The stakes involved in avoiding war have now, however, become so enormous that a definite ending of the war system is clearly required if humanity is not to go on living in grave risk of sudden extinction or at least of destruction of the material and intellectual accumulations of centuries of human culture.

Historically the only more or less reliable alternative to the war system has been the system of enforced law, under which members of a group regulate their relations to one another according to specific rules (not only general principles) and are subjected to an external authority to decide whether or not a rule has been broken and a penalty is required.[6] Even this system has breakdowns, as previously indicated, in the form of civil wars, but the likelihood of such wars is greatly reduced if the society possesses both a democratic ethos and a strong centralization of constitutional authority and military power.[7]

It is difficult to see how nations could be induced to renounce sovereignty and to accept a rule of law in their relations. Political scientists have generally assumed that this development would require a world government, which the nations are as yet patently unwilling to accept and the nature, constitution, and selection of which pose apparently insoluble problems. I

[6] There do exist examples of long-continued periods of peace and lack of hostility between interacting nations (such as the United States and Canada) despite retention of sovereignty, but such situations probably reflect explicit or implicit alliances or balance-of-power situations. The dynamic power struggle going on between rival blocs does not separate the two nations in question, but on the contrary makes them reciprocally dependent and hence peaceful in their interrelations. Such peaceful relations between them would not, however, be assured—in the absence of a peacekeeping authority—unless these nations were involved in a power struggle somewhere else.

[7] Few instances can be cited of a revolutionary war internally generated in a truly democratic society. The most dramatic instance, that of the American Civil War, would probably not have occurred if the military power of the Federal government had been anywhere near as strong as that which the states could raise, as it has subsequently become, and if anarchic notions about the sovereign powers of the individual states had not been given so much apparent support in the U.S. Constitution.

do not believe that a government, in the usual sense, would be a necessary or desirable form of authority for the enforcement of world peace.[8] I would be the first to admit, however, that a "nongovernmental" peace authority with the power to enforce a world treaty against offensive armaments and aggression would also be extraordinarily difficult to organize and administer and would pose problems that have not yet been solved. Under these circumstances the U.S. government commitment to general and complete disarmament represents an implicit act of faith that if concurrence could be obtained from other nations on the broad goals of a disarmament treaty, it would be possible to find or develop mutually acceptable political institutions and mechanisms for its implementation.[9] I concur in this act of faith but believe that quite unorthodox methods, some of them entirely outside the sphere of traditional political theory and governmental practice, will probably be necessary to achieve this objective.

The record, it must be admitted, is not too encouraging with respect to the likelihood of such basic reforms being accepted quickly, even if the intellectual problems of the required structure of the new institutions can be solved. We should, however, be prepared for the possibility that such acceptance may be greatly hastened, if not precipitated, by a major crisis of some sort, for example, a serious unexplained atomic explosion, a confrontation that goes far enough to occasion panicky attempts to effect an exodus from major cities, or the diffusion of atomic

[8] Emile Benoit, "An American Foreign Policy for Survival," *Ethics, International Journal of Social, Political and Legal Philosophy*, July, 1946.

[9] In fact, "United States Program for General and Complete Disarmament in a Peaceful World," submitted to the United Nations in September, 1961, leaves the International Disarmament Organization to the later stages of disarmament and is entirely vague as to its powers, selection, and method of work.

weapons to countries with clearly irresponsible (if not, indeed, absolutely paranoic) leadership. Such events may finally create an emotional awareness of the abyss on the edge of which man has now become intellectually accustomed to living and could create a public opinion prepared to accept and insist on the necessary drastic political changes. Unless, however, workable techniques for handling the problem had already been thought through, publicized, and assessed and unless there was at least a nucleus of political support for them, then the anxieties aroused by the crisis might result in action of a traditional and reactionary sort, reinforcing rather than averting self-destructive trends. Because a time of exaggerated anxiety is not well suited to the thoughtful and objective consideration of genuinely novel solutions, it becomes especially important that such solutions be prepared, publicized, and discussed well in advance.

In the present essay we shall examine the possible effects of economic fears in deterring or discouraging the adoption of disarmament even if the political problems of achieving disarmament can be solved. Two types of fear, in particular, may be important: the fear of "disarmament impacts" and the fear of "coexistence in a disarmed world." The first fear is that a reduction in defense expenditures would lead to a serious decline in economic activity with losses of jobs and incomes, often concentrated in particular industries or localities. The second fear is that, once disarmed, a country might find it impossible to survive in the ensuing struggle between competing economic and social systems and so lose the way of life and set of values under which it is determined to live.

The Fear of Disarmament Impacts

While it is widely assumed that fear of disarmament impacts is an important force in maintaining a high level of armament expenditure and discouraging disarmament, there exists very little objective information indeed about the strength and influence of such fears. I do not know of any study that has been addressed directly to this question [10] nor would such a study be easy to make. In the United States decision-making on defense spending is shared by the President and Congress with either having the power to spend less than the other approves. Both the President and Congress are influenced to an undetermined degree by the rival pressures, on the one hand, of procurement services seeking more and better weapons and defense contractors seeking larger orders and, on the other hand, by the economy bloc seeking to reduce government expenditures, by the rentier bloc represented by banking, insurance, and real estate interests and fearful of inflation, and by the peace bloc opposed in general to arms spending and pursuing the goal of a *détente* through diplomacy, compromise, and slowdown of the arms race.

Even those elements in our population that stand to gain economically from an enlarged defense effort are not necessarily so single-minded in pursuit of their short-term economic interests as to be unaware of the grave dangers of modern armaments or unalterably opposed to constructive efforts to achieve disarmament if possible.[11] Moreover, a democracy such as ours

---

[10] The still-confidential study on the economic effects of disarmament made by Senator Humphrey's Disarmament Subcommittee of the Senate Committee on Foreign Affairs did not contain direct information on this topic. It investigated the defense contractors (whose influence on the size of the defense program is at best only partial), their degree of present dependence on defense contracts, and the extent to which they had prepared plans for alternative activities in the event of disarmament. These matters, while useful to know (and it is mystifying why this study should still not have been made public), bear only obliquely on the question here at issue.

[11] Nobel was not the last of the armament makers who sought to subsidize peace efforts out of the profits of defense contracts. Several major defense

is well accustomed to balancing competing interests and over-riding those which are judged incompatible with the general interest. After 1945 we put through defense cuts relatively far greater than those now in prospect, and the net defense cuts after the Korean War represented about the same proportion (5 percent) of the then GNP as would disarmament (after offsets) on the basis of the model used in our research program.

Fears of disarmament impacts seem strongest in those labor unions whose members work in defense industries, in small business, especially those sectors deeply involved in defense sub-contracts, in sectors of business and labor that are already unemployed or unprofitable or that feel themselves to be insecure (whether or not involved in defense work), in sections of the country that are exceptionally dependent for their livelihood either on defense production or servicing large defense installations, and generally in less well-informed and less sophisticated segments of economic opinion. The managements of big defense firms have shown little concern. It is by no means clear, however, whether those who are less concerned base their optimism mainly on a belief that adjustment to disarmament would be easy or on the concealed premise that disarmament is unlikely to occur. In many cases they obviously have failed to make the distinction and would be much more concerned than they are if disarmament suddenly appeared imminent.

Thus, even if it is true, as I believe, that fears of disarmament impacts have up to now had relatively little influence on disarmament negotiations or disarmament policy, it could well be

---

firms are now accepting research and development contracts from the Arms Control and Disarmament Agency on disarmament problems. One of the chief recommendations made on the basis of my research has been that government-sponsored research and development efforts of this kind should be greatly expanded.

the case that once the political obstacles to disarmament were surmounted, economic fears of disarmament could at that point become much more serious and could exercise a highly deleterious influence on subsequent negotiations and on the political campaign for ratification of a disarmament treaty. Not that such fears would be in most cases openly cited as the grounds for rejecting disarmament! Rather, we would anticipate that a significant sector of public opinion would become more worried about the inevitable residue of politico-military dangers in even a well-thought-out disarmament agreement and less responsive to its politico-military advantages than it would have been were it not tacitly concerned about the economic dangers of disarmament impacts. It is for this reason that research on disarmament impacts may have significant policy implications.

Research conducted by myself and several associates in the "Program of Research on Economic Adjustments to Disarmament" appears to have established a presumption that disarmament in the United States, on the basis of a probable pattern more or less consistent with U.S. government proposals, would not create unsurmountable adjustment problems, assuming reasonably sensible adjustment policies were adopted by government, industry, and labor.[12] The adoption of sensible policies is, to be sure, a relatively optimistic assumption, and the study does suggest that misguided government policies—for example, the attempt to use a substantial portion of defense saving to reduce

[12] See Emile Benoit and Kenneth Boulding, eds., *Disarmament and the Economy* (New York: Harper and Row, 1963), especially my concluding chapter. Other less comprehensive treatments appear in *Economic Impacts of Disarmament,* U.S. Arms Control and Disarmament Agency, Economic Series 1, Publication 2, January, 1962; "Economic Adjustments to Arms Control," *Journal of Arms Control,* Vol. 1, No. 2 (April, 1963); "Would Disarmament Mean a Depression?" *New York Times Magazine,* April 28, 1963; "Disarmament: Its Politics and Economics," ed. by Seymour Melman, *Daedalus,* Winter, 1962.

the national debt—could, in fact, have extremely unfavorable results, with a real depression as a possibility and a period of slow growth with mounting unemployment as a serious likelihood. Yet the study considers it unlikely in practice that such misguided policies will prevail.

The study also calls attention to significant structural maladjustments that would inevitably be created or intensified by disarmament and suggests certain new programs helpful in coping with them. At the same time it notes that on a merely quantitative basis (ignoring certain qualitive aspects that are undoubtedly important) the potential structural maladjustments to be created by disarmament appear no worse than those arising continuously from other sources—growth of the labor force, changes in the pattern of final demand, technological displacement of labor by automation, changes in industrial patterns arising from competition by imports, and technical substitutes for existing materials.

Some commentators have remarked [13] that the relatively optimistic results of the foregoing study depend heavily on the assumption of an extended (twelve-year) disarmament period. It deserves to be emphasized, however, that the reason for assuming this long a period was not in the least to make the economic problems of adjustment appear easier to solve but solely to provide a militarily and politically realistic basis of analysis. The need for an extended period for the implementation of disarmament may be more readily grasped when it is remembered that we refer to "multilateral" rather than "bilateral" disarmament, that is, not merely a cutback in the national defense forces of the disarming nations but a transfer of preponderant force to a peace enforcement authority (the "International Disarmament Organization" in the words of the

[13] For example, see Edward T. Chase, "How to Recover from Disarmament," *New Republic*, June 1, 1963.

U.S. government's disarmament proposal). The establishment of a supranational inspection and enforcement authority of this type would inevitably be a subtle and difficult if not dangerous task, and in the light of what we know about setting up international agencies a twelve-year period for the transfer of decisive military power from national forces to an international authority would seem to be an absolute minimum. It may be relevant to note that the European Economic Community, which aimed to endow its administrative agency, the Commission, with only a relatively small amount of supranational authority—and one that would be exercised in an infinitely less vital area—was planned to be established over a period of twelve to fifteen years.

Nor, in any case, does our study cast any doubt on the capability of the U.S. economy to adjust to a more rapid pace of disarmament if it were politically sensible. The strain of adjustment will depend on when and how fast the crucial *economic* variables change. These are by no means identical with the crucial military variables. From a military viewpoint the crucial element in the speed of disarmament may be how rapidly existing stocks of armaments are destroyed or transferred to the peace enforcement authority. From an economic point of view, however, this element has little importance. What mainly counts here are reductions in national military manpower, reductions of employment in national defense agencies, and especially the rate of cutback in expenditures for new procurement, construction, maintenance and operation, and research and development. The economic impact is also determined by the size and rate of build-up of the national contributions to supranational inspection and enforcement and the extent to which such contributions are merely financial or are matched by flows of real goods and services.

On the whole, the main results of our study would appear to

be consistent with the conclusion that disarmament could be considerably speeded up without any economic crisis, provided that sufficiently vigorous monetary-fiscal policies were followed to maintain adequate total demand in the economy. On the other hand, structural problems would inevitably be more serious in a quick disarmament, and it would seem unrealistic to assume that they could be settled in a wholly satisfactory manner within an extremely brief period, say, two to four years. Inability to solve the structural problems that quickly would not necessarily result in a general decline in activity, but such an outcome could be avoided only by maintaining the incomes and purchasing power of those suffering from structural unemployment. This might require such measures as large termination payments, liberalized social insurance, temporary substitution of civilian for military contracts, liberal education and resettlement grants and loans for demobilized personnel, and expansion both of traditional public works activities and of new government programs designed to utilize the specific human and physical resources being released from the defense program. Some programs of this sort would be helpful in any case, but considerably larger ones would be needed in the unlikely event of a really precipitant disarmament.

Assuming economics can provide answers to the adjustment problems of disarmament, will these answers be politically adopted? Samuelson has asked [14] whether the U.S. government, which has failed in recent years to restore rapid growth rates and to reduce unemployment below 5 percent even with the economic stimulus of a large defense program, can be counted on to do so when the stimulus of big defense is removed.

This is a disturbing question, but certain things should be

[14] In a private communication.

borne in mind. First, the U.S. defense program, while absolutely large, was in real terms *contracting* over the period 1953–60. (The contraction was about 30 percent.) In fact, the slowdown in our economy may be attributable in considerable part to the fact that this contraction occurred and that no adequate offsets were provided. Federal nondefense purchases were also cut back, and the 1954 tax cut was too small to halt the rise in Federal tax revenues. Consequently there was a budget surplus of 11.5 billion dollars on income and product account over the three calendar years 1955, 1956, and 1957 and another of 3.5 billion dollars in 1960.[15] With any reasonable multiplier, these surpluses would suffice to account for much of the economic slowdown actually experienced since 1955.

The projected net cutbacks (after offsets) under disarmament are about 5 percent of GNP—no worse than those which occurred in the post-Korean defense cuts—and the cuts would probably be less precipitant than the cut of 1953–54.

Would our policy responses be even as bad as those of 1953–60? I doubt it. We probably have begun to learn that cost inflation cannot be effectively controlled by general deflation of demand and a slowing down of growth,[16] at least not without making enormous sacrifices. Also, we must bear in mind that

[15] The comparable amounts are only 6 billion and 3.6 billion dollars on a cash budget basis, but the national income account basis cited provides the best measure of the budget's actual impact on the economy, since taxes are credited to the period in which they affect economic activity.

[16] Because with a lower operating rate in the economy and with a slowdown in industrial re-equipment, there is a lower rate of productivity advance, resulting in rising unit costs even if wage rates do rise somewhat more slowly under the pressure of excess unemployment. Thus, prices, as measured by the GNP price deflator, rose by an annual average of 2.1 percent in the period 1953–59, compared with 2.3 percent in the period 1948–53. The 0.2 percent improvement was bought at a remarkably high cost. See Emile Benoit, *Europe at Sixes and Sevens: The Common Market, the Free Trade Association, and the United States* (New York: Columbia University Press, 1961), pp. 164–65.

the 1953–54 arms cut was not really recognized as a major economic change for which definite policy adjustments would be required to maintain stability.[17] In a way, a future disarmament program, precisely because it would be of such self-evident political importance and novelty, would be much more likely to be taken seriously on the economic side as well and to have various adjustment measures prepared for it. Indeed, the exaggerated economic fear it arouses would itself assure that much attention would be given to allaying the economic ill effects.

One further observation must be made on this point. One cannot expect that even wholly successful adjustment measures could do more than restore the economy to the *status quo ante*. Disarmament itself will certainly not *create* full employment and rapid growth if the economy did not have them before disarmament began. Its initial impact will be deflationary, and adjustment policy must be adjudged successful if it counteracts this deflationary impact without introducing new distortions into the economy. Disarmament adjustments cannot be expected to clean up a mess that was already there before disarmament started. Clearly the economic policies applied to 10 percent of the economy will have less influence on its general prosperity than the policies applied to the other 90 percent.

We remain, therefore, hopeful that the need to maintain adequate over-all demand and to prevent a major depression will not be ignored in the event of disarmament and that helpful policy measures will be adopted even if, perhaps, not promptly or forcefully enough to prevent some slowing down of the growth rate.

[17] This point was well made in the ACDA memorandum on *Economic and Social Consequences of Disarmament*, U.S. Reply to the Inquiry of the Secretary General of the United Nations, Part II, March, 1962.

A good deal depends, nevertheless, on the public's confidence in the will and the power of the government to protect prosperity. If such confidence is lacking when disarmament is announced and if a decade or more of defense cuts looms ahead, then the outlook will be bleak and major declines in investment and consumer durables purchases might occur. For this reason, the seriousness of the government's attack on rising unemployment and low growth rates and its capability of taking vigorous action to reverse such trends ought to be demonstrated *before* disarmament. From this point of view, great importance attaches to the success of current efforts to raise growth rates by major tax cuts and other measures.

In this connection it must be noted that Congressional hostility to the expansion of federal nondefense expenditures could create serious difficulties in providing adequate offsets to defense cuts. In the popular mythology, defense expenditure appears in the "free enterprise" column, whereas an expansion of nondefense federal expenditure, even if the work is also done by private contractors, appears as a growth of the public sector, threatening to free enterprise. Public misconceptions about the trend of federal nondefense expenditure are serious. Far from running wild, as popularly supposed, federal nondefense expenditures on goods and services, adjusted for price changes, are now considerably lower than they were before World War II. (On a per capita basis they were a third lower in 1963 than in 1939.) And nondefense purchases of *all* government units—including state and local—have declined from 17 to 12 percent of GNP over the same period. Moreover, since 1953, even with defense spending included, the share of GNP absorbed by the Federal government alone has declined from 17.5 to 11.3 percent.

Congressional hostility to nondefense public spending could

be dangerous, since if tax cuts alone were utilized to stabilize the economy during disarmament, the cuts (and the ensuing budget deficits) would have to be so large as to be clearly outside the possibility of serious political consideration. Moreover, income would be stimulated so much more than employment that tax cuts large enough to provide new employment for all those losing defense employment would create severe inflationary pressure.[18]

The structural problems of disarmament, while less critical than the problem of adequate markets, are likely to be harder to solve, particularly because the low U.S. growth rate since 1953 has already created severe structural disbalance in the U.S. economy. These structural difficulties take the form of major concentrations of protracted and sometimes permanent unemployment, sometimes leading to unemployability, among workers who lack the skills, training, and abilities required for modern industry, who are outside the preferred age groups, or who are in permanently depressed areas or occupations. These conditions, if not alleviated before disarmament begins, would undoubtedly make it harder to effectuate a smooth transfer of the released manpower to new nondefense activities. The structural backlog would clog up the retraining, relocation, redevelopment, and other structural adjustment mechanisms and might even create labor-supply bottlenecks, preventing a sufficiently rapid expansion of output in fields where demand was more than adequate.

The most fundamental structural problem of all, however, will be how to preserve the highly specialized type of economic activity developed within defense industry, involving collaborative scientific-technical-industrial research and development

---

[18] See Emile Benoit, "The Role of Monetary and Fiscal Policies in Disarmament Adjustments," *Journal of Finance*, May, 1963, pp. 116–19.

aimed at breakthroughs on the most crucial and difficult technical problems. Can this precious new national resource (massive
research and development teams using systems analysis to solve
problems of great difficulty and practical import), created as a
byproduct of national defense, be preserved without support
from national defense? In our judgment it will require a bold
new approach to cope successfully with this problem. [19]

International Impacts of Disarmament

Countries other than the United States seem less concerned
about disarmament impacts than we do and will generally experience far smaller economic adjustment problems from their
own disarmament. For one thing, the share of their total economic activity involved in defense activities is generally smaller,
as is evident from the estimates in Table 1. Hence, disarmament
would involve a smaller reduction in expenditure and also a
smaller structural problem of resource transfer.

Only the USSR appears to have a substantially larger proportion of its domestic resources committed to defense activity
than the United States. While doubts have sometimes been expressed about the ability and willingness of the USSR to make
economic adjustments involved in disarmament,[20] I accept the
more usual view that disarmament adjustments would not constitute a major economic problem for the USSR. The main
reasons for this optimistic appraisal are as follows:

1. The USSR has and is likely to retain a substantial degree
of suppressed inflation in its economy, which would create
considerable demand for civilian products as soon as they became available in larger quantities.

---

[19] Benoit and Boulding, *Disarmament and the Economy*, pp. 295–300.

[20] A notable expression of this view was given in an unpublished paper by
John Hardt of the Institute for Defense Analyses in a conference on disarmament organized by Seymour Melman at Columbia University in 1961.

Table 1. *Burden of Defense in Selected Countries*

	Approximate defense expenditure out of domestic resources [a] as percent of GNP, 1958	Armed forces as percent of population, 1960
World total	9.4	0.7
United States	10.2	1.4
USSR	10.2[b]	1.7[c]
Mainland China	4.6[d]	0.4
United Kingdom	7.4	1.1
France	7.1	2.3
Federal Republic of Germany	3.1	0.5
Japan	1.5	0.2
Yugoslavia	7.3	3.0
India	2.1	0.1
Indonesia	5.5	0.2
Brazil	3.2	0.3
Australia	3.8	0.5
Iran	5.2	0.6

Source: "The Burden of National Defense," Appendix to Emile Benoit and Kenneth Boulding, eds., *Disarmament and the Economy* (New York: Harper and Row, 1963), pp. 301ff., prepared by Mary Painter on the basis of national budgets, I.C.A. data, and other sources.

[a] "Out of domestic resources" here signifies after deducting any net receipts from foreign military assistance.

[b] Expenditure in 1960 as a percent of GNP at factor cost. Approximate estimate by Stanley Cohen, "GNP in the Soviet Union," in *Dimensions of Soviet Economic Power*, Part 2, Hearings, Joint Economic Committee, 1962, No. 92043, based on Morris Bornstein, Soviet National Income Accounts for 1955," *Review of Economic Statistics*, XLIV (1964), 452–55.

[c] As of January, 1960, reduction of forces envisaged in law of January 15, 1960, would reduce this to 1.1 percent of the population.

[d] Based on data from unofficial sources.

2. The USSR retains sufficient power to direct labor and to restrain public criticism so that personal inconveniences arising from the overcoming of structural difficulties would not create substantial political problems.

3. The willingness of the USSR to provide liberal retirement allowances to demobilized military personnel and the fact that most industrial administrative posts are under the control of the

government would facilitate reasonably satisfactory financial and other arrangements for demobilized defense personnel.

4. Owing to the exceptionally high quality of the inputs of resources devoted to defense industry (management, skilled labor, research and development, machinery, etc.), disarmament would be particularly welcomed in other areas of Soviet industry and would do much to step up productivity in these areas, thereby avoiding some of the structural difficulties of rapid expansion which would be likely to plague the United States.

The greater confidence of other non-Communist countries that they could handle disarmament impacts without difficulty is connected with their economic ideas and political organization as well as with the generally lower proportion of their resources devoted to defense and the lesser structural specialization and immobility of their defense sectors. Most countries do not have the serious emotional resistances prevailing in the United States to expansion of nondefense government expenditure programs and to budget deficits. They can therefore more readily undertake compensatory public programs or tax cuts as defense expenditures are reduced. Moreover, most countries have more responsive, less decentralized governmental institutions, in which the political will of the nation can be more promptly translated into action and where such action is not so subject to checks imposed by political figures occupying strategic political positions without either broad popular mandate or support from the national leadership. It is partly for these reasons that countries other than the United States are usually more confident than we that they could move promptly and effectively to counter the deflationary impact of arms cuts.

In most of these countries the purely structural problems of reconversion would be smaller than ours, not only because of the smaller portion of the national product devoted to defense, but also because of the less highly specialized character of defense industry, the smaller place in the defense program of defense *industry* and highly trained specialist forces, and the larger proportion of the total representing merely conventional military forces.

In the less well-developed countries, however, the demobilization of their military forces might often create secondary problems of a socio-political character not hitherto much examined. In some Latin American countries, for example, the governments are highly dependent on the support of the military for their existence and might lack the political strength to disband the military even if they wished to do so. Indeed, in some countries the real purpose of the defense establishment is less to defend the country against external foes than to support a regime in power within the country and to prevent a latent social revolution. In some other underdeveloped countries, especially in Asia, the demobilization of the national military force might very likely result in the revival of banditry and the restoration of a regime of local war lords.

Thus, for some and perhaps most underdeveloped countries the maintenance (in some cases even the strengthening) of existing defense forces might be desired, even under conditions of world disarmament, as a means of strengthening the control of their central governments over the nation and avoiding the dangers of revolutions, secessions, reversion to tribalism, and anarchy. For such countries, disarmament might best be conceived as involving not so much the demobilization of their military forces as the endowment of these forces with secondary objectives and functions in the field of economic development, which might increasingly occupy their attention and increasingly dilute their original security goals. Thus, over the course of time their purely military functions could become considerably attenuated, and their primary function might become that of spearheading the nation's effort of economic development.

Lessons in this respect may likely be learned from the civil works responsibilities of the U.S. Corps of Engineers, from the nonmilitary activities of the Israeli, Swiss, and other defense forces, and from the development work undertaken in the past by the French army in Algeria under the Constantine plan.

Disarmament would also affect trade and the balance of payments, but these impacts are difficult to forecast. Much depends on how the defense program changes between now and the time disarmament begins, as well as on the particular sequence of disarmament measures undertaken. Our own studies on these subjects have not yet proceeded far,[21] and the following generalizations should be taken as provisional and speculative.

It has been generally assumed that disarmament would end the balance-of-payments difficulties of the United States by eliminating the debit item "foreign military expenditures," which have been around 3 billion dollars in recent years, an amount recently somewhat in excess of the deficit. It now appears, however, that the favorable balance-of-payments effects may not be quite as prompt or as strong as anticipated. First, the U.S. government is making strong efforts to reduce foreign defense expenditures in order to improve the balance of payments immediately. To the extent these efforts succeed, they will leave smaller cutbacks to be made after disarmament begins. Second, the United States has been building up an important

[21] This subject will be studied in greater detail in the program: Research on International Economics of Disarmament and Arms Control (RIEDAC). A good preliminary survey may be found in Robert Stevens' chapter, "Balance of Payments Adjustments" (Chap. 13), in Benoit and Boulding, *Disarmament and the Economy*.

commercial export market in armaments, which would be lost immediately in the event of disarmament. Third, it now seems less likely that most U.S. overseas defense installations and forces would be demobilized in the early stages of disarmament. Even though the bases might be denuclearized, they might still be kept operational as deterrents against outbreaks of conventional or limited war during the early stages of disarmament. Fourth, the import content of the defense program is being steadily reduced, with the diminished importance of procurement relative to research and development and other services.

These points are also relevant (in reverse) for the analysis of the balance-of-payments positions of other countries, most of which will not be so badly affected by disarmament as has often been feared. Any adverse effects on the European countries may do no more than reduce their recent large surpluses. (They might be much harder hit, however, if these surpluses have by that time disappeared as a result of improvements in the U.S. competitive position!) There are a small number of underdeveloped countries that even under present conditions might be seriously hurt either from the loss of dollar earnings on sales to U.S. foreign military installations, through the loss of defense-support aid, or through the decline in exports of materials (mostly minerals) more heavily utilized in defense than in nondefense final purchases.

Stevens [22] has estimated direct military and defense-related U.S. foreign payments in 1958 as 3.9 billion dollars, of which about 1.3 billion dollars was outside Europe and Canada, and indirect defense-related merchandise imports at 615 million dollars, of which 330 million dollars was outside Europe and Canada. He also estimated about 900 million dollars of defense-

[22] *Ibid.*

related aid going to areas other than Europe and Canada. Receipts from defense-related aid were higher in 1958 than receipts from exports of goods and services in Korea, Laos, Vietnam, and Jordan and were also high in Cambodia, Taiwan, Pakistan, and Bolivia. If we include receipts from U.S. foreign military expenditure together with defense-related aid, we find heavy balance-of-payment dependence on defense programs also in Turkey, Spain, Iceland, the Philippines, Greece, Libya, and Morocco.

It is these countries with heavy dependence on defense-related aid or on military receipts, as well as those heavily dependent on the export of strategic minerals (such as steel, copper, aluminum, nickel, lead, tungsten, manganese, chromium, petroleum, and certain "exotic" materials, especially those with heat-resistant qualities) that seem likely to be most adversely affected.[23]

These adverse effects could be quite serious for some countries. It will be important that additional foreign aid and improved access to export markets for civilian items be made available to ease the transition.

Economic Hopes of Disarmament

A brief mention must also be made of economic *hopes* as well as the economic fears in connection with disarmament. Indeed, except perhaps in the United States the hopes are much stronger than the fears. Such hopes are particularly strong in the underdeveloped countries, which have often jumped to the conclusion that disarmament would involve a 120-billion-dollar world saving on defense efforts, the bulk of which could be readily

[23] U.S. uranium imports, formerly so important, are likely to be negligible in view of the vast stockpiles of nuclear fuels already in existence and the pending cutbacks in production of missile warheads.

turned into additional development aid, thereby assuring the prompt achievement of their development goals. This hope is sometimes bolstered by the notion that this course is the only one that could prevent disarmament from having a seriously depressing effect on the economies of the developed countries. Under analysis, such expectations appear rather unrealistic.

First, the real cutback in world security expenditures would be far less than 115–120 billion dollars of estimated defense expenditure if allowances are made for residual national forces to be maintained, the contributions required to a supranational world security force, and the expansion of certain defense-related civilian activities in space and atomic energy. (In a U.S. disarmament model studied by the writer the net cutbacks after such offsets was only 54 percent of initial expenditures.) The situation in other developed countries with relatively smaller defense programs and less spending on strategic weapons may be similar, and many underdeveloped countries may desire to retain substantial military establishments to check revolutionary, sectionalist, and disintegrationist tendencies.

Second, the real cost of world defense to the *civilian economy* is far less than is suggested by the usual 115–120-billion-dollar estimate of the world's defense bill. A quite large sector of the present cost goes to supply substitutes for civilian goods and services, which would still have to be supplied if the defense programs were eliminated (food, clothing, and shelter; basic education; transportation equipment; and military public works having nondefense uses). The conversion of such expenditures to civilian purposes would not add commensurately to real living standards. It should also be noted that defense totals are inflated by a certain amount of double counting; thus, most military aid comprises equipment donated from stockpiles. Such equipment enters the total of defense expenditure of the donor country when it is originally manufactured, and it is recorded again as a defense expenditure when transferred from the stockpile to the recipient country.

Third, the research and development element in national defense, which is a substantial and rapidly growing segment of total defense expenditures, particularly in the United States and other industrial economies, contributes very largely to civilian progress through its indirect "fall-out," or side effects. Many key elements in modern life, such as jet transportation, atomic energy, and electronic devices, have been largely developed through defense-financed research and development. Indeed, the world's defense programs may in the end more than pay for themselves in relation to the civilian economy by indirect contributions of this sort. The elimination of this segment of the defense program (if not replaced by additional nondefense research and development expenditures) would, over the long run, reduce the capability of the advanced economies to contribute to the less well-developed economies.[24] While civilian research and development could undoubtedly have done more for the civilian economy than equivalent amounts of military research and development, it seems entirely unlikely that, lacking the sharp spur of the threat to national survival, civilian

[24] The high costs of the space program and the disorganizing effects of new competition for intellectuals on the traditional academic markets for brains are producing a reaction against the expansion in defense and defense-related research and development. One aspect of this reaction is a tendency to deny the value for civilian life of the research and development financed by defense or the space program. In fact, the payoffs are becoming more indirect and long-range but not necessarily on that account less weighty. It is hard to imagine, for example, what a communications revolution may be implicit in the new laser technology and the use of microelectronic equipment. Similarly, the revolution in transportation implicit in the slotted-wing and in the VTOL (vertical take off and landing) aircraft may be as great in practical terms as was the change from propellers to jets (which was also financed by defense research and development).

programs of the size, vigor, and daring of the defense research and development programs would have evolved so soon.

Fourth, the amount of foreign aid is fundamentally limited by the amount of growth in the economy and the share of it we are politically willing to make available for this purpose. The U.S. economy has for several years been wasting in unemployment and underutilization of equipment nearly as much as the total cost of the defense program and enough to expand the aid program many times over, were there a willingness to do so. It seems politically unlikely that we would be willing to tax ourselves nearly as heavily to expand our foreign aid programs as we are to maintain an accustomed level of defense. A public opinion survey prepared for the READ program (Research on Economic Adjustments to Disarmament) by the Survey Research Center of the University of Michigan showed that an expansion of foreign aid was the *least* favored use for defense savings in the event of disarmament.[25]

Finally, there is some reason to be skeptical that a very rapid increase in capital flows for development would bring about a corresponding acceleration in development progress and living standards in the developing countries. There are other missing ingredients for development besides capital, such as managerial capabilities, the presence of institutions and attitudes conducive to decision-making, saving, and investment, and orderly political change. Such missing ingredients may create bottlenecks in the development progress which more development aid will not easily or quickly overcome.[26]

For these reasons and others the underdeveloped countries

---

[25] See Emile Benoit, "The Propensity to Reduce the National Debt Out of Defense Savings," *American Economic Review*, LI (1961), 456.

[26] See Albert Hirschman, *The Strategy of Economic Development* (New Haven: Yale University Press, 1958).

may derive less additional foreign aid from released defense resources than they have been hoping to get. Even so, the amounts of resources that would be freed by general and complete disarmament are so huge in relation to the amounts now going to development aid that rather dramatic expansion in foreign aid programs would undoubtedly become possible. The crucial issue in this regard is how disarmament might affect the political willingness to make such increases. This is a matter that may be much influenced by the type of coexistence achieved after disarmament, a matter we shall be discussing in the next part of this essay.

We must first note, however, that the economic benefits of disarmament would vastly transcend an expansion in foreign aid. While the gap in living standards between the developed and underdeveloped countries is enormous, large numbers of persons in developed countries, even in the United States, are living in great poverty. The upgrading of *their* living standards should also have a high priority, both on a welfare basis and because of the great increases in average productivity that it might bring about. Moreover, even those in the middle-income brackets in the developed countries are hard-pressed to maintain the living standards to which they have become accustomed, so that they do not feel as "affluent" as they have sometimes been alleged to be. In addition, there are large unmet needs in the public services, such as education, public welfare, housing, urban renewal, transportation, and resource development, which could contribute greatly to both welfare and productivity in the developed countries.

It is also worth noting that a significant stimulus to the development of the underdeveloped countries may be provided in ways other than by foreign aid and particularly by government support of programs of research and development within developed countries in such fields as unconventional energy sources, population control, teaching machines and other communication devices, desalinization of water, new building materials and techniques, public health (especially attacks on tropical disease), and improved agricultural methods. Such work may provide information of vital significance for eliminating existing bottlenecks on economic development in underdeveloped countries.

Fears of Coexistence under Disarmament

Disarmament is sometimes distrusted as a trap that would permit the conquest of a given socio-economic system by its rivals through some nonmilitary type of combat. The fear that by denuding itself of weapons a society might lose its capacity to resist political, economic, and ideological assault and penetration and might lose out under the competitive conditions of a disarmed world is very likely more powerful as a deterrent to disarmament than the fear of disarmament's economic impacts. For one thing, it appears to affect the Communist as well as the non-Communist world.

Just what it is that is feared is not easy to identify. The Communist world seems mostly to fear ideological contagion and disillusionment, with a relapse into individualism; the non-Communist countries worry more about the danger of paramilitary and military intervention, political warfare, and economic competition. Both sides fear subversion, propaganda, espionage, and political and economic warfare.

It may be helpful to identify briefly some of the alternative interaction patterns that may give rise to fear: [27]

---

[27] The disarmament model here assumed contains virtually unlimited inspection with a wide margin of security. See Benoit and Boulding, *Disarmament and the Economy*, pp. 31–34.

MILITARY AND PARAMILITARY INTERVENTION

Forbidden military activities may be carried on in concealed forms by supplying military personnel, supplies, training, and guidance to other countries in which internal military conflicts are occurring. Such intervention may be even better hidden in guerrilla warfare, where the combatants are disguised as civilians when not in action. Still less easy to spot are paramilitary activities involving the training or supply of assassins, saboteurs, terrorists, mob leaders, and other specialists in revolutionary direct action.

POLITICAL WARFARE

This would include giving financial or other material help of a nonmilitary or noncombat nature to revolutionary movements or parties in another country; bribing journalists, politicians, educators, or others; planting propaganda so as to obscure its origin and make it appear to be emanating from internal sources—in general, any tactics designed to influence the political decisions of another country while hiding or disguising the true source of the influence.

PROPAGANDA

In its simple form, unmixed with political warfare, propaganda involves the publicizing of ideas favorable to one's own country or sytem or adverse to or destructive of another country or system without necessarily disguising the source but usually by appeals to emotions and the repetitive use of simple ideas and slogans with no concern for the truth of the ideas being diffused; that is, exaggeration, distortion, or even outright falsehood may be used if considered effective (but may be used sparingly to protect the credibility of the source).

ESPIONAGE

This consists in collecting information about another country
which that country endeavors to keep secret, typically by
means of secret organizations that are illegal in the country
under surveillance.

ECONOMIC WARFARE

This is the use of economic measures to damage or harass an
opponent. Included are trade embargoes, selective trade controls on items judged helpful to his military potential or economic growth, preclusive buying (to keep others from supplying him) plus boycotts to achieve the same result, dumping in
order to disrupt international markets and cause losses to normal
suppliers, and establishing a strong position in a given national
market in order to be able to exert political pressure by the
threat of sudden withdrawal either on the buying or selling
side. Essentially, economic warfare covers the use of economic
measures directly to achieve hostile political objectives.

ECONOMIC COMPETITION

In contrast to economic warfare, the means here do not involve deception or direct damage to the opponent. Economic
competition works primarily through a rise in production and
trade, guided by economic criteria of costs, productivity, value,
or welfare. The effort is to demonstrate the superior capabilities
of one's own form of economy and *thereby* (and only in-
directly) to gain a political advantage. It is feared by those on
both sides who believe the opponent's system has more to offer
in at least some specific ways but that the attempt to adopt these
features into one's own system would result in its decay or
breakdown.

ECONOMIC COOPERATION

The expansion of trade and contacts, the freer flow of information, the tackling in common of certain vast projects (like polar and space exploration, building of facilities for advanced nuclear research, and world economic development), and the convergence of rival systems are all forms of economic cooperation. They tend to be viewed with misgivings by conservatives, officials, and apologists of both systems who fear (possibly with good reason) that contacts with the opposing systems may impair the blind loyalty with which their populations support their own systems and impair the power, prestige and influence of these officials, apologists, or powerholders within their own systems.

Outlawing Indirect Aggression

There seems to be a real and pronounced difference between military (or paramilitary) interventionism and political warfare, on the one hand, and the other interaction patterns mentioned above on the other. The first two are essentially attempts to do away with the opponent by force or by secret or dishonest means. They are not truly modes of coexistence but, so to speak, "a continuation of war by other means," or what has been called "cold war." They seem essentially incompatible with the basic ethic of coexistence, or non-ethnocentrism, which acknowledges that the stranger, the "other," as a fellow human, has the right to exist and to exist even in his "strangeness," that is, within a different socio-political system, and that we have no right to try to impose our own system on him against his will, although we have the right to try to persuade him. Only by abandoning indirect as well as direct aggression can we transcend the cold war and arrive at a condition of fully peaceful coexistence.

Suppose we grant that the first two categories are indeed forms of indirect aggression; is it conceivable that a prohibition against them could be enforced? While a confident affirmative answer is not yet possible, the difficulties will appear far less than they do now when and if the nations come to accept the desirability of multilateral disarmament with a ban on direct aggression enforced by a supranational peace agency trusted by both sides. It would appear irrational to accept so much and yet balk at the elimination of another sort of conflict equally likely to lead to general war.

This might perhaps be accomplished by a ban on the transmission of persons, money, goods, or other material things (but not communications, propaganda, etc.) across the boundaries of any nation without the knowledge and consent of its government. (In case of doubt, the World Peace Authority would decide which was the legitimate government.) If any government felt the rule were being infringed, it could request comprehensive inspection by the World Peace Authority not only of the border territories, but also of the territory from which the illegitimate assistance was thought to be emanating. If such charges were sustained, the government officials implicated in the indirect aggression would be subject to established penalties and the aggrieved government would be given military assistance.

Such a ban might result in somewhat fewer revolutions, but since under disarmament national governments would retain only tactical and defensive weapons and limited forces, popular revolutions against unbearable tyranny could still occur and with some hope of success. Moreover, revolutionary movements, if and when successful, would be more likely to follow an independent course thereafter, thus limiting the dangers they would pose to the bloc from which they defect.

The chief objective, after all, is the avoidance of direct major-power confrontations arising from involvement on opposite sides of revolutionary struggles. Some limitations on the pace of revolutionary change may be justified as a contribution to human survivability in the nuclear age. Indeed, fewer revolutions may be necessary, to the extent that governments become increasingly sensitive to the pressures of unfavorable world public opinion expressed through UN condemnation and intervention in the event of flagrant violation of the human rights that they are pledged to uphold. There will also be less incentive to resort to revolution if the richer countries intensify their cooperative efforts to accelerate the progress of the underdeveloped countries.

Propaganda and espionage, which are included in the list of feared activities, do not, I believe, require specific regulation. Propaganda is too elusive a thing to be easily regulated. Presumably the more virulent varieties would tend to disappear in an era of increasingly cooperative coexistence, but no attempt should be made to restrain criticism of each other's systems, even though such criticism will often seem unbalanced and unfair to those who are the targets of the criticism and will indeed often *be* unbalanced and unfair. Trust will have to be put in the public's ability to distinguish between truth and falsity. In any case, the most dangerous kind of propaganda (that which is planted, with its true sponsors hidden) would be cut off by the ban on secret transfers of funds. To some extent, this (and the ban on secret transfer of persons) would also tend to reduce the amount of national espionage, which would be largely abandoned as an unnecessary expense in any case as the voluminous inspection activities of the world peace authority got under way.

We come now to the most awkward question. Could Communist countries, inheritors of the Marxist-Leninist revolutionary ideology, abandon indirect aggression as a valid and even "traditional" instrument for advancing their objectives? A few years ago it would have been difficult to be optimistic on this score, despite Khrushchev's remark that revolution cannot be made by rockets and Red China's five principles of coexistence (nonintervention) of the Bandung Resolution.

Recently, however, the widening split between Russia and China has brought out into the open a major change in doctrine that seems to be developing in Russia on this subject. The realization that fomenting and aiding revolution could touch off a major war is creating a frame of mind in which coexistence begins to be taken seriously not just as a propaganda line but as an operating policy offering new possibilities for solving difficult and dangerous problems. The Chinese and Russian policy statements on their controversy provide extremely interesting reading in this connection. Just how far this change of heart has really gone and how much further it is capable of going are unsolved riddles of enormous practical importance.

Essentially the Soviet government appears to wish to limit, although apparently not entirely to abandon, its Leninist (perhaps one should say Trotskyist) international revolutionary commitments. This could result in time in a willingness to abandon in fact as well as in verbal claim the various forms of indirect aggression mentioned, so long as the way were left open for continuing competition and even struggle within the broad field of coexistence. The latter field, as we shall see, is by no means devoid of possibilities for conflict, but they are types of conflict far less likely to lead to war.

Peaceful Coexistence

This term has been used in the past primarily for popular political discussion and often with propagandistic purposes. It has, therefore, lacked precision in meaning; it not only covers a wide field but also often involves a degree of deception, or self-deception, in its use. As used here, the term will cover all types of national interaction other than overt violence and the various forms of indirect aggression discussed above.

It is not possible to apply any abstract concept, such as "peaceful coexistence," to characterize a given historical period, such as the present era, since in practice elements of peaceful coexistence and of cold war tactics are found conjoined in varying proportion in different areas. While peaceful coexistence has been advocated as a goal by the Soviet leadership for a number of years, there has been only gradual progress toward the abandonment of certain forms of indirect aggression. There has apparently been no clear-cut decision as yet to abandon such activity, even though at the present time there is an apparent wish to move in this direction even if this requires the sacrifice of certain traditional attitudes and practices. It should be added that peaceful coexistence will remain precarious until cold war measures have not only ceased but have been outlawed by enforceable agreements as part of a general disarmament and peace enforcement arrangement.

While the term "peaceful coexistence" has often been used as if it were a simple homogeneous reality, it does in fact include a variety of types of activity and relationship, not all of which are by any means harmonious and friendly. Indeed, peaceful coexistence may be viewed as having three main forms: hostile, competitive, and cooperative. Hostile coexistence may appear to be a contradiction in terms and would be so were the hostility absolute. As we know from modern psychiatry, however, hostility is present in some degree and from time to time in most human relationships, even familial. It would be too much to expect to see interbloc rivalry suddenly purged of hostility or freed from hostile interactions and tactics. What is crucial is only that such hostile relations and activities be so limited in severity and in type that they cannot readily develop into more serious forms of combat. Hostile coexistence is intended to do limited but not irreparable damage to the opponent, recognizing that if the damage done is too great, coexistence might be imperiled and grave dangers created for both sides. It is more like quarreling than homicide, more like bringing a punitive lawsuit than like murder. It is in a sense a "no win" policy, in which the goal of complete triumph over the opponent has been given up as unrealistic and even dangerous but in which the struggle is continued in safer forms in the hope of limited gains.

The second form of coexistence, competitive coexistence ("May the best system win") involves attempts to demonstrate in actual performance the working superiority of one's own system in meeting human needs and thereby to win popular support in third countries and even among the people of the rival country. It implies rivalry but not necessarily enmity; it is compatible with mutual respect and even a degree of admiration.

The third form of coexistence, cooperative coexistence ("Let us look for what we have and can do in common without worrying too much about who will ultimately win") attempts to recognize and even enhance the similarities, parallels, and convergencies between the two systems, to improve contacts, communications, and trade, and to work on joint projects where advantageous. It is relaxed about the degree of similarity or difference between the two systems, not desiring to abandon its own essential character but recognizing that both realities are somewhat mixed in practice and not hesitating to adopt elements from the other's system where they can be assimilated with profit.

Clearly these three forms of coexistence are themselves coexistent; examples of all three types already exist in several fields. Moreover, they are somewhat inconsistently interspersed with surviving cold war elements. One may hope that these and even the remaining elements of hostile coexistence will more and more give way to competitive and even cooperative forms. It may help to clarify the meaning of these modalities of co-existence if we examine how they would be expressed in various fields: international trade, world economic development, and domestic socio-economic policies and ideologies.

COEXISTENCE IN TRADE

Under hostile coexistence in trade we may include embar-goes, freezing of funds, diversion of shipping, blacklisting, strategic exports controls, preclusive purchasing, regional autarchy as a means of political isolationism and domination, dumping or offering abnormal prices or conditions of purchase with primarily disruptive intent, and offering supplies or markets with the intent of establishing a dependence subject to later political manipulation.

Competitive coexistence in trade might include normal trade promotion; improvement in trade financing or servicing; and price-cutting or overbidding for "commercial" reasons, that is, with the intent of expanding the seller's or buyer's permanent share of the world's markets; and the inauguration of special trade arrangements designed to win the friendship of under-developed countries (for example, commodity agreements and acceptance of their currencies in payment). On the part of the Communist countries trade promotion might well include efforts to develop more satisfactory quality standards and guar-antees of timely and regular delivery, with adequate replace-ments, spare parts, and services.

Under cooperative coexistence in trade we might include

attempts to expand East-West trade by relaxation of quantitative and currency controls, by offering liberal terms of financing, and by a progressive lowering of trade barriers (both on underdeveloped country exports and on East-West trade), as well as a willingness of state trading organizations to play the game by the relevant GATT provisions on state trading, and possibly by the formation of government trading organizations in private-enterprise countries for certain special purposes or products.

COEXISTENCE IN WORLD ECONOMIC DEVELOPMENT

Under hostile forms of coexistence foreign aid will be mainly unilateral and based on ideological and political criteria, intended to support and strengthen friendly governments and to win votes in UN resolutions.

Under competitive coexistence there may be a fundamental shift over from ideological and political to economic criteria in giving aid, seeking the maintenance of high standards and proper cooperation in assuring the most efficient use of aid resources, but with much aid still remaining unilateral and clearly identified so as to redound to the credit of the donor. Development treaties with specific growth goals and mutual performance guarantees may be offered to demonstrate the efficiency and productivity of one or the other form of economy.[28]

Under cooperative coexistence, on the other hand, we would probably have multilateralization of most aid programs to assure more efficient use of aid and to prevent exploitation of the developed by the underdeveloped nations. We might also see

---

[28] See my testimony before the Subcommittee on Foreign Trade Policy of the House Ways and Means Committee, *Hearings on Private Foreign Investment*, Eighty-Fifth Congress, Second Session, December 5, 1958, pp. 495–99.

joint East-West research and development programs on space technology, oceanic industries, polar development, nuclear fusion power technology, and research and development on removing impediments to economic development.

COEXISTENCE IN DOMESTIC ECONOMIC POLICIES

Under hostile coexistence, domestic economic programs are heavily influenced by considerations of ideological orthodoxy, with blind hostility in Communist societies toward private economic activities (even in agriculture, services, and small-scale manufacturing, where they are particularly useful) and a tendency to concentrate heavily on power-sustaining economic sectors (that is, defense and heavy industrial investment). A parallel jealousy and distrust of the public sector and an ex-aggerated emphasis on traditional forms of private investment may occur in private enterprise economies. Ideologically mo-tivated portrayal by each side of the other's economy will tend to preserve misunderstanding and prejudice, partly by accept-ing each other's dogmatists as giving true descriptions of their own economies and of the differences between the systems. Propaganda, censorship, and various pressures may be used to help preserve the orthodox impressions against objective dis-cussion or confrontation with contrary evidence. In countries with tyrannical governments, persecution or hostile reception of dissenting opinion and nonconformist art products will be likely.

Under competitive coexistence one may expect more con-cern for actual economic results (rate of growth, real output of goods, real consumer satisfaction, maintenance of low unem-ployment, and freedom of consumer and employee choice) and a willingness to disregard, sidestep, or override ideological barriers to their attainment with also a greater willingness to pursue those economic values being relatively neglected, such as freedom of choice in Communist economies and adequacy of employment in private-enterprise economies.

In the cooperative phase of coexistence one might even find a willingness of systems to learn from each other by exchange of technical missions and visitation and by freeing channels of communication and art. This could be helped also by recognizing (and possibly even strengthening) the significant parallels that exist between the rival systems, for example, by exploring the similarities between socialistic centralized production planning and modern monetary-fiscal policy and projective, decentralized, voluntary industrial planning for growth in private-enterprise economies. Similarly, socio-political convergences might be emphasized through better implementation by the Soviets of existing constitutional guarantees of individual rights and freedom of dissent under such formulas as "socialist legality" and "freedom from politics for the arts." In the Western nations, further attempts might be made to achieve equality of educational and vocational and voting opportunity and to reduce the concentration of power implicit in private ownership of mass communications media and private financing of election campaigns.

Coexistence and Disarmament

These will be somewhat startling perspectives for many readers, nor need they fear that the swing toward cooperative coexistence would proceed very rapidly even if disarmament were achieved. The real differences in values are serious, and the tradition of hostility, distrust, and rivalry is too strong. Yet only those with a vivid sense of historical change may be capable of realizing how transient the cold war atmosphere in which we have lived since 1946 may turn out to be. And we should not be surprised that the real revolution in military technology that has made the world unsafe for warfare should finally be having some limited recognition on the political and economic plane. In a way the surprising thing is how long it takes the world's statesmen to see and digest the obvious.

All this will fail to satisfy the fanatics of both systems, for in fact certain risks of coexistence remain. In the end no guarantees can be given as to which system will win. Coexistence would put the issue up to history, making sure only that certain Marquis of Queensbury rules (the barring of direct and indirect aggression) were observed in the struggle. Proponents of each system will feel confident that at least its own central values will survive. Some degree of convergence seems likely, a priori, with the emerging realities resembling very little the artificial, oversimplified abstractions portrayed by the dogmatists and dialecticians of both sides.

Perhaps the best indication of the depth and calmness of a man's faith in the worth of the system under which he lives is his willingness to leave it to be judged by future generations in free and peaceful contact with other societies. The achievement of disarmament requires the recognition that the survival of humanity and even of modern civilization is more important than the temporary triumph of *any* party, ideology, group of leaders, or socio-economic system and that for humans the highest loyalty must be to the survival of mankind and to the culture (material and spiritual) that makes it human.